GENDER DIFFERENCES

Recent Titles in
Contributions in Women's Studies

The Question of How: Women Writers and New Portuguese Literature
Darlene J. Sadlier

Mother Puzzles: Daughters and Mothers in Contemporary American Literature
Mickey Pearlman, editor

Education for Equality: Women's Rights Periodicals and Women's Higher
Education, 1849–1920
Patricia Smith Butcher

Women Changing Work
Patricia W. Lunneborg

From the Hearth to the Open Road: A Feminist Study of Aging in Contemporary
Literature
Barbara Frey Waxman

Women, Equality, and the French Revolution
Candice E. Proctor

Serious Daring from Within: Female Narrative Strategies in Eudora Welty's
Novels
Franziska Gygax

Verging on the Abyss: The Social Fiction of Kate Chopin and Edith Wharton
Mary E. Papke

The Feminization of Poverty: Only in America?
Gertrude Schaffner Goldberg and Eleanor Kremen, editors

The Dominion of Women: The Personal and the Political in Canadian Women's
Literature
Wayne Fraser

Successful Career Women: Their Professional and Personal Characteristics
Cecilia Ann Northcutt

The Life of Margaret Fuller: A Revised, Second Edition
Madeleine Stern

The Sea of Becoming: Approaches to the Fiction of Esther Tusquets
Mary S. Vásquez, editor

GENDER DIFFERENCES

Their Impact on Public Policy

Edited by
MARY LOU KENDRIGAN

CONTRIBUTIONS IN WOMEN'S STUDIES,
NUMBER 121

Greenwood Press
New York • Westport, Connecticut • London

Library of Congress Cataloging-in-Publication Data

Gender differences : their impact on public policy / edited by Mary
Lou Kendrigan.
  p. cm. — (Contributions in women's studies, ISSN 0147–104X ;
no. 121)
  Includes bibliographical references and index.
  ISBN 0–313–24875–3 (lib. bdg. : alk. paper)
  1. Sex role—United States. 2. Sex discrimination against women—
United States. 3. United States—Social policy. 4. Equality—
United States. I. Kendrigan, Mary Lou. II. Series.
 HQ1075.5U6G46   1991
 305.3'0973—dc20   90–43381
      74334
British Library Cataloguing in Publication Data is available.

Library of Congress Catalog Card Number: 90–43381
ISBN: 0–313–24875–3
ISSN: 0147–104X

First published in 1991

Greenwood Press, 88 Post Road West, Westport, CT 06881
An imprint of Greenwood Publishing Group, Inc.

Printed in the United States of America

The paper used in this book complies with the
Permanent Paper Standard issued by the National
Information Standards Organization (Z39.48–1984).

10 9 8 7 6 5 4 3 2

CONTENTS

1

UNDERSTANDING EQUALITY: THE PUBLIC POLICY CONSEQUENCES

MARY LOU KENDRIGAN

Differences permeate society. Gender differences affect all aspects of life. Because inequalities are so pervasive, they are reflected in all issues, not simply in policies designed specifically to affect women. Each chapter in this book illustrates the durability and complexities of existing inequalities. Public policy has a different impact on men and women not only in the areas traditionally treated as feminist concerns: day care, pay equity, equal access to credit. Gender differences touch all aspects of life. The focus here is on issues not usually seen as feminist, but which will reflect gender differences because men and women are differently situated in society. Attention must be directed to tax policy and plant shutdowns as well as to reproductive rights and the question of comparable worth. Feminist analysis should consider programs of compensation for victims of crime as well as rape counselling and domestic assault centers. Women's lives have been profoundly altered by corporate and governmental policies that facilitate the large-scale and most likely permanent loss of thousands of manufacturing jobs in their industries and communities. Women have a special stake in tourism policy and in programs to help victims of head injuries.

Because inequalities are best demonstrated in policy outcomes, this book examines the impact of existing gender differences in public policy outcomes. It asks: which policies lead to more and which to less equality among members of the society? The impetus for this work was research that my colleague and I did on compensation programs for victims of crime (Chapter 2). We found that the impact of such programs on female victims was significantly different than on male victims. Women are victims of different kinds of crime. This book also contains studies of gender differences in factory shutdowns, programs to help the unemployed, tax policies, tourism, veterans' benefits, and the care of differently abled persons.

Equality is very elusive. In our very unequal world, it is difficult to imagine what such equality would look like. Since it is easier to identify illustrations of inequalities than it is to create conditions for equality, a first step toward better understanding of equality is to understand the complexity of existing inequalities. If we are to make any progress toward greater equality between the sexes, our understanding of equality must direct us toward evaluating public policies in order to learn their impact on existing inequalities and to evaluate what effectiveness they might have in lessening such inequalities. I do not intend to make further contributions to the debate about the nature of differences between the sexes. Nor will I discuss the actual causes of sex differences.

My intent is not to answer every question about such differences but rather to give some indication of the complexity of the issues and to indicate the relationship between these complexities and an understanding of equality. Rather than offer justification for equality, I will evaluate the prerequisites of greater equality. I want to draw attention to the impact gender differences have on public policy. My intention is to show why equality of results matters. In the conclusion I will further define equality of results, show how each chapter points to the need to understand equality in this way, and show the advantages of such a conception.

In order to evaluate the nature of existing inequalities it is essential to understand how social stratification, institutional racism, and institutional sexism operate in contemporary society. Each of the chapters in this book presents illustrations of their operation. A system of social stratification implies that social inequalities are connected: inequalities in one dimension are related to inequalities in another. Further, these inequalities may be assumed to be interactive: the net effect of such inequalities is greater than the sum of individual inequalities. These concepts are useful analytical devices because they direct us to examine how various institutions interact with each other and reinforce each other's influence. They illustrate why any analysis of equality must consider differences. They also illustrate why such a definition must concentrate on outcomes.

Since the normal functioning of social institutions leads to the perpetuation of privilege, then social stratification, institutional racism, and institutional sexism explain how the institutions of society work to increase the inequalities already existing between the haves and the have-nots. For example, people who can afford to live in the more affluent neighborhoods are able to provide their children with the best neighborhood schools with little financial sacrifice. Such children receive a better education, which is reinforced by cultural advantages in the home. These students qualify for the "right" institutions of higher education, where their parents can afford to send them. People who have had such training get entry-level positions of higher status, better salaries, and more opportunities for advancement. Meanwhile, equity in their houses grows at a much higher rate. Parents thus have greater financial resources to assist their college educated, professional offspring when they also wish to move into similar neighborhoods.

Likewise, those who cannot afford to live in the "right" kind of neighborhood cannot "qualify" for the right schools, even if they could afford the costs. Thus, when scholarships are available, it becomes "difficult" to find qualified candidates eligible for the scholarship. Poor schooling leads to poor jobs with poor pay and little room for advancement. When, after many well-publicized battles, well-paying jobs are opened to the formerly excluded, it is difficult to find well-qualified employees for the job. The inequalities are perpetuated, and the system justifies and perpetuates itself. Jim Croce sang about the losing end of the stratification system in his "Car-Wash Blues." It is difficult to get an "executive position" if your experience has been at a car wash—or rearing children. And it may be almost as hard to think you deserve such a job as it is to gain the credentials.[1]

By far the best indicator of the status a male will attain in American society is the status his father had held.[2] It is not necessary to exaggerate the mobility for other groups in the society, however, to argue that the cycle that maintains privilege for the privileged and the lack of privilege for the unprivileged works with more rigidity for blacks, other minorities, and women than for white males. Stokely Carmichael and Charles Hamilton developed the concept of institutional racism to deal with the racial inequalities that continually derive from the ordinary operations of society's organizations and institutions and stem from the actions of established and respectable persons.[3] Kirsten Amundsen's concept of institutional sexism shows that the system functions similarly with women.[4] Institutional racism and institutional sexism are social stratification with a "double whammy." All of the society's institutions make life harder for the less privileged and most difficult or impossible for minorities and women. Social stratification explains, for example, how all the institutions of society hampered Abraham Lincoln's chances of becoming president of the United States at the same time that they enhanced the ambitions of John Quincy Adams. Abraham Lincoln had not gone to the right schools or to Harvard. He did not have a father who could help him financially, give him advice, and use his influence in his son's behalf. Success was not impossible, but much more difficult for Abraham Lincoln. It was only with a greater deal of hard work and luck that he achieved his success. Now think of the chances of Booker T. Washington and Susan B. Anthony! With all the hard work and luck they could muster, they could not have made it to the presidency—or even to many positions of considerably lower status. They suffered the "double whammy." (Susan B. Anthony was never able to vote!)

An analysis of both existing inequalities and the direction of social change requires an analysis of the manner in which various institutions operate to perpetuate the existing discrimination against women. It is the role the family plays in perpetuating inequalities that most clearly illuminates how inequalities are interrelated and reinforced in women's lives. Women have the cultural mandate to give priority to the family. Women are brought up to think of themselves primarily as mothers and wives. Even when a woman is working, she is expected to be committed to her family first.[5] Because women are expected to bear the major responsibilities of home and child care, much of the discrimination women face both in jobs and in policies is assumed to be appropriate.[6] Deitch, Nowak, and Snyder explain that since the majority of women continue to combine both family and paid work while men do not, and since paid work is organized on the assumption that all workers can adapt to male work patterns, women are at a disadvantage in both the labor market and at home (Chapter 3). Richard reports that variations in earnings, occupations, lifetime employment patterns, and responsibilities for home and child care are among the most salient differences between men and women in the labor market (Chapter 6). She finds that in job-training programs women are less willing to relocate because of family responsibilities. She also stresses the importance of child care if job-training programs are to meet the needs of women. Because of their family responsibilities, many women prefer jobs that require little or no overtime work or traveling.[7]

The evidence of segregation of the job market on the basis of sex and the lack of social mobility available to women demonstrate that institutional sexism is a more rigid and more discriminatory form of social stratification. The major cause of economic inequality for women is the sex-segregated job market. Half of all working women are in occupations that are over 70 percent female, and more than a quarter are in occupations that are over 95 percent female.[8] Within manufacturing, as within much of the economy, there is a dual or segmented labor market. Women and minorities work disproportionately in low-paying industries and small firms. Furthermore, sex segregation in employment has not decreased significantly over time. The index of sex segregation in the labor market has stayed about the same since 1900. Women work for low wages in weak or nonunion shops.

Again, it is important to see the interconnection between various aspects of the social system. Occupational segregation stems from many sources: discrimination, cultural conditioning, and the personal desires of the women themselves. Women have been conditioned to believe that these usually low-paying, low-status jobs are the only proper jobs for them. Most higher-paying jobs are seen as unfeminine. Such patterns are substantiated by

Richard in her study of job-training programs. Women were training for traditionally female jobs. Such jobs were, of course, lower in pay and lower in status. Richter explains how cultural characteristics are used to trivialize women and limit their influence on the tourist industry (Chapter 8). Willenz finds cultural conditioning limiting women in their ability to gain veterans' benefits (Chapter 9). Women veterans tended to dismiss the value of their contributions to the service of their country. Slavin discusses how cultural expectations lead women to assume the role of caretaker for the victims of head injuries (Chapter 10). She also evaluates how such a role is diminished in importance and political efficacy because it is primarily a female role.

Employers will not hire women for "lifetime" jobs because they believe women are not attached to the labor market. Such expectations become self-fulfilling prophecies. Monk-Turner (Chapter 5) and Ruttenberg and McCarthy (Chapter 7) explain how the myth still persists that women work for "pin money." If, for instance, men and women are convinced that women are not career oriented, then it becomes much easier to fire women when the staff has to be cut back, to give women the dead-end jobs, or to relegate them to jobs that pay less. Attitudes of employers, Richard explains, are usually reinforced by government programs that provide job training. Furthermore, employers are unwilling to invest resources in on-the-job training for women. They resist placing women in training or management positions that will lead to higher pay.[9] Thus, Deitch, Nowak, and Snyder explain that women are often the last hired and the first fired, the first laid off, the last recalled. Women are in occupations in which each individual worker is defined as replaceable. They are not in occupations that are seen as demanding a full-time commitment or requiring independent judgment and decision making.[10] Although the average married woman with children will spend about thirty years in the labor force, employers continue to view women as less stable workers than men.[11] Women can thus anticipate thirty or more years of the least interesting, most tedious, lowest-status, lowest-paying, dead-end jobs.

Women make up about two-thirds of the "discouraged workers," those unemployed who have ceased looking for work and are therefore not counted in official unemployment statistics. Meanwhile, the unemployment insurance program is structurally biased against these workers.[12] Beckett points out that women are less likely than men to get another job after a period of unemployment (Chapter 4). Compared to their white male counterparts, women and minorities remain disproportionately employed by smaller and less capital-intensive firms that lack the stability and resources to provide employment security. Women are less likely to get on-the-job training, less likely to have continuous work experience, more likely to drop out of the job market.

Thus, it is not necessary that there be a deliberate conscious conspiracy among male bosses and colleagues to prevent the advancement of women into more profitable fields—no more than the admissions officers at major universities need be composed of racists. The effectiveness of sexism in the labor market, as with racism, depends on the effectiveness of sexist differentiation and sexist controls in other institutions of society. Is it any wonder that both men and women are reluctant to work for a woman boss? Discriminatory behavior has become so well institutionalized that individuals generally do not have to exercise a conscious choice to operate in a racist or sexist manner.[13] The choices have already been prestructured. The individual has only to conform to the operating norms of the organization with which he is involved and the institution will do the discriminating for him.[14] And as with college board entrance examinations that treat the suburban student identically with the inner-city student, such discrimination often takes place under the guise of equal treatment.

Ideology operates so effectively in the United States that, despite all the evidence, there are serious cultural constraints against analyzing such oppression. Nonetheless, there is a systematic hierarchy of social position in American society. We do treat occupants of different positions as superior, equal, or inferior in socially important respects. Social stratification, institutional racism, and institutional sexism are useful analytical devices because they direct us to examine how various institutions interact with each other and reinforce each other's influence. These concepts help to explain how privilege builds on privilege and the lack of privilege reinforces existing disadvantages. Social stratification, institutional racism, and institutional sexism illustrate why any analysis of equality must consider differences. It also illustrates why such a definition must concentrate on outcomes.

We are undergoing significant changes in the economy and in the family. We can anticipate that the impact of such change will fall most heavily on the most vulnerable members of society. The privileged are better able to adapt to such change. Thus, for example, it should not come as a surprise to read in Monk-Turner that the percentage of women who are professional workers has declined—or that three-fourths of the women who are professional workers are secondary-school teachers or nurses, both lower-paying and lower-status occupations. Beckett points out that women are less likely to get other jobs. Furthermore, displaced blue collar women who are reemployed are more likely to skid downward into occupations that tend to have lower wages and fewer benefits. While unemployment compensation differences between men and women have lessened, the disadvantages of single women as heads of households have increased.[15] It is not simply that change comes when people press for extension of their rights. Expanded opportunities for women to move into some of the better-paying manufacturing jobs in the 1970s were also an important source of movement toward greater sexual equality, higher incomes, and occupational mobility for women. In the 1970s, women entered blue-collar durable-goods-manufacturing jobs at a faster rate than they entered the more rapidly growing service sectors. In the 1980s, however, this trend was reversed. A decline in the number of women employed in manufacturing accompanied a slow but continuing rise in the service-sector jobs for women. Deitch, Nowak, and Snyder explain that just when women were able to gain admittance to well-paying blue-collar jobs, the deindustrialization of society accelerated. Better-paying blue-collar jobs that women gained in the 1970s are disappearing, while women's employment in lower-paying, nonunion, predominantly female, service industries is expanding.

Furthermore, such changes must not be seen in isolation. Changes in one aspect of life will be related to changes in many other aspects as well. For example, with more low-paying jobs the need will increase for better health care and different kinds of funding for day care and housing. Feminists must understand that these complex interrelations will affect their efforts to deal with social change.[16]

If public policy is to be effective in creating more equality, we must be as clear as possible about the meaning of equality. The intent of this book is to expand the definition of equality. A feminist understanding of equality should offer more than a critique of existing inequalities. It should provide some notion of the desirable goals and the action necessary to achieve them. The chapters of this book illustrate why such an understanding of equality must take differences into consideration, must focus on outcomes, and must not see any one public-policy issue in isolation. Any understanding of equality that does less cannot be useful in achieving more equality. In the conclusion I will argue that if feminists seek a society in which being female is no longer sufficient justification for unequal treatment, they must demand equality of results.

NOTES

1. Kay Deaux and Tim Emswiller, "Explanation of Successful Performance Sex Linked Tasks: What is Skill for the Male is Luck for the Female," *Journal of Personality and Social Psychology* 29, no. 1 (1974): 80–85.

2. William H. Sewell, "Social Mobility and Social Participation," *Annuals of the American Academy of Political and Social Sciences* (January 1978): 230–231; also see Peter M. Blau and Otis D. Duncan, *The American Occupational Structure* (New York: John Wiley & Sons, 1967).

3. Stokely Carmichael and Charles V. Hamilton, *Black Power* (New York: Vintage Books, 1967), p. 3.

4. Kirsten Amundsen, *A New Look at the Silenced Majority: Women and American Democracy* (Englewood Cliffs, N.J.: Prentice-Hall, 1977), chap. 5; also see Onora O'Neil, "How Do We Know When Opportunities Are Equal?" in *Sex Equality*, ed. Jane English, p. 151. (Englewood Cliffs, N.J.: Prentice-Hall 1977).

5. Rose Lamb Coser and Gerald Rokoff, "Women in the Occupational World: Social Disruption and Conflict," *Social Problems* 18 (September 1971): 538.

6. Mary Lou Kendrigan, *Political Equality in a Democratic Society: Women in the United States* (Westport, Conn.: Greenwood Press, 1984).

7. Sandra Stencel, "Women in the Work Force," *Congressional Quarterly* (June 1977): 29.

8. Deborah Bachrach, "Women in Employment," *Clearinghouse Review/National Clearinghouse for Legal Services* 14 (February 1981): 1041.

9. Mary Corcoran and Greg J. Duncan, "Work History, Labor Force Attachment, and Earnings Difference between the Races and Sexes," *Journal of Human Resources* 14 (Winter 1979): 4.

10. Coser and Rokoff, "Women in the Occupational World," p. 551.

11. Ralph Smith, *The Subtle Revolution* (Washington, D.C.: Urban Institute, 1979), pp. 58–59.

12. Diana Pearce, "Toil and Trouble: Women Workers and Unemployment Compensation," *Signs* (Spring 1985): 439–459.

13. Virginia Sapiro, "Equality and Preferential Treatment: A Social Psychological Perspective on Equal Employment Policies for Women" (Paper presented to the European Consortium for Political Research, Florence, March 1980).

14. Amundsen, *The Silenced Majority*, p. 22.

15. Pearce, "Women Workers and Unemployment Compensation."

16. Kendrigan, *Political Equality*, pp. 47–64.

2

COMPENSATION FOR VICTIMS OF CRIME: THE GENDER DIFFERENCES

MARY LOU KENDRIGAN AND MARY ANN E. STEGER

Programs to compensate victims of crime were developed to assist all victims of crime, but the major crimes that victimize women were virtually excluded from the programs. Benefits were often determined in ways that were of greater advantage to male victims. Eligibility was determined in ways that was disadvantageous to women. Kendrigan and Steger studied compensation programs for victims of crime in Michigan and Wisconsin. They found that a program that gains much of its support from concern with women's issues does not serve women nearly as well as it does men. Women are often less aware of benefits and less knowledgeable about how to get them. Women expect to get little and make few demands on the system. Women victims do not know of the program and do not demand that it meet their needs. Thus the programs are set up to help all victims of compensable violent crimes, but help is most readily provided to victims of crimes that affect males more than females—murder and assault. However, victim-compensation programs do less well in compensating crimes that affect large numbers of women—the crimes of sexual assault and domestic violence.

If public policy is to be effective in creating more gender equality, we must be as clear as possible about what we mean by equality.[1] Inequalities are so deeply entrenched in society that it is essential that any definition of equality must be similarly pervasive. One way to begin to clarify our understanding of equality is to analyze the manner in which the complexity of existing gender inequalities operate in specific policies and institutions. Our intention in analyzing crime-victim compensation programs is to show that they must be evaluated in a larger perspective which seeks not comparable worth, affirmative action, or compensation to victims of rape, but rather a truly democratic notion of equality.[2]

Compensation for victims of crime is usually not considered part of the feminist agenda. However, such programs provide one illustration of the dimensions that a feminist definition of equality must encompass. Gender differences can be identified in most public policy areas. Because inequalities are so pervasive, they are reflected in all issues—not simply in policies that specifically impact on women. As demonstrated in this chapter, the interactions among existing inequalities are so complex that any definition of equality must be similarly comprehensive. To understand the complexity of existing gender differences, we must evaluate compensation for victims of crime programs as well as rape counselling and domestic assault centers.

Although crime victims number 15 million annually, and are found in one in three households, comparatively little is known about them.[3] In the last two decades, the plight of crime victims has been recognized by public policymakers, criminal justice agencies, the legal community, and the general public. Most victim-compensation programs were created in the 1970s during a time when both the chances of victimization and the costs of such victimization rose dramatically.[4] States initiated these programs recognizing that crime victims might need financial help because of medical costs they incurred and earnings or support they lost. The criteria developed to determine eligibility for compensation differ from state to state. The intent of the legislation has been to assist victims of violent crimes in covering medical expenses and other monetary losses resulting from injuries incurred. Coverage generally extends to both victims and dependents of victims, and the laws usually define both terms broadly. Most of the statutes require that the victims report the crime to the police, and some also require that the victims cooperate in the investigation and prosecution of the case.

All victim-compensation programs establish policies that strictly limit both the classes of victims eligible for compensation and the levels of benefits available to them. All programs cover persons injured or killed as the direct result of a crime. Most of the programs (85 percent) will also compensate someone who is injured or killed in the course of coming to the aid of a crime victim, or in apprehending someone suspected of committing a crime. Dependents of a victim who dies are also eligible.

Compensation is provided for unreimbursed medical expenses, funeral expenses, loss of earnings, and support of dependents of victims who die. Property loss generally is not reimbursed. A few states provide compensation for psychiatric services, occupational training, and household help. Most of the laws set a ceiling on the amount of recovery by an individual claimant, in a few states up to $50,000, but more commonly in the range of $10,000 to $15,000.

Victim-compensation programs have been narrowly conceived and are limited in scope. Only a small fraction of eligible victims are aware of these compensation programs and apply for assistance.[5] It has been estimated that only one percent of the victims receive money from victim compensation and civil tort actions. With over 12 million index crimes reported annually, victim compensation programs reach less than 25,000 victims. These programs appear to have low visibility in most jurisdictions.[6] Furthermore, very little information is available about the impact of compensation programs upon victims.[7]

While many legislators approve of bills to assist victims of crime, they tend to be cautious in designing these programs and do not want to sign a blank check. The cost-containment procedures incorporated in victim-compensation legislation often have an ad hoc quality. Typically, these restrictions are not derived from the broad principles used to justify the program, but they are often necessary to get the bill passed.[8] As we will see, many of these restraints have severely limited the effectiveness of such programs for women.

What public consciousness there is about problems faced by victims is largely due to what is known as the victim's rights movement. This movement encompasses a number of different organizations and individuals with a common commitment to improving the treatment and position of victims in our society.[9] Much of the impetus for the movement has been attributed to women's rights organizations, whose leaders are especially concerned about the rights of rape victims and the victims of domestic abuse.[10] Although the victim's rights movement covers a wide variety of issues in addition to victim compensation programs, much of the attention focused on victims of crimes was stimulated by feminist concerns.[11]

We wish to show that a program that gains much of its support from concern with women's issues does not serve women nearly as well as it does men. Women are often less aware of benefits and less knowledgeable about how to get them. Women expect to get little and make few demands on the system. Women victims do not know of the program and do not demand that it meet their needs. Thus the programs are set up to help all victims of compensable violent crimes, but help is most readily provided to victims of crimes that affect males more than females—murder and assault. These crimes produce victims easily compensated within the rules of compensation programs. For victims who are killed, there is money for funeral expenses and loss of support. For assault victims, there is money to cover the medical expenses and lost wages. However, as we will see, the victim-compensation programs do less well in compensating crimes that affect large numbers of women—the crimes of sexual assault and domestic violence.

The point is not that the programs are inequitable if men get greater benefits from the programs than women do. Men are twice as likely to be victims of violent crimes, but women are also victims of violence.[12] The issue is whether crime victim compensation programs meet the needs of female victims of crime as well as they meet the needs of male victims. Are victims of domestic abuse or rape taken as seriously as the victims of bar-room fights? Does the distribution of program benefits reflect inequalities in the society? For example, since men tend to earn higher salaries than women, do compensation programs build these differences into their awards? The important question is not whether women get less money from the programs than men do, but rather how victim compensation programs can be structured to effectively meet the needs of both female and male victims.

When the female victim of rape or domestic abuse does file a claim with a compensation agency, she often finds that the program is not structured to fit the injuries she sustained or the remedies she requires. It has been estimated that every year between 1.8 and 3.3 million women are the victims of some form of violence by their husbands.[13] Women are victims of family violence at a rate of three times that of men.[14] Research on these victims concludes that, while women who have been subject to abuse by a partner need many types of assistance, a primary need is for safe shelter.[15] In all the initial projects that deal with violence between spouses, shelter was the primary benefit provided.

Although victim-compensation programs provide for compensation for loss of support, few programs have translated that into providing safe shelter for victims of domestic violence. In addition, the individuals typically excluded from compensation are relatives of the offender, persons living in the same household as the offender, and/or persons engaged in a continuing (sexual) relationship with the offender. If persons related to the offender or living in the same household with the offender are automatically excluded from program eligibility, battered women and their children may be victims of crime but receive no benefits.

All of the early compensation programs had such an exclusionary clause. This automatic exclusion produced many anomalies. For example, a separated wife attacked by her husband qualified for benefits, but a wife living with her husband did not, even though she was so severely slashed by her husband that she did leave him. Several alternatives to policies of summary denial in case of relation or common residence have recently been instituted around the country. One of these is simply to add a clause to the statute allowing the program to waive this restriction "in the interest of justice." This allows a program to compensate, for instance, small children left orphaned as a result of their father murdering their mother—a claim that otherwise would have to be denied. Wisconsin adopted this approach in 1981. Another option is to allow compensation when the victim separates from the offender and cooperates in the prosecution. A third way to provide aid for needy victims of familial violence is to restrict payment of expenses to the service providers; this is the policy in Hawaii and Michigan. This alternative helps to keep victims from going into serious debt as a result of a violent incident. Perhaps the most far-reaching way of ensuring that victims will not be denied compensation on a technicality, a way being used in many states, is to establish a policy that proscribes only those awards that would unjustly benefit the offender, rather than unconditionally disqualifying certain arbitrary classes of victims.

Next to murder, rape is the most feared crime and the most devastating to the lives of its victims.[16] Rape victims are, of course, mostly women. The 1980 National Crime Survey found that the victimization rate for rape of females age 12 and over was 1.6 per 1,000—a figure that has not changed significantly since 1973.[17] Unfortunately, victims of such crimes are not well served by compensation programs. Women are often less aware of benefits and less knowledgeable about how to get them. One study of rape victims found that three out of four women in the study had not heard of the available compensation.[18]

The issue is not that women get smaller compensation for rape than men get for barroom brawls. Rather, the issue is that rape victims have needs that are not being met. In all existing state victim-compensation programs, victims of sexual assault can seek reimbursement for their crime-related physical injuries. However, in states with minimum-loss requirements, these victims may not receive any financial assistance because their physical injuries are not costly enough to qualify for reimbursement. One study concluded that 91 percent of rape victims and 60 percent of attempted-rape victims reported physical injuries.[19] In general, rape takes longer to commit than other crimes, and there is more opportunity for injury because of this.[20] However, other than the actual injury of rape, most injuries sustained during a rape are relatively minor: cuts, bruises, and black eyes. One government study found that most rape victims (60 percent) had between $50 and $250 in medical expenses, and another 13 percent had expenses of less than $50.[21] Rape, when compared to other crimes, is a "cheap" crime, and the "cheapness" of the crime affects the amount of compensation the women receive. Consequently programs with minimum-loss requirements often discriminate against certain classes of victims, especially rape victims, the elderly, and the disabled.[22]

When the needs of rape victims extend beyond costs due to physical injuries, compensation is not often available. Sexual assaults usually produce victims with few physical injuries but severe emotional stress. Neither the extent of the injuries nor the relatively inexpensive medical costs should

detract from the emotional trauma suffered by such victims. The initial
reaction of most rape victims is severe. For the first month, the majority
are clinically distressed on measures of fear, anxiety, paranoia, depression,
confusion, interpersonal relations, sensitivity, self-esteem, and social adjustment. Some problems persist far beyond the initial reaction, and evidence
of trauma remains as long as a year after the rape.[23] Although victims of
many types of violent crime are likely to suffer emotional stress, rape produces the most trauma. In addition, attribution of blame to the victim may
leave her feeling doubly victimized.[24]

Victims' services can both reduce the psychological stress and help the
victim deal with that stress. To meet the needs of rape victims, counseling
should be an eligible expense in victim-compensation programs, and it
should be adequately compensated. For many women, the circumstances of
rape mean that they must find new, safer housing, change locks, change
jobs, or otherwise alter their lives. Such changes may be painful, hard to
arrange, and expensive.[25] Compensation programs have not been helpful
in assisting with these types of expenses.

When public policies fail to consider the concerns of women, eventually
some of the dimensions of such discrimination are recognized. For example,
while programs of compensation for victims of crime initially ignored the
needs of rape victims, more recent legislation has been adapted to accommodate some of those victims. A recent federal law requires that state victim-
compensation programs provide psychological counseling if the states are
to supplement their programs with federal funds.

VICTIM-COMPENSATION PROGRAMS IN WISCONSIN
AND MICHIGAN

Our research analyzed the victim-compensation programs in Wisconsin
and Michigan to test how gender differences in victimization affect the
distribution of program benefits and to learn how they reflected the gender
differences existing in the society.[26] We studied Wisconsin and Michigan
because we had access to the records in these states. Victim-compensation
programs were created in Wisconsin and Michigan in 1976 by their respective state legislatures. Michigan's program is administered by a Crime
Victims Compensation Board, which consists of three members appointed
by the governor. This board is housed in the state's Department of Management and Budget, but it is an independent entity and not integrated into
the work of this department. Wisconsin's program was originally housed
in the state's Department of Industry, Labor, and Human Relations. In 1980
the program was transferred to the Department of Justice, and the executive
director now answers to the attorney general of the state.

Michigan's program has consistently handled more claims than the program in Wisconsin. This may be because of Michigan's larger population

and higher crime index total. In 1980, the crime index total for Michigan was 616,065, compared to a total of 224,619 in Wisconsin.[27] In this same year, Michigan received 1,760 compensation claims and Wisconsin received 903. In 1981, 1,712 claims were received in Michigan. Even though Wisconsin changed the start of its program year from January to July in 1981 and reported an 18-month rather than a yearly figure, 1,386 claims were received in this period, which is still lower than the figure for Michigan's 12-month period.

For a comparison of the eligibility requirements in Michigan and Wisconsin, see Table 2.1, which lists the reasons for denial of a crime victim compensation claim used by each state from 1977 to 1983. This comparison shows that Michigan and Wisconsin have some common requirements, plus a few unique to each state. Both states have reporting requirements, specifying some period within which the claim must be filed and reported to the police. Both states require victims to cooperate with the police, and there are similar rules about situations where compensation will be denied because no crime occurred or the crime causing the injuries was not compensable. Michigan has two requirements not found in Wisconsin—a financial hardship requirement and geographic restrictions; and Wisconsin has one category not found in Michigan—the claimant must have eligible costs.

METHODOLOGY OF THE STUDY

This discussion is based on an analysis of systematic samples with random starts of two types of claim resolution—awards and denials—taken from the total claims received and processed by the Michigan and Wisconsin victim-compensation programs in 1983.[28] In that year, Wisconsin awarded benefits to 335 victims or their surviving dependents, and Michigan to 952. Of these award cases, a sample of 213 cases was analyzed from Wisconsin and 317 from Michigan. In this same year, there were 852 cases in which compensation was denied in Michigan, and 217 in Wisconsin. Of these denial cases, a sample of 283 denials was analyzed in Michigan and 144 from Wisconsin.

Since we were concerned with the impact of gender differences, an obvious first step was to compare the percentages of female and male applicants. In 1983, 50 percent of the awards in the Wisconsin sample and 46 percent of the Michigan sample involved female victims. Victims were females in a smaller percentage of the denials than males: 39 percent in Wisconsin, 45 percent in Michigan. (See Table 2.2.)

The Awards

In Wisconsin, those eligible for benefits are persons who are victims of the 29 violent crimes listed in the enabling legislation and persons injured

Table 2.1
Reasons Applicants to the Crime Victim Compensation Programs in Wisconsin and Michigan Were Denied Benefits

Denial Reasons in Wisconsin	Denial Resons in Michigan
Cost Requirements: - Did not meet $200 minimum	- Did not suffer minimum out-of-pocket loss of $100 - Did not lose at least two continuous weeks earnings or support
Reporting Requirements: - Did not file within 2 years - Not reported to police or not reported within 5 days	- Did not file within 30 days or 90 days from death of victim or within 1 year with extension - Not reported to police within 48 hours - Did not provide requested information to Board
Lack of Cooperation: - Did not cooperate with police	- Did not cooperate with police
Contributory Conduct: - Committed a crime causing injury - Conduct contributed to injury	- Committed or was accomplice to crime causing injury - Conduct contributed to injury
No Crime/Crime Not Compensable: - Crime not compensable under the Act - No crime occured	- Crime not compensable under the Act - No crime occurred - Loss/damage to personal
Relationship with Offender: - Related to and living with offender - In a sexual relationship with offender - Living in same household with offender's relative, or accomplice - Victim is spouse, parent, child, brother, or sister of offended	- Living in same household with offender
No Eligible Costs: - No Claim: no medical expense, lost wages or dependency	
	Geographic Restrictions: - Not a state resident; did not suffer injuries in Michigan **Financial Hardship:** - Victim will not suffer Financial hardship if not granted financial assistance by program

while aiding victims or police officers attempting to apprehend a suspected criminal. Dependents of victims who are killed are also eligible. Wisconsin gives awards of up to $10,000 to victims with medical costs or lost wages not covered by another source, and the maximum award for funeral expenses is $2,000. Michigan defines victims as those injured or killed as the direct result of a crime, but no list of specific crimes is included in the enabling legislation. The state also extends benefits to those injured or killed

Table 2.2
Percentage of Cases Awarded and Denied Compensation, by Sex of Victim

	Wisconsin			Michigan	
		Victim's Sex			
	Female	Male		Female	Male
1983 Awards	65%	55%		53%	52%
1983 Denials	35%	45%		47%	48%
	100%	100%		100%	100%
	(n=162)	(n=195)		(n=273)	(n=237)
	$X^2=3.31$			$X^2=.04$	
	p<.10			N.S.	

while intervening in a crime and to the dependents of victims killed. Both states give benefits in similar categories: lost wages, medical expenses, funeral expenses, and loss of support. In addition, Wisconsin will compensate for clothing used for evidence and will make homeworker awards, emergency awards, and awards to cover attorney's fees (which can be 10 percent of the total award, but not an additional 10 percent). Only Michigan has emergency awards for expenses on this list.

One of the ways we expected apparently neutral laws to reflect discrimination against women was in granting male victims higher compensation for lost wages due to their generally higher wage levels. (The average awards to female and male victims in 1983 by both states are reported in Table 2.3.) Our expectations were met in Wisconsin, which based lost-wage benefits on the net wage of the victim.[29]

In Wisconsin, employed victims must have a physician declare that they cannot work for a period of time because of the injuries sustained. The compensation for lost wages is computed from the person's net wage and the number of days lost work (with a doctor's approval). Consequently, amounts received are a function of both the seriousness of the injuries (since more serious injuries mean more days lost from work) and the net wage of the victim. Since the average lost-wage award for males was $323 higher than the average for females in this state, male victims have higher net wages, more disabling injuries, or both.

However, our expectations were not met in Michigan. Societal differences in the wages of men and women were not evident in this state because the eligible pool of victims is poor by definition and there is a ceiling of $100 weekly on lost wages. (The administrator of the Michigan program ex-

Table 2.3

Mean (Average) Awards Given to Female and Male Crime Victims in 1983

	Wisconsin		Michigan	
	Female Victims	Male Victims	Female Victims	Male Victims
Type of Award				
Lost Wages	$230 (n=12)	$533 (n=26)	$969 (n=15)	$776 (n=36)
Medical Expenses	$676	$792	$1,452	$2,347
Funeral Expenses	$1,862 (n=15)	$1,884 (n=20)	$1,174 (n=77)	$1,181 (n=29)
Loss of Support	$6,660 (n=2)	$3,400 (n=1)	$13,500 (n=2)	$13,500 (n=1)
Other Awards	$48 (n=33)	$49 (n=9)	$1198 (n=32)	$364 (n=36)
Total Awards	$972 (n=106)	$1,122 (n=107)	$1,705 (n=139)	$2,048 (n=166)

For Wisconsin, the "Other Awards" category consists of payment for clothing used as evidence. In Michigan, this category includes all money paid directly to the victim (or the victim's dependents).

plained that if the benefits were raised to $200 a week or if the program were to cover all costs, the costs would be prohibitive and the program would be forced to shut down within three years.)[30] The average award is $886 higher in Michigan, and this may be due to the fact that this state compensates only people who demonstrate that they will suffer serious financial hardship if compensation is not granted. So, those who received compensation probably recouped all allowable expenses. In Wisconsin, financial hardship does not have to be demonstrated, and the program only covers expenses not covered by some other private or public source. It is much more likely that compensated victims in Wisconsin have insurance coverage and need less compensation from the program than is the case in Michigan.

In Michigan victims must have lost two weeks of work because of crime-related injuries to qualify for lost-wage compensation, but those who qualify receive the amount of their loss up to $100 per week. Since there is this ceiling, net wages are less important in this state, and there may be few differences in awards to employed male and to employed female victims. In addition, Michigan's financial hardship requirements disqualify victims of both sexes with good jobs. Employed victims who qualify are very likely to be employed in marginal, low-paying jobs.

Nonetheless, in both states male victims receive higher average total awards than females. Since men are more likely than women to be victims of battery crimes and crimes that inflict serious physical injuries, the programs in both states appear to respond to the needs of these seriously injured male victims.[31]

Eligibility Requirements

There are differences in eligibility requirements in the two states. First is the means test, required only in Michigan. This state's victims must demonstrate that they will suffer serious financial hardship if denied compensation, and applicants must report all financial resources, including all income and its sources, liquid and illiquid assets, and all monthly expenses. In Wisconsin, applicants must have exhausted all other sources of assistance before applying to the program, but no means test is employed. If victims have private insurance coverage or other public assistance, compensation is not denied but reduced by the amount of money received from these sources.

In the first years of the program, both states had minimal loss requirements. In Michigan, victims had to incur a minimum out-of-pocket loss of $100 or lose at least two continuous weeks' earnings or support; this minimum could be waived when the victim was retired because of age or disability. In the first few program years, Wisconsin had a $200 loss requirement, but in 1980 this was waived for victims of sexual assaults. In 1981, the Wisconsin legislature eliminated the minimal loss rule for all victims. Michigan retained its requirement, but in 1985, amendments were made to the enabling legislation that allowed program administrators to waive this minimum for victims of sexual assault as well as for retired or disabled persons. The minimum for all other victims, however, was raised from $100 to $200.

We anticipated that cost-containment provisions built into victim compensation programs would have a particularly negative impact on women. The most controversial class typically excluded from compensation comprises relatives of the offender, persons living in the same household as the offender, and/or persons engaged in a continual (sexual) relationship with the offender. In order to keep offenders from benefiting from compensation awards, both Wisconsin and Michigan have rules that make it hard for persons living with the offender to receive compensation. In Wisconsin the number of male and female victims denied compensation because they had some sort of personal relationship with the offender was very small. The Michigan statute has no provisions against providing compensation to persons who have had sexual relations with the offender or to relatives of the offender, but Michigan will not allow persons who live with the offender to be compensated—although the Michigan program will pay a service provider. This affects women who have left abusive husbands, since they were living with the offender at the time of the crime and do not qualify for benefits paid directly to them.

According to the Michigan law, loss of earnings is not covered if a wife is injured by her husband. What should the policy be if the woman is willing to cooperate in the prosecution of an abusive husband? The Michigan Compensation Board has tried to interpret the law as broadly as possible in this kind of case. If the husband is in custody or in jail, the board will make payments. It will not do so, however, if he is simply out of the house.[32] The Compensation Board believes that the Michigan law requires that the provision against the offender living in the same household with the victim should be interpreted to mean at the time of the offense, not at the time the claim is filed.[33]

In the early years of the program in Wisconsin, victims related to (or residing with) the offender and victims maintaining a sexual relationship with the offender were denied benefits. In the 1981 legislative session, compensation to these victims was authorized if judged to be in the interests of justice. Because of these changes, some victims previously ineligible for any compensation could now qualify. The program staff has the discretion to make or deny compensation in each case. Currently, if the victim is related to the offender or living in the same household with the offender, responsible for committing a crime that caused or contributed to the injury, or if the victim is known to have engaged in conduct that substantially contributed to the injury or death (or which the victim should have reasonably foreseen could lead to injury or death), a judgment is made. These factors may result in a denial, but they do not automatically require one.[34]

In comparing the reasons female and male victims of crimes other than sexual assault were denied compensation in Wisconsin, we found that the main reason female victims were denied compensation was because of no eligible costs. (See Table 2.4 for the full list of percentages.) It is unlikely that most of the female victims whose claims were denied because their expenses were minimal or nonexistent have their expenses covered by sources outside the compensation programs. If it is the case that they do not have this outside coverage, these figures verify that female victims incur physical injuries that are less costly than those of their male counterparts.

In Table 2.5, sexual assault victims and victims of crimes other than sexual assault in each state are compared on the reasons for denial. The denial category that contains most of the sexual assault cases is "no costs." These victims were most frequently denied compensation because they did not have sufficient medical costs, lost wages, or other eligible costs.

Some victims in this category may have been denied compensation because their expenses were covered by another source (most likely an insurance

Table 2.4
Gender Differences in the Percentage of Cases Denied Compensation, by Reason
for Denial (for crimes other than sexual assault)

Reasons for Denial	Wisconsin		Michigan	
	Female Victims 1983 (n=44)	Male Victims 1983 (n=36)	Female Victims 1983 (n=118)	Male Victims 1983 (n=156)
1) Minimum Cost Requirements	a ---	---	29%	25%
2) Reporting Requirements	3%	6%	14%	17%
3) No Cooperation/ Contributory Conduct	19%	48%	15%	13%
4) No Crime/Crime Not Compensable	25%	16%	29%	41%
5) Relationship With Offender	6%	3%	---	---
6) No Costs	47%	26%	---	---
7) Geographic Restrictions	---	---	13%	4%
	100%	99%*	100%	100%

* Rounding error.

a When the broken line appears, the reasons for denial in that category do not apply.

plan). Since Wisconsin has initiated the award for clothing replacement, fewer victims of sexual assault have been denied compensation because they failed to show sufficient losses. Clothing replacement is less likely to be covered under private insurance plans. It is impossible to determine the number denied compensation because no authorization was given for counseling. Although some of Wisconsin's sexual-assault cases were denied compensation because of reasons of conduct, this reason was more likely to be associated with cases involving the other crime categories. The program administrator and claims specialists do not believe that contributory conduct can be grounds for denying compensation in sexual assault cases.[35] In addition, no sexual-assault victims were denied compensation because of a

Table 2.5

The Percentage of Cases Denied Compensation by Reason for Denial:
A Comparison of Sexual Assault Victims and Victims of Other Types of Crime

	Wisconsin		Michigan	
	Sexual Assault Victims	Other Victims	Sexual Assault Victims	Other Victims
	1983 (n=20)	1983 (n=123)	1983 (n=9)	1983 (n=274)
Reasons for Denial				
1) Minimum Cost Requirements	a ---	---	33%	27%
2) Reporting Requirements	10%	5%	33%	16%
3) No Cooperation/ Contributory Conduct	20%	40%	11%	14%
4) No Crime/Crime Not Compensable	10%	19%	11%	36%
5) Relationship With Offender	0%	4%	---	---
6) No Costs	60%	32%	---	---
7) Geographic Restrictions	---	---	11%	8%
	100%	100%	99% *	101% *

* Rounding error.

a When the broken line appears instead of the percentage, the category is not applicable. In 1983, Wisconsin did not have a minimum cost requirement, and Wisconsin has never had geographic restrictions comparable to those in Michigan. In Michigan, there are no requirements comparable to Wisconsin's requirements concering the relationship the victims has with the offender and the denial category that is labeled "no cost."

personal relationship with the offender, which might involve a prior sexual relationship, being related to the offender, or living in the same household with the offender.

The Wisconsin claims specialists and the Director of the Wisconsin Crime Victims' Compensation Program recognize that sexual assault is often a "cheap" crime. They are aware that many male applicants involved in fights, especially bar fights, incur medical costs significantly higher than those associated with sexual assault.[36] This difference may account for the higher average medical compensation that men receive from the Wisconsin program. Since both Wisconsin and Michigan spend half their compensation totals on medical expenses, the fact that males receive higher medical compensation also carries over and affects the total.

In Michigan, only nine sexual-assault victims were denied compensation in 1983. One third were denied because of the minimum cost requirements, and another third were denied under the state's reporting requirements. In comparison, over a third of the victims of other crimes were denied compensation on the grounds that no crime had occurred or that the crime causing the injuries was not compensable. (The financial hardship requirement is not listed in the table because that provision was not given for any denials.)

Nonetheless, the awards for victims of sexual assault were very low in Michigan. This may be because Michigan will list any crime in which a homicide occurs as homicide, even if a rape occurred. It may also be due to the lack of visibility of the compensation program. The Michigan Board estimated that only about 30 percent of the potentially eligible crime victims apply for compensation. Board members believe that there are many victims of crime in Michigan who are still not aware of the program.[37] Although statistics on victims are very difficult to compile, the Michigan Compensation Board attempted to compare their claims with the National Crime Survey statistics for Michigan. They found that many more homicides than assaults appear to lead to claims filed with the board. The program administrator speculated that this is because the funeral homes—particularly in Wayne County (Detroit)—aggressively inform their customers of the program. The compensation program does provide information at hospitals, rape counseling centers, and shelters for battered women. However, the publicity does not seem as effective as that conducted through the funeral parlors. The program administrator also speculated that perhaps rape victims are unwilling to report their experience to even more agencies than they already must.

At this time, the Michigan Compensation Board will not cover moving costs, costs of changing locks, or other such costs that are commonly incurred by victims of rape. The Michigan program will and does provide for counseling. The program director spoke of a case where a minor had been raped by a member of her family. The program did provide for costs at the treatment center. A program has recently opened in a Lansing hospital to treat and counsel crime victims. Although the program was too new to have had any applicants, the program administrator of the Michigan program explained that much of the incentive for understanding the need of victims of violent crimes to receive counseling, especially counseling some time after the crime, is based on the research on postshock syndrome among Vietnam veterans. Qualifying for counseling may be a problem because of the requirement that the claim be filed within a year of the crime. However, the board has been willing to reopen cases when there is evidence that psychological counseling is needed for delayed reactions.[38]

In Wisconsin, the program director is also conscious of the sexual victims' needs for counseling. One of the steps he is taking is the drafting of a manual for hospital personnel and people in the state's Victim and Witness Assistance Program who refer victims to the compensation program. The manual would make it very explicit that counseling is an eligible expense. Physicians in Wisconsin also need to be made aware that counseling for victims of rape can be covered only with their authorization.

The program administrators in Wisconsin have continued to change that state's requirements to meet the needs of rape victims. At the present, they are working to increase the maximum clothing replacement award to $200 and to include additional money for the replacement of bedding or linens held for evidence. A proposal has also been drafted to request authorization for payment to cover clean-up costs associated with crimes. Although the program director of the Michigan program was convinced when first interviewed that the minimum-loss requirement was not a serious factor in limiting the number of rape victims eligible for compensation, this requirement has now been eliminated. In addition, Michigan rape victims are not responsible for the costs of forensic exams.

It does not appear that counseling is being authorized to any great extent in either state. In Michigan, a very small number of the victims who file claims ask the board for money, and of those who do, few ask for counseling. Even when states do not have minimum-cost requirements, the fact that so many female victims and victims of sexual assaults are denied compensation because they are judged to have no eligible costs raises the suspicion that victims suffering psychological trauma are not being recognized. If a sizeable number of these victims in either state were being compensated, there would be a stronger relationship between crimes of sexual assault and compensation awards. If a realistic evaluation of the needs of rape victims were considered in the award procedures, rape would not be perceived as a "cheap" crime.

Although both the Wisconsin and Michigan programs provide compensation for loss of support, neither program has translated that into providing safe shelter for victims of domestic violence. In Wisconsin, loss-of-support awards are given when the victim dies and is responsible for supporting one or more dependents. The amount is figured by computing four times the victim's net yearly income, and from this total all life insurance, other insurance and Social Security benefits are deducted. The amount awarded cannot exceed $10,000. Michigan's loss-of-support awards are based on the needs of the dependents and the resources of the victim. In Michigan, to recover out-of-pocket loss, a person must show at least $100 in medical expenses. To recover lost earnings or lost support a person must have lost at least two continuous weeks of earnings or support. A victim is compensated for actual lost wages but not more than $100 for each week of lost earnings or—in the case of death—lost support. When the victim has an injury that leads to more than two weeks of lost wages, she or he is compensated for the time of the disability. In 1984, the Michigan Supreme Court ruled that the board should take into consideration "services in kind" when computing lost wages. In the particular case, a victim's husband sued for loss of child care and housekeeping. The Court ruled that the board should consider such losses.[39] Recent Michigan legislation has attempted to rule out such claims by defining support as actual monetary payment.

Nonetheless, there has been no movement to compensate women for loss of shelter when they are victims of domestic violence. Loss of support from physically abusive husbands is not considered a compensable claim. When the suggestion was made to the Michigan Board that it should be, the board members responded that such consideration would bankrupt the program.[40] In case of domestic violence in Michigan, persons living with the offender at the time of the crime are eligible only for compensation paid directly to health-care providers. In Wisconsin, before program administrators were given the authority to make decisions "in the interest of justice" in cases where the victim had some personal relationship to the offender, battered women and their children could receive no benefits at all.

In Wisconsin, which bases compensation for lost wages on the net wage of the victim, the amounts awarded reflect societal differences. Since Wisconsin also bases its loss-of-support payments on income, the same dynamic is at work. Gender differences in income produce higher loss-of-support payments for the dependents of male victims than for the dependents of female victims. In Michigan, however, because of financial hardship requirements, minimum work-loss requirements, and a very low weekly ceiling on compensation for lost wages, we found that gender differences were not reflected in amounts awarded. Michigan's requirements appear to restrict eligibility to only those victims who are both needy and seriously disabled, and the same financial hardship criteria are used to judge the needs of the victim's descendents. Gender differences are less easily identified among the most impoverished.

CONCLUSION

Although compensation programs vary from state to state in structure and eligibility requirements, such programs do indeed mirror gender differences found in American society. Compensation programs were developed to assist victims of crime, but the major crimes that victimize women were virtually excluded from the programs. Benefits were often determined in ways that were advantageous to male victims. Although both the Wisconsin and Michigan program provide compensation for loss of support, neither program has translated that into providing safe shelter for victims of domestic violence. Loss of support from physically abusive husbands is not considered a compensable claim. When the suggestion was made to the Michigan Board that it should be, the board members responded with concerns about the costs of such services.

Victim-compensation programs are not created to correct imbalances between men and women in their rates of employment, earning power, and income levels. These societal differences, however, become important when compensation benefits are based on financial need, employment status, and wage levels, and are restricted by some minimum-cost requirements. Since women are less likely to be the victims of crime than men, a program to compensate victims of crime can be expected to provide more assistance to men than to women. The issue is not that women get smaller amounts of compensation for rape than men get for barroom brawls. The issue is that rape victims and victims of domestic abuse have needs that are not being met. The reasons why they are not being met can help us to understand the complexity of existing inequalities. Furthermore, such understanding makes clear the importance of understanding equality as equality of results.

While an understanding of equality as equality of results will not solve the problems created by existing inequalities, this understanding of equality is more appropriate than other understandings of equality because equality of results directs those concerned with equality to take into consideration differences, to look to what a program accomplished, and to avoid excessive commitment to any one program. A policy of equality of results does not mean that equality requires identical outcomes in all situations. However, a policy of equality of results does mean that there will be a concern with minimizing differences in the outcomes of policies. Thus, it looks at policy outcomes: what public policies lead to more equality and which policies produce less equality between members of the society.

One of the lessons we can learn about equality from our analysis of compensation programs is that treating people the same, when their situations are not the same, will lead to increased inequalities. An evaluation of compensation of victims of crime programs clearly illustrates that treating men and women the same will not solve the problem of inequalities between the sexes. Rules that are applied similarly in different situations cannot ensure equality. Women are victims of different kinds of crimes. Such differences lead to other differences that make any program that does not consider gender differences inadequate in meeting the needs of women who are victims of violence. Equality does not involve treating people the same. Rather, equality requires treating people equally well. But what is equally well? There is, of course, no precisely correct answer to that question. However, we do know that sometimes it is necessary to consider differences in order to treat citizens equally well.

A second lesson provided by this analysis is that women and men who are feminists must be involved in the development of policies, in their im-

plementation, and in the evaluation of their effectiveness. Certainly movements towards equality require the removal of obstacles to greater
participation in public life. Women's lack of representation in shaping policies means that public policy is not as effective as it might be in meeting
women's needs. While men and women are differently affected by policies,
those differences are not only ignored, but the problem is usually defined
in simply male terms. When women are not involved in the shaping of
policy, the right questions are not asked. This was evident in the analysis
of programs of compensation for victims of crime. While many legislators
approve of bills to assist victims of crime, they tend to be cautious in
designing these programs and do not want to sign a blank check. Several
of these cost-containment procedures have severely limited the effectiveness
of such programs for women.

No one asked: "But what about victims of rape or domestic abuse?" This
omission could be seen both as a failure of imagination and as a direct result
of the exclusion of women from policy-making positions. When the suggestion was made that compensation programs should provide support for
victims of domestic abuse, board members raised questions about fiscal
responsibility. Such constant budgetary complaints conceal an excellent example of institutional sexism. In effect, the policy analyst or bureaucrat
who says, "We don't have enough money to compensate women for domestic violence" is really arguing that scarce available funds should be spent
on men's problems (bar fights) rather than women's (domestic abuse). Why?
If funds are limited, why not introduce *limited* compensation for domestic
abuse and drop bar fights off the list?

Such discrimination is usually not noticed because women are often invisible in the conception, development, and evaluation of such programs.
While public policy usually ignored the concerns of women, eventually some
dimensions of such gender discrimination are recognized. For example, the
compensation programs for victims of crime initially ignored the specific
needs of rape victims. More recent legislation has been adopted to accommodate some of those needs. Nonetheless, these programs are seldom quite
as effective for women as they are for men. If such programs are to be more
effective for women, women and men who are feminists must be involved
in the development of policies, in their implementation, and in the evaluation
of their effectiveness. Women should be involved in state legislatures and
be members of compensation boards. They should be directors of programs—as well as in staff positions.

A third lesson that this analysis offers is that it is not, however, simply
participation that counts but certain kinds of participation with specific
results. Participation is a necessary but not a sufficient condition for equality
of results. Because treating people differently in order to treat them equally
well is far more challenging than treating everyone the same, it is essential
to look at the outcomes of public policies.

If race and gender are not to be obstacles to access to the advantages of society, public policy must be directed towards lessening the obstacles of race and gender. African-Americans should have no more obstacles than the average white person. The average woman should have no more obstacles than the average male. Thus, the desired outcome of compensation programs is the elimination of all internal and external barriers to women being helped as much by the programs as men are helped. It is not absolutely clear what this would involve.

We are so far from equality it is difficult to see what it would look like. We could not identify either the Michigan or Wisconsin program as better suited to achieving equality. We could identify less gender differences in the Michigan program but that is because Michigan has a means test. As a result only the poorest citizens receive benefits. It is more difficult to find gender differences in the awards that are granted since this population does not reflect the societal differences between male and female incomes. It would seem to be more egalitarian to not require a means test. In that case, the Wisconsin program would seem to be more egalitarian. However, since the Michigan program eliminates so many of the claims that the Wisconsin program would include, it then is able to compensate the most destitute at higher levels of compensation.

Thus, the interactions among inequalities are complex. No one program alone can correct existing inequalities; we must try to keep programs from reinforcing them. We must attempt to make modest improvements while avoiding blatant discrimination. To do this, we must be flexible and continually experiment. The only check on increased inequalities is constant awareness of goals and constant evaluation of policies. Thus, a proper understanding of equality requires that any one program must be evaluated in a larger perspective that is not obsessively committed to any one program or group of programs but rather favors equality.

Equality of results is not the whole answer to the problems of the perpetuation of inequalities, but that does not mean we have no answers. Some policies are steps toward equality or away from it. An analysis of one program can help us to locate the parameters involved in a proper understanding of equality. Such an understanding would require *both* Wisconsin and Michigan to make extensive changes in their programs.

For example, if feminists were effective participants in the development and implementation of crime victim compensation programs, certainly the program would not exclude major crimes that affect women. Victims would not be excluded merely because they had been sexually involved with an offender; certainly rape victims would be compensated for counseling, and possibly for loss of clothing and for moving expenses. Perhaps some support would be provided for victims of domestic abuse.

The result of all of this would not, of course, be equality of total outcomes. This understanding of equality does not mean absolute equality of outcomes.

Such an understanding would possibly lessen existing inequalities. It would certainly resist adding to them. At this time it is most important to work towards greater gender equality. Today differences do exist between the treatment of men and the treatment of women. Will gender differences disappear at some future time? Any commitment to differences must not be static. Under equal treatment differences will certainly change and perhaps some gender differences will lessen. Maybe then other differences will require more attention. Probably there will still be some differences, although gender differences may not be as important as some other differences—family position, social class, or political ideology. Perhaps if racial differences lessen, class differences may become more important.

Thus this research demonstrates that inequality of outcomes is produced by policies that do not take socially significant differences into account. The significance of this insight is not limited to unequal outcomes based on gender. It may well be that these programs are not well designed to serve the needs of other special populations. The programs have been criticized, for example, for not serving the interests of the elderly in that victims may not be compensated for loss of such property as eyeglasses. (The Michigan Board will cover the loss of dentures or glasses because they are considered "optional prosthetic devices.")

The point is not to create specific programs for women, the elderly, and other special populations, although that may be precisely what is done in special demonstration projects. While such programs create the perception that women and the elderly receive "special" attention, the larger programs primarily benefit males. We must recognize that program rules will have different impacts on different groups of victims. This recognition should lead to provisions in victim-compensation programs that take into consideration the needs of all groups of victims. Also we must continually reevaluate the outcomes of these programs. The goal should be to create programs for all citizens—not all of whom are nonelderly white males.

NOTES

We would like especially to thank David Zimny for his assistance with data analysis and editing. We are also grateful to Katherine McCracken for her editing assistance. In addition, we would like to thank Margaret Gillis for her help in research and collecting and coding the Michigan data, and Kristin Steger for her help in collecting the Wisconsin data.

1. Mary Lou Kendrigan, *Political Equality in a Democratic Society: Women in the United States* (Westport, Conn.: Greenwood Press, 1984).

2. The primary impetus for this research was a project I participated in while a Research Associate for the Wisconsin Legislative Reference Bureau: see Mary Lou Kendrigan, *Compensation for Victims of Crime* (Madison, Wisc.: Legislative Reference Bureau, August 1972).

3. Deborah P. Kelly, "Delivering Legal Services to Victims: An Evaluation and Prescription," *The Justice System Journal* 9 (1984): 64.

4. U.S. Department of Justice, *Policy Briefs: Crime Victim Compensation* (Washington, D.C.: Office of Development, Testing and Dissemination, National Institute of Justice, 1980), p. 1.

5. Paul S. Hudson, "The Crime Victim and the Criminal Justice System: Time for a Change," *Pepperdine Law Review* 11 (1984): 23.

6. Daniel McGillis and Patricia Smith, *Compensating Victims of Crime: An Analysis of American Programs* (Washington, D.C.: U.S. Department of Justice, National Institute of Justice, Office of Development, Testing and Discrimination, July 1983), p. 52.

7. Daniel McGillis, Patricia Smith, and Albert D. Biderman, "Sources of Data for Victimology," *Journal of Criminal Law and Criminology* 72 no. 2 (1981).

8. McGillis and Smith, *Compensating Victims of Crime.*

9. Josephine Gittler, "Expanding the Role of the Victim in a Criminal Action: An Overview of Issues and Problems," *Pepperdine Law Review: Victims' Rights Symposium* 11 (1984): 149.

10. Richard Aynes, "Constitutional Considerations: Government Responsibility and the Right Not to Be a Victim," *Pepperdine Law Review: Victims' Rights Symposium* 11 (1984): 115.

11. Sandra Wexler, "Battered Women and Public Policy," *Women, Power and Policy*, ed. Ellen Boneparth (New York: Pergamon Press, 1982).

12. Melitta Schmideberg, "Criminals and Their Victims," *International Journal of Offender Therapy and Comparative Criminology* 24, no. 2 (1980); Stephanie Riger, "On Women," in *Reactions to Crime*, ed. D. A. Lewis (Beverly Hills, Calif.: Sage, 1981).

13. Patricia Resick, "The Trauma of Rape and the Criminal Justice System," *The Justice System Journal* 9, no. 1 (1984): 53.

14. United States Department of Justice, Bureau of Justice Statistics, *Family Violence*, April 1984.

15. Wexler, "Battered Women and Public Policy."

16. Lisa Brodyaga, Margaret Gates, Susan Singer, Marna Tucker, and Richardson White, *Rape and Its Victims: A Report for Citizens, Health Facilities and Criminal Justice Agencies* (Washington, D.C.: Government Printing Office, 1975).

17. United States Department of Justice, Bureau of Justice Statistics, *Criminal Victimization in the United States, 1972–80 Trends*, September 1983.

18. Kelly, "Delivering Legal Services to Victims," p. 64.

19. Charles W. Dean and Mary DeBruyn-Kops, *The Crime and Consequences of Rape* (Springfield, Ill.: Thomas, 1982).

20. Riger, "On Women."

21. U.S. Department of Justice, *Criminal Victimization in the United States* (Washington, D.C.: National Criminal Justice Information and Statistics Services, Law Enforcement Assistance Administration, 1979), p. 56.

22. McGillis and Smith, *Compensating Victims of Crime.*

23. Resick, "The Trauma of Rape."

24. Riger, "On Women."

25. Mary E. Baluss, "Services for Victims of Crimes: A Developing Opportunity," *Evaluation and Change*, 1980.

26. Mary Lou Kendrigan and Mary Ann E. Steger, "Compensation of Victims of Crime: A Feminist Issue" (Paper presented to the Annual Meeting of the Academy of Criminal Justice Sciences, Chicago, March 28–30, 1984); Mary Lou Kendrigan and Mary Ann E. Steger, "Gender Differences in Denying Compensation to Victims of Crime in Wisconsin" (Paper presented to the Annual Meeting of the Midwest Political Science Association, Chicago, April 11–15, 1984); Mary Ann E. Steger and Mary Lou Kendrigan, "The Impact of Compensation Programs for Victims of Crime on Women" (Paper presented to the Annual Meeting of the American Political Science Association, Washington, August 30–September 2, 1984).

27. U.S. Department of Justice, *Policy Briefs: Crime Victim Compensation* (Washington, D.C.: Office of Development, Testing and Dissemination, National Institute of Justice, 1980).

28. The Michigan samples were taken from computerized summaries of the case files. Separate random samples were drawn from the claims denied and the claims granted. The claims had been filed according to the case number assigned to them on arrival in the Lansing office, and a table of random numbers was used to choose the claims for the samples. Every third one of the claims denied and every third one of the claims granted were included in the sample.

The Wisconsin samples for 1983 were taken from the actual case files stored in the Madison office. The same procedure described above was used to create a sample of claims granted and a sample of claims denied. The 1979 denials are all cases decided on in the year that were recorded in the summary report prepared by Wisconsin's Department of Industry, Labor, and Human Relations.

29. Due to the small size of the case samples, the cell frequencies in Tables 2.3–2.5 are too small to warrant the usual statistical tests for independence or difference of means. These tables are presented here for their heuristic value, not to test any statistical hypothesis.

30. Michael Fullwood, Program Administrator, Michigan Crime Victims Compensation Board, interview, May 1986.

31. Empirical verification of this is found in an article on the Wisconsin denials: Mary Ann E. Steger, "The Impact of Eligibility Rules on Females and Male Crime Victims in a State Victim Compensation Program," *The Justice System Journal* 10 (1985): 193–212.

32. Fullwood interview.

33. Ibid.

34. State of Wisconsin, "Victim and Witness Services, 1981–1982 Annual Report," *Family Violence*, April 1984.

35. Richard H. Anderson, Executive Director of the Office of Crime Victim Services, interview, Madison, Wisc.; February 1985.

36. Ibid.

37. State of Michigan, Crime Victims Compensation Board, Annual Report, 1982–1983.

38. Fullwood interview.

39. Jerome v. Crime Victims Compensation Board, 29 June 1984.

40. State of Michigan, Members of the Crime Victims Compensation Board, interview July 1986.

3

MANUFACTURING JOB LOSS AMONG BLUE-COLLAR WOMEN: AN ASSESSMENT OF DATA AND POLICY

CYNTHIA DEITCH, THOMAS C. NOWAK, AND KAY A. SNYDER

Job displacement for women is significant. Furthermore, the difficulties surrounding job displacement are different in some respects for women than for men. Women who lose their jobs have greater difficulties finding other jobs. Displaced blue-collar factory women workers, when they are reemployed, are more likely to skid downward into occupations which tend to have lower wages and fewer benefits. Yet when the human plight of displaced workers is chronicled by the media and addressed by policymakers, displaced women workers are rarely, if ever, mentioned. Women are the invisible displaced workers. The authors of this chapter argue that without a full employment policy, equal opportunity employment and affirmative action policy could do little to protect women workers or their short-lived gains. Since it was market mechanisms which created the employment or inequality problem in the first place, they advocate policies explicitly aimed at redirecting market forces to institute equality, restructure social relations, and supersede market allocations.

The decline of manufacturing production within the United States, and consequent job loss, has given rise to wide-ranging and intense policy debates on employment, industrial, and import policies. When the human plight of displaced workers—that is, workers who have lost jobs due to partial or total plant closings or relocations—is chronicled by the media and addressed by policymakers, displaced women workers are rarely if ever mentioned. The silence on women is not because women are unaffected, but rather, we believe, because the dominant imagery associated with displaced workers is of smokestack industries and the *male* blue-collar worker. Although women are a significant segment of dislocated workers, they have been ignored to a large degree in the media and in academic research. Women have been the invisible displaced workers, in part because their jobs, including their blue-collar jobs in manufacturing, tend to be in the least privileged sectors of the economy. Women are disproportionately located in low-wage jobs in smaller firms or plants with weak or no unions—workplaces that receive little publicity when they close down. Yet clearly such job loss is significant, for women as well as men.

The purpose of this chapter is to show that the decline in manufacturing jobs has, indeed, seriously affected significant numbers of women workers and that the economic problems and prospects facing these women merit attention. We analyze the situation of displaced blue-collar women in relationship to economic change and public policy affecting employment opportunities for women, as well as manufacturing employment for both sexes. We show that in the 1970s, small but significant numbers of women entered higher-wage, blue-collar jobs in manufacturing and improved their positions within these industries. These gains were then undermined by manufacturing job loss in the 1980s. Much of this chapter focuses on the wave of plant closings and layoffs in the relatively high unemployment years of the early 1980s. The trends and patterns that we analyze have long-term implications for women's employment and public policy. Plant closings and large scale layoffs have become a continuing fact of economic life in the United States, in "good" times as well as bad.

At the same time that women were winning access to some of the better-paying, blue-collar jobs in the 1970s, fundamental changes were occurring in the United States and world economy which produced a decline in manufacturing jobs in many industries in the United States. These changes, associated with the term "deindustrialization," have included a shift in capital investment from older industrial areas of the northeastern United States to newer areas in the South and West, from the United States and more developed capitalist countries to lower-wage areas of the world; a shift from productivity increasing investment to wage decreasing investment strategies, including a rapid increase in mergers and acquisitions. For some industries, this has meant that the more labor intensive aspects of production were moved abroad while new technologies decreased the demand for labor in those manufacturing jobs which remained in the United States. In other industries, such as steel, jobs were lost in the United States because corporations failed to modernize and remain competitive. Overall, the dynamics of deindustrialization have resulted in large scale job loss for blue-collar workers in many manufacturing industries.

What diverse political perspectives on deindustrialization have made clear, from Harrison and Bluestone (1988) to *Business Week* (1986), is that the United States lacks a consistent industrial policy for planning and coordinating economic change. We argue that without a *full employment* policy, *equal opportunity employment* and affirmative action policy could do little to protect women workers or their short-lived gains. At the same time that deindustrialization, economic restructuring of traditional industries, and a recession induced by tight monetary policy were leaving millions of workers without employment in the early 1980s, social welfare safety net policies were dismantled or curtailed, and significant reversals in affirmative action and equal employment policies were initiated. This is the economic and policy climate in which significant manufacturing job loss, for women and men, occurred.

The material presented in this chapter is organized in four parts. First we discuss why blue-collar manufacturing jobs are a significant source of employment opportunity for women. We examine aggregate level national statistics indicating the increasing significance of women's economic contributions to families, the extent and location of women's employment in manufacturing, the gains made by women in better-paying, traditionally male industry sectors and occupations within manufacturing in the 1970s, and the overall employment reduction sustained by many manufacturing industries in the 1980s. Next we briefly consider the case of one particular industry—basic steel—because it represents a prototypical case of a male-dominated, good-paying manufacturing industry which reluctantly opened its gates to women in the 1970s. Women made substantial numerical gains over just a few years; but the precipitous decline of steel manufacturing and employment in the 1980s virtually wiped out women's gains. Subsequently, we turn to individual level data from a special national survey of displaced workers conducted by the U.S. Department of Labor (1984). These data, along with the findings of several different case studies of displaced workers from specific plants and industries, enable us to discuss the differential impact of the loss of manufacturing jobs on women and men, focusing on some of the particular difficulties facing women, as well as the patterns of economic loss common to women and men. In the final section we discuss policy, critiquing the limitations of existing policy and indicating sources of constraint on future change, both for women's employment and for broader economic policies affecting employment in manufacturing.

THE IMPORTANCE OF BETTER PAID MANUFACTURING JOBS FOR WOMEN

The loss of better-paid, blue-collar jobs in manufacturing during the 1980s was especially problematic for women because it occurred at a time when women's economic contributions to families had become increasingly significant. As Bell (1983, p. 7) notes, the depression of 1982–1983 was "the first to occur since the breadwinner vanished and the typical family appeared which receives income from two or more earners." Whereas in 1960 less than one third (31.6 percent) of husbands who were employed had a wife who was actively seeking work or actually working for wages, this figure had nearly doubled by 1983. By then, a full 59.6 percent of employed husbands had wives in the labor force (U.S. Bureau of the Census 1985, p. 399). As the percentage of families with a full-time homemaker continues to decline, the dependence of families on women's earnings could be even more important in subsequent recessions.

The high rate of unemployment in many economically depressed regions of the United States in the first half of the 1980s also meant that as married men lost their jobs, such families had to rely more and more on the earning power of women. In 1960, for example, only 40.1 percent of unemployed husbands had a wife who was working at or actively seeking a paid job, whereas a full 62.1 percent did by 1983 at the peak of a recession—even though the number of unemployed husbands during this time period had more than doubled (U.S. Bureau of the Census 1985, p. 399).

Increasingly, the multiearner family has become typical, as well as necessary, to meet family financial need. Only one third (33.9 percent) of wage earning, married couple families in 1982 received a wage or salary solely from the husband (U.S. Department of Labor, *Earnings of Workers and Their Families*, 1983, Table 1). Additionally, more than two and one half million wives in 1982 were the sole employed member of their families— an increase of nearly 44 percent since 1978. By 1986 the median income of married couple families with the wife in the paid labor force was 50 percent higher (or about $12,500 greater) than the median income of families with a nonworking wife (U.S. Department of Labor, Women's Bureau, 1988). These income differences have been growing over time.

Women's income is important not only because most families no longer are supported solely by a male breadwinner, but also because more women than ever before are responsible for maintaining families. By the height of the recession in the early 1980s, for example, one out of three breadwinners (defined as the sole job holder in a family) was a women (Bell 1983, p. 3). The number of women maintaining families on their own, with no spouse present, more than doubled from 4.5 million in 1960 to 9.7 million in 1982 (U.S. Department of Labor, *The Female-Male Earnings Gap*, 1982, p. 1). By 1987, 16.6 percent of families were maintained by women (U.S. Department of Labor, Women's Bureau, 1988). Characteristically, families headed by women suffer from high unemployment and low income: in 1986, for example, one-third (34 percent) of the families maintained by women (no husband present) had incomes below the poverty level. As Bell (1983, p. 10) notes, wage loss tends to have a severe impact on family income when unemployment strikes a family maintained by a woman. For such families, job loss is generally not cushioned by someone else's paycheck.

Clearly, the loss of better-paying factory jobs dealt a serious blow to women, both in their efforts to support themselves and their families and to contribute adequately to family income. Rosen (1987, Chap. 8) has found that married blue-collar women do not drop out of the labor force when they lose their jobs. Both married and single women continue looking for work when they are laid off because their paychecks are not expendable.

In this chapter, we focus specifically on blue-collar manufacturing jobs for several reasons. First, blue-collar women are neglected in much of the writing on gender and public policy. Disproportionate attention has been focused on the minority of women who are highly educated professionals. The 1980 census shows that only 15 percent of all employed women (and 20 percent of men) had completed the basic four years of college. Even among the age group with the highest educational attainment—25 to 34 year olds—only 24 percent of the employed women (and 27 percent of the men) had completed four years of college. Thus, the vast majority of women in the U.S. labor force lack the credentials and training to compete for high status professional jobs. Second, blue-collar manufacturing jobs, particularly in durable goods industries such as steel, auto, and machinery, have traditionally paid much higher wages than the service industry jobs in which most women are located, as shown in Table 3.1. Therefore, the expanded opportunity for women to move into some of the better paying manufacturing jobs in the 1970s was an important source of movement toward greater sexual equality, higher earnings, and occupational mobility for women. We focus on manufacturing industries because this is where most, though not all, blue-collar women are employed.[1] Although the number of manufacturing jobs held by women as well as men declined in the 1970s, women's share of the existing blue-collar manufacturing jobs has not diminished (see Table 3.2).

The data in column "a" of Table 3.1 demonstrate the economic importance of production jobs in manufacturing relative to nonsupervisory jobs in other sectors. Weekly earnings for workers in most manufacturing industries are higher than the average for all industries, and are considerably higher than in the predominantly female, growing service sectors where most women find jobs. In 1985, 72 percent of all women on private, nonagricultural payrolls in the United States were in the three service categories (retail trade, finance, and "services") shown in Table 3.1; 18 percent were on manufacturing payrolls (U.S. Department of Labor, *Employment and Earnings*, March 1986). Actually, the difference in economic rewards between blue-collar manufacturing jobs and others tends to be understated in Table 3.1. The better-paying manufacturing jobs also generally have better health and welfare benefits than do the service sector jobs. Many jobs in retail sales and personal services include no benefits or very limited ones.

Table 3.1

Wages, Percent Female, and Employment Trends for Selected Industries

	Weekly Earnings 1985	Percent Female 1985	Thousands of Jobs Lost or Gained	
			1979-85	1979-89
	(a)	(b)	(c)	(d)
Private sector total	$301.16	43.9%	+5547	+13158
All Manufacturing	385.56	32.5	-1854	-1691
Durable goods manufacturing	415.71	26.3	-1418	-1422
Selected Durable Categories:				
Primary metals	481.31	12.7	- 338	- 389
—Steel	548.69	9.0	- 263	- 237
Transportation equip.	541.45	18.1	- 124	- 148
—Motor Vehicles	584.64	19.2	- 110	- 98
Machinery, except electrical	427.04	21.8	-1216	- 334
Fabricated metal products	398.96	22.1	- 182	- 226
Electrical & Electronic Equip.	384.48	41.8	- 11	- 188
Instruments & Related				
Products	376.79	42.8	- 7	+ 7
Nondurable Goods manufact.	343.73	41.5	- 407	- 269
Selected Nondurable Categories:				
Petroleum & coal products	605.12	15.8	- 28	- 31
Food & kindred products	340.75	31.1	- 31	+ 1
Printing & publishing	365.31	42.1	+ 112	+ 195
Textile mill products	367.06	47.7	- 177	- 143
Leather & products	216.50	59.4	- 75	- 92
Apparel & other textile				
products	207.64	80.4	- 165	- 196
Selected Nonmanufacturing Categories:				
Retail Trade	177.31	51.8	+2431	+3849
Finance, insurance and				
real estate	289.02	61.2	+ 798	+1161
Services	260.76	59.8	+4894	+8281

All of the data in this table are annual figures based on the Bureau of Labor Statistics quarterly survey of establishment payrolls. Columns (a), (c), and (d) are for production workers in manufacturing and nonsupervisory workers in nonmanufacturing categories, on private nonagricultural payrolls.

Source: Employment and Earnings, January 1982, January 1986, January 1990.

Column (b) is calculated from payroll data on women and all employees.

Source: Employment and Earnings, March 1986.

For the growing number of women who support themselves or maintain families and have no other source of health benefits, the lack of a decent benefits package is a very real problem.

Several significant patterns are evident in Table 3.1. First, among the selected industries shown, generally the higher the percentage of women in an industry, the lower the wages. This appears within both the durable and nondurable goods categories in Table 3.1. Second, the *durable* goods producing industries tend to be more predominantly male and better paying than the nondurable goods industries. The dual economy and labor market segmentation literature discussed briefly below suggests why these patterns appear. Third, the vast majority (over 90 percent) of the manufacturing jobs lost between from 1979 to 1985 were never replaced in the subsequent "recovery" years.

Durable goods industries are more likely to be capital intensive, with fewer firms dominating the market, and employers placing more value on a relatively experienced, stable production labor force—which typically meant a more male work force (e.g., Edwards et al. 1976; Tolbert et al. 1980; Gordon et al. 1982). In the post–World War II decades of economic growth, unions in many durable goods industries such as steel and autos succeeded, until recent rounds of concessions, in tying wage increases to productivity increases. In recent decades, however, the stability and solvency of many durable industries such as steel eroded in the face of intense international competition. Consequently, durable goods industries face market pressures previously characteristic only of nondurable industries and have responded by seeking employment reductions and wage concessions. Job loss in these industries is evident in columns "c" and "d" of Table 3.1.

In nondurable industries such as textiles, clothing, and shoes, there are a larger number of smaller shops; production tends to be more labor intensive; labor is less organized; unions are weaker, wages are lower, and more women are employed. These industries have been affected by lower-priced foreign competition, including the contracting out of production to low wage factories overseas, for several decades (e.g., Nash and Fernandez-Kelly 1983). Thus, within manufacturing as in much of the economy, a dual or segmented labor market exists, with women and minorities disproportionately concentrated in the lower-paying industries and smaller firms. The growth of low-paying service sector jobs employing large numbers of women and minorities has reinforced the dual labor market, as suggested by Smith (1984) and as evident in the wage and employment figures in Table 3.1.

Durable goods manufacturing averages a higher ratio of skilled to semi-skilled blue-collar jobs than does nondurable manufacturing. Within both manufacturing sectors, skilled workers earn more and are more predominantly male than is the case for semiskilled workers. The 1970 census shows the following median annual earnings for women (not restricted to full time or year round): In durable goods manufacturing, women in crafts earned

$4917 and operatives earned $4262; in nondurable goods, women in crafts earned $4364 and operatives earned $3375. We are interested in seeing what gains women made in entering the three higher-paying, more predominantly male categories since the early 1970s.

Trends in Blue-Collar Manufacturing Employment for Women

The data in Table 3.2 show that between 1972 (the first year for which this data series is available) and 1979 women gained in both skilled and semiskilled durable goods manufacturing, and in skilled nondurable manufacturing.[2] In contrast, women experienced a net decrease in the semiskilled nondurable category in the 1970s and the 1980s. The trends noted above were in absolute numbers of women and women's relative share of total employment. The largest concentration of blue-collar women, however, remains in the lower-paying semiskilled nondurable category.

In absolute numbers, the most significant *gain* evident in Table 3.2 was in semiskilled durable goods manufacturing between 1972 and 1979, with a net increase of 524,000 jobs for women. This is also the category which shows the greatest job *loss* for women after 1979. Between 1979 and 1985, women lost all of the previous gain and then some—a total of 635,000 jobs. Only a small portion of this loss—113,000 jobs—was recouped in 1985–1989. Women's share of the remaining semiskilled durable goods jobs by 1989 was less than it had been in 1979. In contrast, women experienced gains, in absolute numbers employed and relative to men, in *skilled* blue-collar manufacturing jobs. The number of women involved, however, is dramatically smaller in the skilled than semiskilled categories. Additionally, women's employment in skilled jobs in durable goods industries—the highest paying of the four divisions examined here—declined somewhat after 1985.

Another way to evaluate the data in Table 3.2 is to calculate the percentage change in the number of women employed for different time periods. For durable goods manufacturing, there was a 42.5 percent increase in women between 1972 and 1979 (from 1,404,000 to 2,001,000). In contrast, there was a 14.9 percent decrease from 1979 to 1989. For nondurable manufacturing there was a 1.4 percent decline from 1972 to 1979, and a 6.2 decline from 1979 to 1989. For comparison, it may be noted that in the nonmanufacturing sector (all services, trade, finance, etc.) the 1972–1979 years witnessed a 32 percent marginal increase in all women's employment; and the 1979–1985 period shows continued, though slower, growth with a 16.4 percent increase. In other words, during the 1970s, women entered blue-collar, durable goods manufacturing jobs at a faster rate than they entered the more rapidly growing services sector (42.5 percent versus 32 percent). In the 1980s, however, this trend clearly reversed, with a decline in the numbers of women employed in manufacturing, and a slower but continuing

Table 3.2
Trends in Blue-Collar Manufacturing Employment for Women[a] (in thousands)

	1972	1979	1985	1989
Durable goods manufacturing Total				
Number of women	1404	2001	1677	1763
Percent female	17.7	22.4	22.6	23.2
Skilled[b]				
Number of women	82	155	466	439
Percent female	3.3	5.4	16.3	15.5
Semiskilled				
Number of women	1322	1846	1211	1324
Percent female	24.4	30.4	26.0	27.8
Nondurable goods manufacturing Total				
Number of women	2265	2234	2023	2095
Percent female	40.1	39.4	39.9	39.2
Skilled				
Number of women	136	184	191	227
Percent female	10.4	12.5	16.4	17.7
Semiskilled				
Number of women	2129	2050	1832	1868
Percent female	54.7	48.9	47.0	46.0

[a]Data are from the Current Population Survey quarterly survey of households, and are calculated from the annual averages published in Employment and Earnings, January issues of 1973, 1980, 1986, and 1990.

[b]Skilled positions are those termed "skilled crafts" by the U.S. Bureau of the Census. Semiskilled positions include machine and transport operatives, handlers and laborers; approximately 95% are operatives.

rise in service sector jobs for women. Overall, the trends we have discussed, and the data we present in Tables 3.1 and 3.2, show that the better-paying blue-collar jobs women gained in the 1970s are disappearing, while the expanding areas of women's employment are in lower-paying, predominantly female, service industries.

GENDER DIFFERENCES

Table 3.3
Women's Employment in Production and Maintenance Jobs in the Steel Industry

	All Reporting Companies and Plants				U.S. Steel Duquesne Works		
Year	No. of Plants	Total Employed	Total Women	Percent Female	Total Employed	Total Women	Percent Female
1974	104	255,626	3793	1.5	3041	0	0.0
1975	161	263,969	5776	2.2	3021	23	.8
1976	154	260,203	8230	3.2	3031	36	1.2
1977	157	246,442	9522	3.9	2962	71	2.4
1978	146	244,967	11491	4.7	--	--	--
1979	139	249,027	14500	5.8	3774	167	4.4
1981	--						
	--	--	--	--	2676	127	4.7
1984	--	--	--	--	1466	16	1.1
1985	--	--	--	--	0	0	0

-- Indicates data were not available.
Source: 1974-1979 data obtained from the United Steel Workers of America (USWA); 1981, 1984 data in Tarasovic (1984) from USWA Local 1256

THE CASE OF WOMEN IN THE STEEL INDUSTRY

In this section we focus on the case of the steel industry as a specific example of the very real and significant gains women made in higher-paying manufacturing jobs in the 1970s, due to affirmative action policy and pressure. The steel industry is also relevant for our discussion of the erosion of affirmative action gains in manufacturing in the 1980s, due to corporate disinvestment policies in steel (Deitch and Erickson 1986) and other industries (Bluestone and Harrison 1982). We begin with the expansion of opportunity for women in the 1970s.

The data presented earlier, in Table 3.1, clearly indicate the financial attraction of employment in the steel industry, with weekly earnings considerably higher than those of most manufacturing or service industries. The national data in Table 3.3 show that in 1974 only 1.5 percent of the unionized production and maintenance workers in the steel industry were female. By 1979, women's employment had nearly quadrupled.[3] The employment gains women made in the steel industry between 1974 and 1979 resulted from what began as a fight for racial equality. The NAACP began filing complaints of racial discrimination in hiring, placement, and promotion policies in the steel industry in the mid–1950s (Fonow 1977). After the passage of the 1964 Civil Rights Act, the NAACP began litigation under Title VII of that act which prohibited race or sex discrimination in employment. In a number of cases, the NAACP won back pay awards and court orders requiring an end to discriminatory practices. The U.S. Department of Justice joined with the NAACP in bringing a suit against U.S. Steel's Fairfield, Alabama plant. Several sex discrimination cases were joined to the other Title VII complaints (Fonow 1977). On the question of sex discrimination, the U.S. government charged the union and the companies with failing to advertise for, recruit, and hire women on the same basis as white males. Sex as well as race discrimination was charged in transfer, assignment, and promotion practices and in the seniority system (Fonow 1977; Tarasovic 1984).

In order to avoid costly litigation and a court-ordered plan, company representatives submitted a voluntary agreement to end discrimination. The government withdrew its complaint. Two consent decrees were signed in April 1974, legally binding the union and nine major steel companies covering 249 plants and 348,000 workers to a seniority, placement, and promotion plan (Consent Decree I) and to a hiring plan (Consent Decree II). The hiring plan provided that 50 percent of all new production employees hired had to be women or minorities (black or Hispanic), and that in the first year, 20 percent had to be women (Fonow 1977; Tarasovic 1984). The consent decree included mandated reporting of "compliance data" on female and minority employment by company and plant. Some of these data on women in production and maintenance jobs in the steel industry are shown in Table 3.3.[4] The consent decree provisions became part of the union contract for the basic steel industry.

At the national level, taking into account the yearly variation in the number of plants reporting, the data in Table 3.3 suggest that about 10,000 women entered the mills between 1974 and 1979. Although women's share of total jobs rose to 5.8 percent nationally by 1979, in some specific plants such as U.S. Steel's Chicago and Gary mills, for example, women were 14 percent and 17 percent, respectively, of the production work force in 1979. Several mills went from having zero women in 1974 to several hundred women in just a few years. The consent decrees provided opportunities for women and racial minorities to learn skilled trades. Although the numbers and percentage of women in the crafts occupations remained very small, Ullman and Deaux (1980) show that in the two large Midwestern steel mills they studied, women moved into the skilled crafts occupations and apprenticeships at a faster rate than total female employment increased.

Table 3.3 also provides data on changes in employment at one specific mill, U.S. Steel's Duquesne works, in the Pittsburgh area. The Duquesne mill had no women at all in 1974, and added women slowly but consistently over the next few years. By 1984, however, total employment was only 39 percent of what it had been in 1979; women's employment was down to only 10 percent of its 1979 level. In June of 1984, the mill was totally shut down (Deitch and Erickson 1986). The impact of last hired, first fired, seniority systems is evident in the disproportionate loss of women between 1981 and 1984. Ultimately, however, it was the closing of the mill, not the seniority system, that left women jobless. Duquesne was not an unusual case. By 1984, U.S. Steel had laid off over 100,000 workers and shut down over 150 plants nationally (Cuff 1985). Other steel companies had also closed plants or substantially cut back employment in many locations. Thus the total closing of many steel mills eradicated the gains women had made over the previous decade. Employment gains in the steel industry in the 1980s occurred in the nonunionized "mini-mill" sector, which is not covered by the 1974 consent decrees.

Steel production in the United States historically was concentrated geographically in areas which tend to have limited employment opportunities for women (Deitch 1986). Metropolitan areas like Pittsburgh, Youngstown, and Gary have considerably lower than average female labor force participation rates, few manufacturing jobs for women, and a larger than average male-female earnings differential (Deitch 1986). This pattern suggests the significance of the advantage women gained when these jobs were lost. Some metropolitan areas which have lost jobs in the steel industry in recent years have also lost large numbers of other manufacturing jobs and have gained service jobs at a slower than average rate (Deitch 1986). With large numbers of unemployed workers looking for any available jobs, it was very difficult for displaced steelworkers, male or female, to find manufacturing jobs in their communities. The crafts apprenticeship programs that some women entered in the mills were generally not recognized elsewhere as apprenticeship training. Thus it was rare for women displaced from the steel industry to move into other jobs that would use their newly gained skills or experience, or provide comparable wages. For example, for the 63 women former steelworkers that Tarasovic (1984) interviewed, yearly earnings at the Duquesne mill had averaged $21,490, with 90 percent earning over $20,000. At the time that they were interviewed, only 12 of these women found full time work, and they earned an average of $8295 in their new jobs.[5]

Although the steel industry is not typical of most women's manufacturing employment, there are broader policy implications to be drawn from this case. Many of the features which made the affirmative action plan in the steel industry effective are the very same policies which courts, the Justice Department, and the Civil Rights Commission, under the Reagan administration, tried to reverse and declare illegal. For example, the steel plan included goals, quotas, and timetables; it covered future hiring, not just the individuals directly discriminated against in the past; it included recruitment, training, placement, and transfers within a plant, and promotion to supervisory ranks; local enforcement committees, data collection, and reporting was mandated.

The 1974 consent decree plan was not a perfect affirmative action policy. Women's share of total employment remained quite small. Women often experienced harassment and unfair treatment from male coworkers and supervisors. As the last hired, women were frequently (but not always) among the first laid off and the last recalled. The consent decree could not provide any protection against plant closings and the decline of the industry. The consent decree model results in policies restricted to specific companies, industries, or time periods. The companies never admitted any past instances of sex or race discrimination. The 1974 settlement included some provisions protested by the NAACP and the National Organization for Women (Fonow 1977). Nonetheless, there were very real and significant gains.

A strong affirmative action policy cannot bring back the jobs women lost in the steel industry when whole shifts, departments, divisions, and plants have closed. There are, however, other policy implications. First, various proposals for state and federal policies to save and restore jobs in the steel industry are not likely to provide opportunities for women unless increased government involvement is tied to increased affirmative action efforts.[6] Second, for other sectors of the economy, renewed pressure for comprehensive affirmative action plans from courts and policymakers might give women the entry they found in steel in the 1970s, in other, more viable industries in the 1990s.

EVIDENCE FROM STUDIES OF DISPLACED WORKERS

Job loss in the steel industry, is only one part of a broader pattern of job displacement among blue-collar women in manufacturing. In order to examine the situation of displaced women more generally, we have analyzed unpublished data from a special Department of Labor survey of workers who experienced job loss due to a shutdown or permanent layoffs between January 1979 and January 1984.[7] Our analysis of these data suggests a number of reasons why it is important to examine job displacement among women. Significantly, a substantial percentage of the displaced workers were female. About one third (31.7 percent) of all full-time workers in the United States displaced between 1979 and 1983 were women—a total of nearly 1.5 million women.[8] Nationally, nearly one quarter (23.4 percent) of all displaced workers were "semiskilled" machine operators, assemblers, and inspectors (21.4 percent of displaced whites and 32.5 percent of blacks). Among displaced semiskilled manufacturing workers, 35.6 percent were women (32.9 percent of whites and 47.7 percent of blacks).

The data in Table 3.4 show that there are gender differences in what happens to displaced, semiskilled manufacturing workers. For both blacks

Table 3.4
Workers Displaced from Full-time, Semiskilled Manufacturing Jobs: 1979–1983

| | Whites[a] | | Blacks | |
	Males	Females	Males	Females
Mean number of weeks unemployed	41.4	44.6	52.0	58.9
Percent reemployed	63.5	51.7	42.7	39.8
Mean weekly wage of former job	$349	$224	$308	$222
Mean wage change per week for reemployed workers	$-84	$-32	$9[b]	$-29
Percent in durable goods industries	76.8	50.3	78.1	57.3
Weighted N[c] (1000)	46,746	21,962	8427	7844

[a]Nonhispanic Whites.

[b]Insufficient "n" to be reliable.

[c]The weighted numbers are the best estimates of the numbers of displaced workers in each of these categories, according to the U.S. Department of Labor. Data are missing for individual categories in the table.

Source: Unpublished data from the national survey of displaced workers sponsored by the U.S. Department of Labor (1985), conducted as a supplement to the Current Population Survey.

and whites, women on the average are unemployed longer and have lower rates of reemployment. Displaced, semiskilled men are more likely than comparable women to have lost jobs in the higher-paying durable goods sector. Consequently, men earned more in the job from which they were displaced; and white men experienced a greater wage drop with reemployment. In general, differences by sex observed in Table 3.4 are similar among blacks and whites. Blacks tend to be unemployed longer and are less likely to be reemployed than are whites of both sexes. Our analysis of data from a second Department of Labor survey (not shown), covering job loss in 1981–1985, shows the same overall patterns of gender and racial difference (e.g., Deitch 1987).

The lack of geographical mobility among displaced workers makes it important to consider the regional context in which job loss occurs. Of the semiskilled factory operatives who were displaced in 1979–1983, the survey data show that only 13.4 percent moved to a different city or county to find or take another job. Only 12.1 percent of the women moved, as compared to 14.1 percent of the men. White semiskilled males who are displaced are more likely to move (16.6 percent) than comparable females (14.6 percent), but black semiskilled men are less likely to move (5.4 percent) than are their black female counterparts (11.3 percent).

A number of conditions limit the labor market mobility of semiskilled factory workers, especially among women and in an economically depressed area. Halle (1984) indicates that home ownership represents a major form of saving for blue-collar workers; consequently, any attempt to sell a house in a depressed community will not only be difficult, but would result in a major loss of savings when property values decline in stagnant communities. Additionally, some blue-collar operatives have ethnic roots in city neighborhoods and small rural towns and can rely on kin for social, psychological, and at times for economic support during periods of economic stress. Extended family support may be very important in helping blue-collar women juggle family and job responsibilities, as extended family members assist with child care, meal preparation, and housecleaning, and thereby make it possible for women to work in paid jobs. Some women do not feel they can move because they have responsibility for elderly relatives who live in the area (Nowak and Snyder 1984). Furthermore, blue-collar operatives rarely engage in national job searches. They lack the professional associations to facilitate a national job search and rely instead on friends, family, the local newspaper, and factory to factory inquiries in order to seek employment. Finally, a number of displaced workers (especially married women and an increasing number of married men) have other family members who are employed and are somewhat able to buffer the income loss suffered by the unemployed.

Since such individuals appear "trapped" in a local and regional labor market, regional differences in the structure of employment opportunity are an important part of the context in which blue-collar women attempt to cope with job loss. Well after the nation as a whole officially recovered from the recessions of the early 1980s, certain regions continued to suffer high unemploymemt, particularly for factory workers in durable goods industries such as primary metals, machinery, and transportation equipment. A large number of displaced workers (according to the 1984 survey, roughly 1.2 million) live in the heavily industrialized East North Central region which includes Ohio, Indiana, Illinois, Michigan, Wisconsin, and Minnesota. A second region with chronic unemployment, the Middle Atlantic, is comprised of Pennsylvania, New Jersey, and New York. In these two regions, only slightly more than 50 percent of all displaced workers had been able to return to work, either in their former jobs or in completely new ones, at the time of the 1984 survey.

The permanent loss of many blue-collar jobs is readily apparent when we contrast the situation faced by displaced workers in the high unemployment Middle Atlantic region to the situation in a region with relatively low unemployment, New England. In 1985, Massachusetts, for example, had the lowest overall unemployment rate in the nation at 3.8 percent (Weinstein and Gross 1985, p. 32). Reemployment rates vary widely by region even though men are more likely than women to be reemployed in both New England and the Middle Atlantic, as well as in the United States as a whole. In New England, for example, 69.4 percent of displaced white and 62.6 percent of black men classified as semiskilled were reemployed when interviewed in 1984, yet only 53.8 percent of their white and 45.4 percent of their black male counterparts in the Middle Atlantic were reemployed. For semiskilled white women, 54.8 percent were reemployed in New England while only 37.3 percent were reemployed in the Middle Atlantic. Insufficient numbers made it impossible to make the regional comparison for black women. Such disparities in reemployment rates suggest that research which examines unemployment or job displacement among women in New England (such as Rosen 1987) may present a more optimistic picture of white displaced women than would a similar study of other regions of the country in the same time period.[9]

Effects of Job Displacement on Women

Although research on unemployment traditionally has focused on men, in the 1980s a small but growing number of case studies demonstrated the importance of examining the economic and psychological effects of job loss on blue-collar women (see, for example, Cochrane 1985; Gordon et al. 1984; Hoffman et al. 1988; Nowak and Synder 1984, 1986; Perrucci et al. 1988, Rayman and Bluestone 1982; Rosen 1982, 1987; Snyder and Nowak 1984).[10] Findings from these studies combined with data from the national Displaced Worker Survey discussed earlier, enable us to assess the effects of job displacement on blue-collar women. In our review of this literature, we find that the effects of job displacement on women vary, depending on such factors as a women's race, age, marital status, family situation, employment options, cultural background, as well as the economic health of the industry and local labor market. On the question of marital status, for example, various researchers (Rosen 1982; Nowak and Snyder 1984; Schlozman 1984) have found that women who head families confront the worst financial problems when unemployed, even though the impact on women in dual earner families is also significant. As Rosen (1987, p. 166) aptly points out, "men's and women's different work and family roles and different labor market opportunities create different options and goals for workers when they are displaced from their jobs."

In the rest of this section, we summarize five general patterns of job displacement effects on women most evident in existing data. All five patterns suggest that the effects of job displacement on women are considerable, and that the difficulties facing women are different in some respects from those facing men.

First, the U.S. Displaced Worker Survey data show that women who lose their jobs tend to have greater difficulty than men do in finding other jobs. Reviews of the literature, as well as studies conducted of plant shutdowns in various industries and regions of the United States, have found a similar pattern at the plant level (Bluestone and Harrison 1982, pp. 58 & 61; C & R Associates 1978, p. 24; Gordon et al. 1984, pp. 22–25; Mick 1975, p. 205; Perrucci et al. 1988, pp. 70–72; Snyder and Nowak 1984). Reemployment patterns will depend greatly on the availability of jobs to both men and women in the local economy. For example, Nowak and Snyder's research (1986) in a western Pennsylvania community indicated that sex differences in reemployment rates were still evident, but were less pronounced about three and one-half years after termination than they had been some two years earlier. It was not that the situation of women had improved so much; rather, the economic situation of terminated men had been adversely affected by the deteriorating local and regional economy. In stagnating economies, the reemployment prospects for both terminated men and women are clearly bleak. In contrast, about half of the reemployed women Rosen (1982) interviewed in Massachusetts were recalled to their former jobs: clearly not an option when a plant shuts down permanently.

Second, displaced blue-collar factory women who are reemployed are more likely than reemployed men to skid downward into low-wage service jobs with few benefits. For example, in an analysis of longitudinal Social Security data on employment trends in the Hartford, Connecticut aircraft industry, Rayman and Bluestone (1982) found that women were more likely than men to have skidded out of durable goods manufacturing—into such jobs as nurses' aide, secretary, or salesclerk—into jobs which tend to provide lower wage and inferior job benefits. Synder and Nowak (1984; see also Nowak and Snyder 1986) found a similar pattern with the Robertshaw (thermostat control) plant shutdown. Terminated men were much more likely than women to regain jobs as crafts workers or as operatives. The vast majority of reemployed women found themselves in positions such as retail sales clerks, food service workers, aides in nursing homes, or cleaners and housekeepers. Those reemployed in sales and service work were much more likely than other reemployed workers to hold only part-time jobs;

they were much less likely to receive fringe benefits; their weekly wage was only one half that of other reemployed workers; and, they were much less likely than other workers to prefer their present job to their Robertshaw position.

Third, studies of specific plant shutdowns have shown that among workers terminated from a single plant or from the same industry, women have faced greater income loss with reemployment than have men (Bluestone and Harrison 1982, p. 61; C & R Associates 1978, p. 24; Mick 1975, p. 205; Nowak and Snyder 1984, 1986; Perrucci et al. 1988, pp. 73–75). In their research on the Robertshaw plant shutdown, Nowak and Snyder (1986) found that these male-female differences in earning losses persisted over time. In contrast, however, to the pattern of women showing greater income loss evident in various case studies cited above, the national sample data from the Displaced Workers Survey (Table 3.4) show a greater wage loss for white males than for women or black men. This apparent disparity between local and national level data is, actually, quite consistent with patterns we have discussed. As mentioned previously, the Displaced Worker Survey data show that nationally, displaced, semiskilled men are more likely than comparable women to have lost jobs in the higher-paying durable goods industries. Consequently, men earned more in the job from which they were displaced; and, in the aggregate, white men experienced a greater wage drop with reemployment (see Table 3.4).[11] Furthermore, the data on earnings loss in Table 3.4 are reported solely for reemployed workers; women are less likely to be reemployed than men and are unemployed longer, on average. If income loss were calculated for all displaced workers, not just for those who are reemployed, the magnitude of the economic loss for women relative to men would appear much greater.

Fourth, studies of laid-off workers have also shown that family income has declined significantly when women have been displaced, especially in areas where unemployment has been protracted. Rosen (1987) found that younger, American born women who were married lost about 15 percent of their families' yearly income. Auto workers in the Gordon et al. (1984) study lost substantially more, a 42 percent household income loss, because they included single workers (who were less likely to be able to rely on the income of other family members) and also because they suffered much longer periods of unemployment. Nowak and Snyder (1986) found that, in spite of the fact that men at Robertshaw had higher wages than did women and therefore could fall further in income, the relative decline in the household income of the terminated women did not differ significantly from that of terminated men during either interview. Similarly, Perrucci et al. (1988, pp. 75–80) found that women displaced from RCA were as likely as men to experience increased economic distress in the household, as measured by the number of categories of consumer items they felt they were unable to afford. Perrucci et al. (1988) also found no difference between men and women in the number or kinds of adjustments made in household living expenses. As more and more men in the United States have wives in the paid labor force, and more women maintain families, we cannot assume that unemployment necessarily has a more detrimental effect on household income for men than for women.

Fifth, the existing research provides evidence that women express a variety of negative emotional and physical reactions to job loss, as do men. Rosen (1987) noted that women felt a sense of anger, betrayal, and powerlessness in response to losing their jobs. The married women whom she interviewed did feel some ambivalence about losing their jobs because unemployment (especially since it tended to be much more short term than in more economically depressed regions of the country) reduced their earnings, but also freed them temporarily from the double burden of a full-time job and taking care of their families. Underlying their sense of relief, however, women were beset by anxiety about their family's financial problems, and about when and how they would find new jobs. In Cochrane's research (1985), the vast majority of women felt generally depressed after nine months of unemployment and, for many, this had an impact on their sleeping and eating patterns. Rayman and Bluestone (1982) found that men and women differed in the physical responses to job loss which they reported, except for a few common experiences. Among the displaced RCA workers examined by Perrucci et al. (1988, pp. 85–94), similar percentages of men and women reported effects on their health, such as headaches and stomach trouble, as a result of their layoff. Men were more likely than women, however, to have increased their alcohol consumption. Regardless of their marital status, women were as pessimistic as men about their economic future.

In contrast to Rosen's research (1987), the women interviewed by Nowak and Snyder (1986) were much less likely to express any positive reactions to their layoff—undoubtedly due to their longer period of unemployment, the lack of any possibility for recall, and the fact that many more were primary wage earners who had no one else to depend on for financial support. In the stagnant local economy of western Pennsylvania, Nowak and Snyder found that negative reactions to job loss persisted over time. In fact, more men and women mentioned negative responses when asked an open-ended question about the shutdown three and one-half years after their termination than was true one and one-half years after. The longterm effects of job displacement for both terminated women and men, especially for primary wage earners, are far-reaching in a stagnant local economy.

To summarize, the effects of job dislocation are significant, both economically and psychologically, for blue-collar women in manufacturing, as well as for men. The research cited above indicates the importance of examining displaced women workers, who receive very little publicity but contribute vitally to household income. In economically stagnant regions of the country, many displaced women and men will never again enjoy economic and job security. The studies examined suggest that the health and psychological costs of the loss of economic security are high as many of these individuals experience depression, suffer low self-esteem, and become demoralized.

Clearly the long-term experiences of both women and men affected by job displacement, and by unemployment in general, should be taken into account in developing policies to deal with unemployment. As the Displaced Worker Survey showed, there are also important differences in the experiences of displaced workers by race and region. Unless policies help to alleviate the serious longterm problems frequently faced by both women and men who lose their jobs, the most vulnerable individuals and communities may disproportionately bear the brunt of economic change.

POLICY PERSPECTIVES

In this section we discuss some of the limitation and constraints upon policy which are likely to affect the future prospects of displaced blue-collar women. First we consider policies aimed at promoting equality in employment of women. Then we turn to broader macroeconomic policies affecting more general employment and economic conditions for blue-collar workers. We focus on some of the broader structural economic problems and on the political constraints which mitigate against viable solutions. We view employment policy in the United States, including equal employment opportunity and affirmative action policy, in relation to the particular historical development and limitations of the American welfare state, and the U.S. political bias against the forms and extent of government intervention in the economy found in many Western European social welfare policies.

Weir and Skocpol (1985) and Ruggie (1984) offer some useful distinctions among types of welfare state policies affecting employment. Weir and Skocpol (1985) distinguish between (a) the development of "commercial Keynesianism" in the United States, where state interventions to manage the economy through tax cuts and public spending adjustments were split off from social welfare policies, with more emphasis on controlling inflation than achieving full employment; and (b) the "social Keynesianism" which developed in Sweden, for example, where the two functions have been integrated and coordinated, aimed at a full employment economy with high levels of public, social welfare income allocation. We suggest that the fragmentation and separation of fiscal and social welfare policy, and the lack of a commitment to full employment, have limited the effectiveness of U.S. policy aimed at equal employment opportunity for women and minorities. Ruggie (1984) analyzes how equal employment policies, in a "liberal" welfare state such as Britain or the United States, are aimed at ameliorating or compensating for the consequence of the market *without* superseding market allocation. Such policies tend to reinforce market mechanisms which created the employment or inequality problems in the first place. In contrast, in what is termed a "corporatist" welfare state such as Sweden, policies are explicitly aimed at redirecting market forces to institute equality, restructure social relations, and supersede market allocation. Ruggie argues, and we agree, that policies aimed at promoting sex equality without challenging existing capitalist market relationships tend to reinforce already existing gender divisions and leave women vulnerable to the business cycle.

Ratner (1980) and Ruggie (1984), employing similar concepts but slightly different terminology, identify three models which represent three different assumptions about sources of female labor market inequality, evident in different national approaches to policy. (1) An individual discrimination model narrowly conceptualizes inequality as resulting from human capital deficiencies—such as inadequate training and experience—in women themselves, and in specific unfair treatment by some employers of women who do have the same qualifications as men. The policies guided by this conception tend to promote programs for women's self improvement on the one hand, and on the other hand, legislation to prohibit specific practices of discrimination and to process complaints of unfair treatment by demonstrably qualified individuals. (2) A role conflict model locates women's employment problems in the conflicting obligations and expectations of women's family and work roles. This approach, most developed in Sweden, for example, emphasizes expansion of child care and other social support services for working mothers, and the modification of social policies that advantage the one earner family (Ratner 1980). (3) A structural inequality model conceptualizes institutional discrimination as an inherent feature of the existing "normal" operation of the labor market regardless of registered complaints and leads to remedial strategies to alter the way women are recruited, selected, assigned, trained, and promoted within work organizations (Ratner 1980). The steel industry consent decrees, discussed earlier, are an example of the structural model, but limited to specific firms within one industry for a limited time period.

Ratner (1980, p. 44) observes that countries tend to "choose the approach that is least threatening to the power relationships among existing groups in the labor market and most consistent with past labor market policy," with most following some combination of the three models. Ratner notes that in countries like the United States (and to some extent Britain)—where unionization of women workers is low, an ideology of individualism prevails, and labor disputes are often resolved in courts of law—the individual discrimination model dominates policy. Unfortunately, this model tends to be least effective, and emphasizes equality of opportunity rather than equality of results (see Kendrigan 1984).

In an analysis of women's rights policies proposed at the U.S. federal level in the 1970s, Gelb and Palley (1982) found that policies perceived as affecting sex role equity rather than sex role change were more likely to win adoption. They define role equity issues as policies which extend to women relatively delineated or narrowly construed rights already enjoyed by other groups, and which may gain policy makers advantage with feminist groups or voters with little cost or controversy. As Gelb and Palley (1982, p. 8) note:

In contrast, role change issues appear to produce change in the dependent female role of wife, mother, and homemaker, holding out the potential of greater sexual freedom and independence in a variety of contexts. The latter issues are fraught with greater political pitfalls, including perceived threats to existing values, in turn creating visible and often powerful opposition.

Boneparth and Stoper (1983) suggest that U.S. government policies on women's employment have been of limited value because they have failed to address the conflict between work and family roles. They argue that since the majority of women continue to combine both family and paid work while men do not, and since paid work is organized on the assumption that all workers can adapt to male work patterns, most women are at a disadvantage in both the labor market and the home. Boneparth and Stoper suggest that the only solution to the conflict is to restructure work patterns for both women and men, because changes affecting women's work alone will reinforce the sex segregation and resultant sex inequality of the labor force. The logic of Boneparth and Stoper's argument clearly points to the limitations of policy goals oriented toward role equity rather than role change, and to the limitations of policies which extend narrow legal rights already enjoyed by other groups rather than policies which help women break out of dependent familial roles.

The limitations of U.S. policies affecting women's employment opportunity also reflect the specific historical evolution of equal employment opportunity (EEO) policy in the United States, which originally was not at all concerned with women's rights. Burstein (1985) traces the origin of EEO legislation back to the early 1940s in concept and in much of the actual wording. Inclusion of sex discrimination in Title VII of the 1964 Civil Rights Act was somewhat accidental (Robinson 1979; Charrad and Deitch 1986). Burstein (1985) shows that before the actual passage of Title VII, there was almost no public demand that women should be protected by proposed EEO legislation; and there was no serious consideration of whether sex and race discrimination could or should be handled by the same legal treatment. Subsequent legislation affecting sex discrimination in employment has basically modified or extended Title VII rather than break new ground (U.S. Department of Labor 1983). Thus those U.S. federal policies most explicitly concerned with women's employment opportunities were not conceived or formulated with the specific needs of women or the likely impact on women in mind.

Burstein (1985, p. 128) describes Title VII as a very traditional piece of legislation, in some respects, with "enforcement procedures closely modeled on those of other statutes, oriented toward protecting the rights of the accused, voluntary conciliation, case-by-case resolution, and heavy reliance on prosecution by individual victims of discrimination." Burstein contrasts this with the 1965 Voting Rights Act which included a *categorical* presumption of discrimination and a direct approach to enforcement. Of all the strategies for enforcing equal employment policies considered in a comparative national perspective, Ratner (1980, p. 421) suggests that litigation of individual cases is probably the most inefficient and ineffective, and also probably more prevalent in the United States than in all the rest of the advanced industrial democracies combined. As in the case of the steel industry described earlier, litigation under Title VII, at times, has been an effective vehicle for change. But it has been effective only when civil rights and feminist movement organizations accompanied court battles with broader political pressure, when the U.S. Justice Department facilitated (rather than opposed) class action suits, and when corporations perceived a threat of costly court action against them.

Such a fortuitous model of policy change leaves women, and the gains women make, highly vulnerable to market fluctuations and transitions in the economy. In periods of economic recession the predominantly female, sex-segregated occupations tend to lose fewer jobs, but fewer women enter the labor market than in periods of growth. Also, the generally higher unemployment rate for women than men in male-dominated industries and occupations is greatest during business cycle downturns (Monk-Turner 1984). Thus, periods of recession reinforce traditional positions of women outside and within paid employment (Smith 1980). In the United States and other Western democracies in recent decades, periods of downturn in the economy have tended to create a policy climate unsympathetic to maintaining, let alone expanding, women's employment and sex equality (Ratner, p. 429). Public works and training programs targeted toward the unemployed tend to continue to serve males more than females (Ratner, p. 428). According to Pearce (1985), women have always been underrepresented among the recipients of U.S. unemployment compensation relative to their proportion of the unemployed; this gap has increased in the 1980s, along with policies decreasing the percentage of all unemployed workers covered by benefits. Thus existing equal employment policy is not equipped to address the problems of displaced blue-collar women; nor is existing social welfare policy.

U.S. Economic and Employment Policies in the 1980s

In this section we briefly discuss some of the government policies which have created or contributed to the depressed economic prospects for dis-

placed male and female factory workers, returning to dynamics of deindustrialization that were touched upon in the introduction to this chapter
and to the limitations of recent U.S. macroeconomic policy. As we have
shown earlier, the fact that some blue-collar women and men are subsequently reemployed in manufacturing jobs should not obscure the loss of
wage and benefits which generally occurs among displaced workers of both
sexes. Those workers able to go back to their old jobs or comparable blue-
collar jobs find wages and working conditions eroded. Weakened labor
unions, aggressively antiunion employers, capital flight to low wage areas,
and an abundance of job seekers all contribute to the disappearance of the
well-paid, unionized industrial jobs that traditionally provided mobility into
the middle class for the sons and daughters of blue-collar workers. As Reich
notes (1986), "If you get a job but lose the ladder, I'm not sure you have
gained much."

During the 1980s the Reagan administration abandoned even ad hoc
efforts to assure fuller employment through government programs and fiscal
policy. That administration's emphasis on deregulation, cutbacks in national
expenditures in many nondefense areas, and refusal to raise taxes to decrease
the deficit are all part of a strategy to increase production in the private
sector and generate employment *through market forces.* Capital credits to
stimulate investment without restrictions on the nature and location of such
investment, lax enforcement of antitrust legislation, and an antilabor posture
were part of a strategy to pressure "over priced" blue-collar labor in heavily
unionized industries such as steel and autos to accept concessions or face
unemployment. The rash of mergers and acquisitions during the 1980s sent
a clear signal to unions that a single product or even industry is no longer
indispensable to corporate profits. Persistent unemployment and the constant threat of shutdowns forced unions to yield wages, benefits, and control
over the shop floor to management. Organized labor had almost no influence
in an administration dominated by monetarists and a commitment to "free"
market principles.

While a post-1983 upswing in business moderated unemployment in some
regions and industries, new waves of unemployment emerged in others—
as in oil in the Southwest and in parts of the microelectronics industry in
California's Silicon Valley. Several economic problems persisted which
threatened to increase the rate of structural unemployment and underemployment in the United States. A persistent international trade deficit—$50
billion in 1985 with Japan alone (Wysocki 1986, p. 29.)—demonstrated
how noncompetitive the United States had become in many areas such as
consumer electronics and precision tools. In an effort to remain competitive
and boost profits, American corporations invested heavily in Third World
subsidiaries or subcontracted much manufacturing and assembly to low-
cost corporations abroad. But wage and benefit concessions by American
workers could not push American labor costs to the low levels found in

such countries as Korea, Singapore, Taiwan, and Brazil. As a consequence of competition from low-wage countries, underemployed and unemployed blue-collar men and women found consumer goods less expensive, but lost their jobs in the process.

With a few exceptions, economic policy makers in the Bush administration—Boskin, Darman, and Sununu—disparaged the idea of an industrial policy dedicated to preserving or creating manufacturing jobs in the United States. In the summer of 1989 Sununu and Darman, for example, halted Commerce Secretary Mosbacher's attempt to promote a domestic high definition television industry. Boskin, Darman, and Sununu felt such subsidies would distort the market and misallocate resources. Cutbacks in national expenditures in many nondefense and defense areas, and refusal to raise taxes to decrease the deficit were all part of a strategy to increase production in the private sector and generate employment through market forces. But the high cost of capital in the United States made further expansion in domestic employment increasingly dependent on foreign investment.

The moderate growth rates achieved in the middle to late 1980s were largely financed by growing public and private debt. Rises in military spending increased the national deficit. In an effort to (in the face of falling real income for many groups) sustain their standard of living, many individuals borrowed more heavily. In "1986 the average family was carrying more than $11,000 worth of outstanding consumer credit, and was spending a fifth of its monthly disposable income to pay it off" (Harrison and Bluestone 1988, p. 27). As the United States found itself more dependent on foreign capital, economic growth became increasingly dependent on Japanese and Western European decisions about global investment opportunities.

Interest rate regulations to stimulate employment became less effective. Economic policy makers in the Bush administration wanted the Federal Reserve Bank to lower interest rates to avoid a recession in early 1990. Federal Reserve Board Directors felt, however, that the underlying rate of inflation was too high and that they had to keep interest rates high to attract international funds (i.e., from the Japanese) to fund our deficit. Rising Japanese interest rates together with the growing capital needs of Eastern Europe forced the Federal Reserve Bank to keep interest rates high in order to attract sufficient capital to the United States. The debt explosion stimulated by Reagan "free market" economic policies clearly narrowed the ability of the Federal Reserve Bank to manage American monetary policy.

Capital credits and Bush's proposal to lower the capital gains tax sought to stimulate investment without restrictions on the nature and location of such investment. While the rash of mergers, acquisitions, and corporate break ups slowed when the junk bond market collapsed and Drexel went bankrupt, corporations continued to downsize and subcontract work—thereby increasing the pool of surplus and contingent labor. According to Bureau of Labor Force Statistics data, the number of American workers whose primary income was earned in temporary jobs increased 77 percent between 1983 and 1986 (Kanter 1989, p. 302). A weak labor movement simply could not mobilize political support for full employment policies in an administration committed to "free" market principles.

The problems described above are the structural dilemmas and contradictions of the global economy. As an alternative to the policies of the Reagan and Bush administrations, a number of corporate and governmental policy directions have been debated. We have already indicated why policies which require extensive labor mobilization or government intervention are not likely to be successful in the present political climate. Below, we briefly consider the provocative solutions to economic displacement suggested by Kanter (1983) and Piore and Sabel (1984)—strategies which rely on new forms of private sector initiative. Kanter (1983) discusses employment security as one important condition for generating the commitment necessary to stimulate innovation and productivity. Kanter points to the models of IBM and Hewlett-Packard, where workers are continually retrained and reassigned when necessary. In the absence of the government's commitment to national full employment, however, corporate commitment to employment security within certain firms could accentuate the disadvantages faced by women and minorities in the labor market. Compared to their white male counterparts, women and minorities remain disproportionately employed by smaller and less capital-intensive firms which lack the stability and resources to provide employment security.

Piore and Sabel (1984) feel that the United States needs to pressure export-oriented countries to absorb more of their own production. To do so, however, would require considerable coordination among countries' economies, and an active and even intrusive role by agencies such as the International Monetary Fund to better prevent countries from depressing internal consumption in favor of exports. Piore and Sabel's proposal points to the limitations of strictly national solutions to global economic problems. They acknowledge, however, that such proposals are unlikely to win acceptance.

According to Piore and Sabel, within the United States, domestic firms must develop more flexible and innovative production techniques to enable them to respond more quickly to rapidly changing consumer tastes as well as changing capital markets. Such a development would require working conditions and wages to be stabilized so that competing firms do not "cheat" by undercutting wages. External suppliers would also have to be treated as collaborators (Piore and Sabel 1984, p. 268) in design and production to encourage innovation, insure quality control, and enhance stability in the market. Such a model might be plausible in certain sectors of the U.S. economy as a result of the growth in subcontracting by large corporations eager to cut costs and a rise in small firm start-ups by highly skilled blue-collar workers or professionals. It is unlikely, however, that gains in employment would provide jobs for women and minorities because such workers are largely absent from the industry and labor market sectors most affected by Piore and Sabel's model, and frequently lack the specialized skills (e.g., welding or software engineering) important to the viability of the small companies Piore and Sabel describe.

The proposals of Kanter and of Piore and Sabel are in many ways "progressive" in the options they would provide to workers. These authors, however, fail to examine how their reforms would affect racial and sexual divisions in the U.S. labor market. In reviewing Kanter's and Piore and Sabel's proposals, we return to a key contradiction in the U.S. policy suggested earlier: Reforms which promote change by reinforcing the market and relying upon private sector initiative are more acceptable ideologically in the United States than those that challenge existing market and social relations; but such reforms tend to reproduce the sex and race divisions and the resulting inequalities already existing in the market. We have suggested ways in which this pattern appears for policies affecting broad employment conditions and for reforms specifically aimed at gender equality.

CONCLUSION

We have focused our discussion on blue-collar women in manufacturing industries. The sex segregation of the labor market and the low pay associated with many predominantly female jobs is central to most analyses of the problems which women, as a group, confront in employment and unemployment. Women displaced from blue-collar manufacturing jobs, even women who have worked in better-paying, traditionally male occupations and industries, are not at all exempt from these problems. As illustrated most dramatically in the case of the steel industry, but also evident elsewhere, it was the pressure of affirmative action and equal employment opportunity policy that helped women move into better paying manufacturing jobs in the 1970s. When they lose these jobs, women's future employment prospects and patterns will be affected by the strengths and weaknesses of policies on sex equality. As blue-collar workers, such women are also affected by class as well as sex dynamics in the labor market and by the future of labor in the U.S. economy. More specifically, their lives have been profoundly altered by the corporate and governmental policies which facilitated the large-scale and most likely permanent loss of thousands of manufacturing jobs in their industries and communities.

Throughout this chapter we have attempted to show how the situation of women who are displaced, blue-collar, manufacturing workers is affected by the combination of two areas of public policy concern. One is antidiscrimination or equal employment opportunity policy, and the other is macroeconomic policy affecting business and employment conditions in general. The separation of these two domains, whereby equal employment opportunity has not been linked to full employment, has severely limited efforts to remedy sex and race inequality with federal policy in the United States. Advances on both fronts are necessary to substantially improve the employment prospects for women, particularly blue-collar women. Throughout the 1980s, public policy was in retreat in both areas. Therefore, a gain in either domain by itself in the 1990s might provide significant relief in the short run. We have warned, however, that employment policies which rely on market forces and private sector initiatives tend to reinforce existing race and gender inequalities. We have argued that, in the long run, fragmented, piecemeal reforms limit progress toward full equality.

NOTES

The authors thank Judy Michaels for library research assistance.

1. Although we shall be using the terms blue-collar and manufacturing interchangeably in our discussion, it should be noted that not all blue-collar women are in manufacturing industries (over a third are not), not all women in manufacturing jobs are blue-collar (approximately half are), and that the majority of blue-collar women are in largely female work settings—in textiles, apparel, or electronics assembly, for example. (These estimates are calculated from U.S. Department of Labor, *Employment and Earnings*, January 1986.)

2. The data in Table 3.2 are annual averages based on the Current Population Survey of Households (CPS). Comparable series data were available and examined for each year beginning with 1972. For presentation in the table, we chose 1979 because it was the last peak year before the current period of decline in manufacturing employment; it was the last year before monetary policies shifted, leading to the high value of the dollar which in turn affected the competitiveness of U.S. produced manufacturing goods; and it is the year for which the Displaced Worker Survey data (also part of the CPS, and discussed later in this chapter) begins. By comparing 1972, 1979 and 1985, we have avoided peak recession years which would bias apparent trends. The combination of skilled and semiskilled occupational categories in manufacturing is the best equivalent, for the household data on individuals used in Table 3.2, to the establishment data on nonsupervisory production and maintenance workers on manufacturing payrolls presented in Table 3.1.

3. In interpreting the data in Table 3.3, it should be noted that the number of plants reporting varies from year to year. Also, the "percent female" statistics in Table 3.3 are for production and maintenance workers and only for companies covered in the 1974 consent decree, as discussed. The figures for "percent female" in Table 3.1 include white-collar workers and are not restricted to specific firms or plants.

4. The data for 1974–1979 were obtained from the United Steel Workers of America (USWA), Civil Rights Division. The 1981 and 1984 data were obtained by Tarasovic (1984) from officials of USWA local 1256, of which she was a member.

5. It is not clear from Tarasovic's paper how long these women had been unemployed.

6. Proposals to revitalize the steel industry with increased federal intervention include federal spending on infrastructure repairs to stimulate demand for steel; some form of protection against imports tied to mandated company investment in

modernization of steel facilities; loans, loan guarantees, or investment incentives for employees, local groups, or others attempting to purchase viable mills and keep them open; and a nationally subsidized steel industry as exists in most other advanced industrial nations (Deitch and Erickson, 1986).

7. This special survey, sponsored by the U.S. Department of Labor's Employment and Training Administration, was conducted in January 1984 as a supplement to the Current Population Survey. Prior to this survey, no studies provided an accurate basis for describing the number and characteristics of displaced workers in the United States as a whole. In reports based on this survey, the Department of Labor uses the term displaced worker to "refer to persons with tenure of 3 years or more who lost or left a job between January 1979 and January 1984 because of plant closings or moves, slack work, or the abolishment of their positions or shifts" (U.S. Department of Labor, 1985). In the descriptive statistics that follow, we use the department's weighted sample results that are inflated to independent estimates of the total civilian noninstitutional population of the United States by age, race, Hispanic origin, and sex in order to provide an accurate portrait of job displacement (see U.S. Department of Labor, 1985, pp. 15–18).

8. We have limited our analysis to full-time displaced workers, since their situation is very different from that of part-time workers. If we had included part-time displaced workers, the percentage of women would be even higher—34.6 percent of all displaced workers (both full-time and part-time) were women. Hispanics are excluded from our analysis because there were too few cases to analyze separately. In subsequent paragraphs, we use the term "whites" to refer to nonhispanic whites.

9. Elsewhere, Nowak and Snyder (1986) further examine regional contrasts in the 1984 survey of displaced workers.

10. Only two of the studies we have reviewed focus solely on displaced women. Cochrane's (1985) study of a plant closing involving women garment workers in rural Oregon, and Rosen's (1982, 1987) research on New England women laid off from traditional women's factory jobs, such as apparel manufacturing. All of the other studies have been of workers terminated in durable goods industries which have generally been dominated by men. The Gordon et al. (1984) study of laid-off auto workers in Michigan, and Rayman and Bluestone's (1982) study of laid-off aircraft workers in Hartford, Connecticut have both included about 80 percent men. Hoffman, et al. found that workers in the closing plants they studied differed substantially from workers in comparison plants: women comprised a much larger percentage of the workers who had already been laid off (36 percent) and who were anticipating their plant's closing (23 percent) than in comparison plants (13 percent).

The Perrucci et al. study (1988) of an RCA television cabinet plant closing in a small community in rural Indiana included about 50 percent women. Nowak and Snyder's research (1986; see also Snyder and Nowak, 1984) on the plant shutdown of the Indiana Division of Robertshaw Controls—a manufacturer of thermostat controls in a small western Pennsylvania community—included about 80 percent women. As shown in Table 3.1, there is a higher percentage of women in the instruments and controls equipment industry than in most other durable goods manufacturing; the Robertshaw plant had always employed mostly women. Only in Nowak and Snyder's research (1986) were terminated women interviewed more than once; in this case they were interviewed about one and one-half years and again three and one-half years after they were terminated by the plant shutdown. (Additionally, Cochrane [1985] did in-depth interviews over time with a small group of the displaced women to whom she had originally sent questionnaires.) All of these studies were done on industries undergoing substantial job loss at the time of the research. Except for the two studies done in New England (Rosen, 1982, 1987; Rayman and Bluestone, 1982), all were done in areas hard hit by local and regional economic decline.

11. For the national displaced worker sample, we cannot make statistically reliable comparisons of wage loss by reemployed women and men displaced from the same specific industry because there are too few blue-collar women in the sample in the higher-wage manufacturing industry categories.

REFERENCES

Bell, Carolyn. 1983. "Job Loss, Wage Loss, and Family Income: Aspects of the Massachusetts Experience." *Working Paper #7*. Wellesley, Mass.: Department of Economics, Wellesley College, September.

Blau, Francine. 1984. "Women in the Labor Force: An Overview." In *Women: A Feminist Perspective*, ed. Jo Freeman, pp. 297–315. Palo Alto, Calif.: Mayfield.

Bluestone, Barry, and Bennett Harrison. 1982. *The Deindustrialization of America: Plant Closings, Community Abandonment, and the Dismantling of Basic Industry*. New York: Basic Books.

Boneparth, Ellen, and Emily Stoper. 1983. "Work, Gender and Technological Innovation." In *Families, Politics, and Public Policy*, ed. I. Diamond, pp. 265–278. New York: Longman.

Burstein, Paul. 1985. *Discrimination, Jobs and Politics*. Chicago: University of Chicago Press.

Business Week. 1986. "The Hollow Corporation: The Decline of Manufacturing Threatens the Entire U.S. Economy." March 3, pp. 57–85.

C & R Associates. 1978. *Community Costs of Plant Closings: Bibliography and Survey of the Literature*. Report Prepared for the Federal Trade Commission, Washington, D.C.

Charrad, Mounira, and Cynthia Deitch. 1986. "Gender and State Policy: A Theoretical Investigation." Paper presented at the annual meeting of the American Sociological Association, New York.

Cochrane, Brenda. 1985. "The Impact of Unemployment on Women Workers: A Cross Sectional and Case Analysis." Ph.D. dissertation, University of Oregon.

Cuff, Daniel. 1985. "Steel's Fierce Domestic Battle." *New York Times*, September 16.

Deaux, Kay, and Joseph Ullman. 1983. *Women of Steel*. New York: Praeger.

Deitch, Cynthia. 1988. "Job Displacement, Labor Market Recomposition and the Structure of Inequality." Paper presented at the annual meeting of the American Sociological Association, Atlanta.

———. 1986. "Women's Employment and the Industry Structure of Urban Labor Markets in the U.S." Unpublished paper. Department of Sociology, University of Pittsburgh.

Deitch, Cynthia, and Robert Erickson. 1986. " 'Save Dorothy': A Political Response to Structural Change in the Steel Industry." In *Redundancy, Lay-Offs and Plant Closures: A Social Impact*, ed. Raymond Lee. London: Croom Helm Ltd.

Edwards, Richard, Michael Reich, and David Gordon, eds. 1985. *Labor Market Segmentation*. Lexington, Mass.: Heath.

Fonow, Mary Margaret. 1977. "Women in Steel: A Case Study of the Participation of Women in a Trade Union." Ph.D. dissertation, Ohio State University.

Gelb, Joyce, and Marian L. Palley. 1982. *Women and Public Policies*. Princeton: Princeton University Press.

Gordon, Avery F., Paul Schervish, and Barry Bluestone. 1984. "The Unemployment and Reemployment Experiences of Michigan Auto Workers." *Report on the Michigan Auto Industry Workers Study*. Submitted to the Office of Automotive Industry Affairs, U.S. Department of Commerce and to the Transportation Systems Center, U.S. Department of Transportation.

Gordon, David, Michael Reich, and Richard Edwards. 1982. *Segmented Work, Divided Workers*. New York: Cambridge University Press.

Halle, David. 1984. *America's Working Man: Work, Home, and Politics Among Blue Collar Property Owners*. Chicago: University of Chicago Press.

Harrison, Bennett, and Barry Bluestone. 1988. *The Great U-Turn: Corporate Restructuring and the Polarizing of America*. New York: Basic Books.

Hoffman, William, Clifford Broman, V. Lee Hamilton, and Deborah S. Renner. 1988. "Impacts of Plant Closings: Wave One of a Study on Autoworkers and Their Families." Paper presented at the annual meeting of the American Sociological Association, Atlanta.

Kanter, Rosabeth. 1989. *When Giants Learn to Dance: Mastering the Challenge of Strategy, Management and Careers in the 1990s*. New York: Simon and Schuster.

———. 1983. *The Change Masters*. New York: Simon and Schuster.

Kendrigan, Mary Lou. 1984. *Political Equality in a Democratic Society: Women in the United States*. Westport, Conn.: Greenwood.

Lekachman, Robert. 1966. *The Age of Keynes*. New York: McGraw-Hill.

Mick, Stephen S. 1975. "Social and Personal Costs of Plant Shutdowns." *Industrial Relations* 14: 203–270.

Monk-Turner, Elizabeth. 1984. *Sex Differences in Unemployment Rates in Male-dominated Occupations and Industries During Periods of Economic Downturn*. Bethesda, Md.: ERIC Document Reproduction Service.

Nash, June, and Maria Patricia Fernandez-Kelly, eds. 1983. *Women, Men, and the International Division of Labor*. Albany: SUNY Press.

Nowak, Thomas C., and Kay A. Snyder. 1986. "Sex Differences in the Long-Term Consequences of Job Loss." Paper presented at the annual meeting of the American Sociological Association, New York.

———. 1985. "Surviving Job Loss: The Long-Term Impact of a Plant Shutdown." Paper presented at the annual meeting of the Society for the Study of Social Problems, Washington, D.C.

———. 1984. "Women's Struggle to Survive a Plant Shutdown," *Journal of Intergroup Relations* 11 (4): 25–44.

Pearce, Diana. 1985. "Toil and Trouble: Women Workers and Unemployment Compensation." *Signs* 10 (3): 439–459.

Perrucci, Carolyn C., Robert Perrucci, Dena Targ and Harry R. Targ. 1988. *Plant Closings: International Context and Social Costs*. New York: Aldine de Gruyter.

Piore, Michael, and Charles Sabel. 1984. *The Second Industrial Divide*. New York: Basic Books.

Ratner, Ronnie S., ed. 1980. *Equal Employment Opportunity for Women*. Philadelphia: Temple University Press.

———. 1980. "The Policy and Problem: Overview of Seven Countries." In *Equal Employment Opportunity for Women*, ed. Ronnie Ratner. Philadelphia: Temple University Press.

———. 1980. "Equal Employment Policy for Women: Summary of Themes and Issues." In *Equal Employment Opportunity for Women*, ed. Ronnie Ratner. Philadelphia: Temple University Press.

Rayman, Paula A., and Barry Bluestone. 1982. *Out of Work: The Consequences of Unemployment in the Hartford Aircraft Industry*. Boston: Social Welfare Research Institute, Boston College.

Reich, Michael. 1986. "Down the Ladder." *Wall Street Journal*. March 12.

Robinson, Donald A. 1979. "Two Movements in Pursuit of Equal Employment Opportunity." *Signs* 4: 413–433.

Rosen, Ellen Israel. 1987. *Bitter Choices: Blue Collar Women In and Out of Work*. Chicago: University of Chicago Press.

———. 1982. *Hobson's Choice: Employment and Unemployment Among "Blue Collar" Workers in New England*. Social Welfare Research Institute, Boston College: Final report to the U.S. Department of Labor and Training Administration.

Ruggie, Mary. 1984. *The State and Working Women*. Princeton, N.J.: Princeton University Press.

Schlozman, Kay Lehman. 1984. "Women and Unemployment: Assessing the Biggest Myths." In *Women: A Feminist Perspective*, ed. Jo Freeman. Palo Alto, Calif.: Mayfield.

Smith, Joan. 1984. "The Paradox of Women's Poverty: Wage-earning Women and Economic Transformation." *Signs* 10 (2): 291–310.

Smith, Ralph. 1980. "Women's Stake in a High-Growth Economy in the United States." In *Equal Employment Opportunity for Women*, ed. Ronnie Ratner, pp. 350–365. Philadelphia: Temple University Press.

Snyder, Kay, and Thomas C. Nowak. 1984. "Job Loss and Demoralization: Do Women Fare Better than Men?" *International Journal of Mental Health* 13: 92–106.

Tarasovic, Marcia M. 1984. "Women of Steel." Unpublished student paper, Chatham College, Pittsburgh, Pa.

Tolbert, Charles, Patrick Horan, and E. M. Beck. 1980. "The Structure of Economic Segmentation." *American Journal of Sociology* 85: 1095–1116.

Ullman, Joseph and Kay Deaux. 1980. "Recent Efforts to Increase Female Participation in Apprenticeship in the Basic Steel Industry in the Midwest." In *Apprenticeship Research: Emerging Findings and Future Trends*, eds. Vernon M. Briggs, Jr., and Felician F. Foltman. Ithaca: New York State School of Industrial and Labor Relations, Cornell University.

U.S. Bureau of the Census. 1985. *Statistical Abstract of the U.S.: 1986.* Washington, D.C.: Government Printing Office.

U.S. Department of Commerce, Bureau of the Census. 1970, 1980. *Census of the Population, U.S. Summary.* Washington, D.C.: Government Printing Office.

U.S. Department of Labor, Bureau of Labor Statistics. 1986. "Average Hours and Earnings of Production of Nonsupervisory Workers on Nonagricultural Payrolls by Industry Division and Manufacturing Group." *Employment and Earnings* 33 (January).

U.S. Department of Labor, Bureau of Labor Statistics. 1985. *Displaced Workers, 1979–1983.* Washington, D.C.: U.S. Government Printing Office.

U.S. Department of Labor, Bureau of Labor Statistics. 1983. *Earnings of Workers and Their Families: Fourth Quarter, 1982.* USDL Release 83–42. Washington, D.C. January 31. Table 1.

U.S. Department of Labor, Bureau of Labor Statistics. 1975, 1978–1986. "Employed Persons by Industry, Sex and Occupation." *Employment and Earnings* 22, 25–33 (January).

U.S. Department of Labor, Bureau of Labor Statistics. 1982. *The Female-Male Earnings Gap: A Review of Employment and Earnings Issues.* Washington, D.C. (September).

U.S. Department of Labor, Bureau of Labor Statistics. 1982, 1988. "Production of Nonsupervisory Workers on Private Nonagricultural Payrolls by Major Industry and Manufacturing Group." *Employment and Earnings* 29, 33 (January).

U.S. Department of Labor, Bureau of Labor Statistics. 1986. "Women Employees on Nonagricultural Payrolls by Major Industry and Manufacturing Group." *Employment and Earnings* 33 (March).

U.S. Department of Labor, Women's Bureau. 1988. *Facts on Women Workers, 1988.* Washington, D.C.: Government Printing Office.

U.S. Department of Labor, Women's Bureau. 1985. *Time of Change, 1983 Handbook on Women Workers.* Washington, D.C.: Government Printing Office.

Weinstein, Bernard, and Harold T. Gross. 1985. "The Frost Belt's Revenge," *Wall Street Journal,* November 19, p. 32.

Weir, Margaret, and Theda Skocpol. 1985. "State Structures and the Possibilities for 'Keynesian' Responses to the Great Depression in Sweden, Britain, and the United States." In *Bringing the State Back In,* ed. Peter Evans, Dietrich Rueschemeyer, and Theda Skocpol, pp. 107–163. New York: Cambridge University.

Wysocki, Bernard. 1986. "Hopes Riding on Nakasone Visit to United States," *Wall Street Journal,* April 10.

4

GENDER DIFFERENCES IN THE IMPACT OF A PLANT SHUTDOWN

JOYCE O. BECKETT

This is a study of the impact of a plant closing on employees in the pharmaceutical industry. Beckett found that policies can matter. Notification of plant closings do have an impact on the affected employees. She also found that differences must be taken into consideration in analyzing the impact on workers. Plant closings do not affect all workers equally. The differences identified here include gender differences and differences on the basis of age. Older workers and women are particularly vulnerable to the effects of such forms of unemployment. Nonetheless, studies of plant closings usually focus on the younger male worker. Thus, when issues are defined in ways that ignore the plight of women, and when women are not represented in shaping policies, policies are usually developed in ways that are not as beneficial to women as to men.

INTRODUCTION AND LITERATURE REVIEW

Is it likely that a plant closing in an area with high unemployment will have few short-term negative effects and in some instances temporary, positive consequences for the displaced workers? This chapter shows that such results are possible within a context of an advanced closing notice and company sponsored programs during a lengthy phase-out period. The workers in this research were not the usual middle-aged, blue-collar, white male respondents often discussed in the literature; instead, they were older men and women representing various occupational levels. Older workers and women increasingly face this form of unemployment, yet are usually neglected in plant closing literature. Moreover, these groups are at high risk for the negative effects of plant closings.

One outcome of recent renewed interest in the process of unemployment is an expressed need to recognize and distinguish various forms of unemployment. Depending on the type of unemployment, differential consequences occur for both workers and the community.[1] Though plant closings are not usually distinguished from other forms of unemployment, estimates suggest that the incidence of this event is significant. Mass layoffs and plant closings have displaced millions of U.S. workers. During 1979–1985, 5.1 million workers lost jobs at which they had worked for at least three years; plant closings and/or plant moves were responsible for half of these losses.[2] In addition, during the first quarter of 1982, a period of economic recession, 14 percent of the unemployed were terminated because of plant closings.[3] In 1987, a better economic time, plant closings accounted for 13 percent of the layoffs.[4]

Though negative financial consequences of plant closings are documented, less definitive attention is given to noneconomic effects.[5] Moreover, empirical studies of the noneconomic outcomes typically fail to consider possible differential gender and age issues or to examine the buffering effects of intervention programs. Previous evidence suggests that the negative economic and noneconomic consequences of plant closings are related. The former tends to spiral into mental and physical symptomotology including depression, anxiety, alcoholism, hypertension, and ulcers; and family and social problems such as withdrawal, violence, and divorce.[6]

As with other phenomena, however, plant closings do not equally influence all displaced workers. For example, women and older workers are often employed in jobs vulnerable to plant shutdowns. Furthermore, they frequently lack the skills required to secure new employment. Consequently, the duration of unemployment for these groups is longer; and, if found, subsequent work tends to be at lower wages and lower occupational status.[7] Although some literature discusses interventions that companies can use to decrease negative effects, little evidence exists on the impact of such programs, especially company sponsored efforts for displaced workers.[8]

For several reasons, two studies of the economic and noneconomic consequences of plant closings are relevant to the research presented in this chapter.[9] First, both show that workers' reactions and adjustment to job loss is characterized by a process of adaptation. For example, Kasl and his colleagues find that workers have elevated levels of physical and mental health symptoms prior to a closing. These symptoms gradually recede and return to baseline within a year following the shutdown. Second, the studies suggest that the context of the closing is crucial in explaining the workers' adaptation. For example, the Kasl study shows the differential impact of geographical area. Buss and Redburn focus on the importance of financial resources (e.g., unemployment benefits, company sponsored supplementary unemployment benefits [SUB], trade adjustment assistance [TAA]), and a labor market that can absorb the displaced workers. The greater the economic supports, the better the displaced workers cope and the fewer the physical and mental health problems.

Third, both studies indicate the need for and value of research based on multiple outcome measures with observations made prior to closing and continuing over time. It is not sufficient to measure only the economic situations or any of the varied noneconomic consequences for the workers. To form a comprehensive picture that aids our understanding, many different situations must be studied. In order to understand the process of adjustment to a plant closing, the situations should be observed longitudinally, beginning before the closing and following the workers for several years following the shutdown.

Fourth, both sets of investigators note that the information obtained from the displaced workers differed depending on the type of research method used. Findings from case study methods, such as personal interviews, were more negative than those from mailed, structured questionnaires. It seems the workers were more likely to admit having problems in face-to-face discussions.

Moreover, the two studies provide evidence that plant closings do not always produce severe negative financial, social, or physical and mental health consequences. When there is limited economic deprivation, some workers' noneconomic situation is indistinguishable from steadily employed individuals.

CONTEXT

This chapter presents findings from a longitudinal investigation of the consequences of job loss among mature persons, age 52 and over, employed in a midwestern pharmaceutical plant which closed in December 1981. Although this case study cannot demonstrate the specific contributions of either the plant, the closing, or the research project, the context is a major factor in understanding the outcomes reported and thus is discussed here. The context highlights specific characteristics that have bearing on the reported outcomes. These include a plant with a history of opportunities for stable employment, located in a high unemployment area, and with a management who provided phase-out programs to help ameliorate the negative consequences of the plant closing.

The Plant

The Washington Plant,[10] established in the mid–1800s was the first unit of what developed into an international pharmaceutical company. In its most productive years, the plant employed 4000 workers. Because of its long history and lack of cyclic layoffs that characterized some neighboring plants, it was an attractive place to work. If often employed several generations of a family. Even before it was fashionable in other industries, the Washington Plant recruited women for work. There were certain jobs requiring counting of pills, quality assurance (spotting inappropriate pills among a group), and manual dexterity that the management felt women did better than men.

In the 1970s, the plant began to cut back its production and staff; and in 1975, Wilson-Bailey, the company that had run the Washington Plant since its inception, was taken over by the Beecher Corporation. By 1980, the Washington Plant's census had dropped to 2000 workers.

The Closing

In sharp contrast to plant closings where employees are given virtually no advance notice of the shutdown, employees of the Washington Plant were given about two years' notice. In September 1979, employees were told that a committee had studied the plant situation and had recommended it be closed. In October 1979, an announcement was made that the board of the Beecher Corporation concurred with the recommendation and that the plant would close, probably in June 1982. Ultimately, this schedule was modified so that the actual close-out occurred in December 1981.

From the time of the initial announcement, management from both the corporate headquarters and the plant itself began phase-out activities. Impact bargaining began in December 1979 with the major union in the plant in order to settle the close-out contract terms. This bargaining was successfully concluded in February 1980. The contract included provisions for severance benefits, early retirement, and transfers to other plants. Between January and April 1980, the plant personnel were reorganized to meet phase-out needs. Communication sessions were held with employees to keep them abreast of the closing schedule and phase-out efforts. By March 1980, the management task force initiated a two-day program for middle management on handling stress; this was the first phase-out activity. Other programs included management development seminars (e.g., sessions covering such issues as motivation and productivity, dynamics of separation, and employee counseling); and employment counseling and out-placement center, located in the plant, for salaried workers; career continuation seminars for salaried employees led by a company specializing in successful plant closing strategies; and a preretirement training program offered to all workers 52 years and older conducted on company time by gerontologists from the Institute of Gerontology at the University of Michigan.

The Research Project

Shortly after being contacted by the corporate management about the preretirement program, the institute became interested in conducting research at the Washington Plant. The number of mature workers affected by the closing, the occupational diversity of the work force, and the number of women in the work force combined to make this plant an ideal place to study the effects of plant closings on older workers. Compared to other plant closing samples, these mature men and women were distinguished by generous salaries and stable employment histories. Many had never worked for another company. The Institute discussed its research interests with both corporate and plant management and they responded enthusiastically.

The Washington Plant provided an opportunity to explore, in a case study, the effect of a specific type of unemployment—a plant closing—on a special population. A longitudinal design was employed to capture the process and outcomes of the closing. Information on the process of the closing and workers' economic and noneconomic characteristics were collected in four phases using multiple research methods. Phase I involved interviews and discussions with plant management, employees, and union officials. Phase II involved a structured questionnaire mailed in fall 1980 to all 633 plant employees who were age 52 and over. The response rate was 58 percent ($N = 364$). Phase III occurred after the closing and involved a structured questionnaire mailed between October 1981 and April 1982 to those who had completed the first questionnaire. A total of 288 questionnaires (79 percent) were returned. Phase IV included in-depth, personal interviews with 20 employees who filled out the second questionnaire. The aim was to gain a deeper understanding of the closing and its consequences. This purposive subsample of 20 was diverse; it was composed of women and men of various marital, occupation, and employment statuses. The interviews were conducted in early 1981 and were audiotaped.

This report focused on the 288 displaced workers who responded to both questionnaires, a group of mature workers and four-fifths (79 percent) of those who responded to the initial questionnaire. Preliminary analyses showed that Phase II and Phase III survey samples did *not* differ significantly from each other or from the plant population of mature workers on demographic variables (e.g., age, gender, income occupation, race), tenure at the plant, or on the outcome measures.[11]

Several features of the study are noteworthy:

• The project focused on mature workers (age 52 to 65) and many (45 percent of the sample) were women. According to the literature, members of these groups are particularly vulnerable to the negative effects of a plant shutdown. These respondents, however, had enjoyed steady employment with an average tenure of 26 years at the plant.

- The data were collected during a time of economic recession in an area marked by high unemployment (15 percent) and several other plant closings during the study years (1980–1982). Unemployment rates in previous plant closing research did not exceed 10 percent.

- This was a longitudinal study with survey data collected at two points in time: (1) a year after the announcement of the closing, yet a year before the scheduled closing; and (2) after workers left the plant (because departments in the plant were phased out, the respondents left the plant at various points in time following the announced closing).

- Data were available on various facets of the worker's life including physical and mental health and economic measures.

DESCRIPTION OF SAMPLE

Respondents were predominantly white, married, Catholic workers with at least a high school education. (See Table 4.1.) All were between 52 and 66 years old and a large portion (45 percent) were women. They were remarkably stable in terms of place of residence and job tenure. All but one currently lived in the plant's metropolitan area. Most (62 percent) had resided there for the major portion of their lives and 89 percent owned their homes. Tenure at the plant ranged from 2 to 44 years ($X = 26$ yrs) with many employees located in production and laborer positions (43 percent). The mean 1979 earnings were $20,000. Most workers appeared financially stable prior to the closing with 63 percent reporting "occasionally" or "never" worrying about meeting "family expenses and bills."

Although males and females had similar tenure at the plant ($X = 26$ years for both), female workers differed from their male co-workers in several ways. Women had less education and tended to be concentrated in lower level occupations. Specifically, women comprised a majority of clerical (87 percent) and production workers (60 percent) while men constituted a majority of marginal (69 percent) and skilled trades (95 percent) employees. On average, women earned $7000 less than men. This income differential was due in part to the fact that males were more likely than females to hold higher paying occupations. There was also an income differential between women and men in the same occupational category. This gap ranged from $1,500 in the technical-clerical positions to $11,000 in the professional-managerial occupations. Another striking difference between men and women was their marital status. Almost all (91 percent) of the men were married but only about half (51 percent) of the women. Women were also more likely than men to have never married (26 percent of women and 3 percent of men).

Table 4.1
Phase II Sample Characteristics in Percentages by Gender

Variables	Male	Female	Total
Race			
White	95	97	96
Nonwhite	5	3	4
	100 (159)	100 (129)	100 (288)
Religion			
Protestant	41	31	36
Catholic	54	63	58
Other	5	6	15
	100 (159)	100 (129)	100 (288)
Education			
Grade	6	4	5
Some High School	23	26	24
High School	36	51	43
<BA	17	10	14
College	18	9	14
	100 (159)	100 (129)	100 (288)

$(x^2=11.4, df=4, p=.04)$

Variables	Male	Female	Total
Marital Status			
Married	91	51	72
Widowed	3	10	6
Divorced/Separated	3	13	7
Never Married	3	26	15
	100 (159)	100 (129)	100 (288)

$(x^2=68.0, df=3, p=.00)$

Variables	Male	Female	Total
Occupation			
Professional Managerial	35	22	30
Clerical/Technical	3	19	10
Skilled Trades	31	2	18
Production Laborers	31	57	42
	100 (159)	100 (129)	100 (288)

$(x^2=68.8, df=3, p=.00)$

The displaced workers completed the second questionnaire approximately one year after they left the plant. At that time, about one-third of the respondents were working (35 percent), one-third retired (32 percent) and one-third unemployed (33 percent). More women than men, however, were unemployed (39 percent versus 27 percent) and fewer (26 percent versus 42 percent) were working. (See Table 4.2.) Almost all the retired and unemployed respondents received income from sources such as pension, severance, social security, and unemployment benefits. For example, two-thirds (68 percent) collected severance payments that averaged $18,000, and nearly all (94 percent) were eligible for pension benefits which average $462 a month. There were no gender differences in the amount of these funds. (See Table 4.2.)

MEASURES

Outcome Measures

Nine outcome variables characterize economic and noneconomic factors. All have been validated at the University of Michigan Institute for Social Research.[12] They include four measures of psychological health, two of physical health, and three of economic circumstances.

Psychological Health. The four measures are life satisfaction, marital happiness, morale, and anxiety. To characterize *life satisfaction*, respondents rated their satisfaction with life as a whole from 1 (completely dissatisfied) to 7 (completely satisfied). *Marital Happiness* was measured on a 5-point scale: "taking things all together, how would you describe your marriage?" Responses ranged from 1 (very unhappy) to 5 (very happy). Bradburn's Affect Balance Scale was used to measure *morale*.[13] Here, respondents indicated whether or not, "in the last few weeks, they had experienced 10 feelings such as "restlessness," "loneliness," "boredom," and "happiness." Ratings on the positive and negative items were added and scores ranged from 0 (low morale) to 10 (high morale).[14] A measure developed by Veroff and his associates was used to measure *anxiety*.[15] Five symptoms (nervousness, headaches, loss of appetite, upset stomach, and problems of sleeping) were indexed on a 4-point frequency scale.[16] Scores on the items were summed and the total anxiety score ranged from 5 (low) to 20 (high).[17]

Physical Health. Respondents rated their *current health* on a 4-point scale ranging from poor to very good. To characterize the amount of *health limitations* in daily activities, they used a 5-point scale (1 = none and 5 = a lot).

Economic Circumstances. Respondents indicated their annual earnings (*individual income*) for 1979 and for 1981. In addition, they indicated the category, ranging from 1 ($15,000) to 6 ($35,000), of their total *family income*. The third economic indicator was *financial worries*. It was measured

Table 4.2
Characteristics of Sample by Gender

Variable	Male			Female			F	Total			Total Range
	N	x̄	SD	N	x̄	SD		N	x̄	SD	
Age	159	58	3.6	129	58	3.2	n.s.	288	58	3.4	52-66
Years Employed	159	26	10.0	129	26	11.8	n.s.	288	26	10.8	2 to 44
Retired—Phase III	159	.30	.46	129	.34	.48	n.s.	288	.32	.48	0 to 1
Working—Phase III	159	.42	.49	129	.26	.44	F=8.58 p=.00	288	.35	.47	0 to 1
Unemployed—Phase III	159	.27	.44	129	.39	.49	F=5.10 p=.02	288	.33	.47	0 to 1
Married	159	.91	.28	129	.52	.50	F=69.80 p-.00	288	.74	.44	0 to 1
$ Pension	88	$487	$310	87	$437	$221	n.s.	175	$462	$270	$33 to $2020
$ Severance	63	$19140	$16725	63	$17348	$13404	n.s.	126	$18244	$15121	$563 to $60375
$ Social Security	42	$711	$228	26	$623	$330	n.s.	68	$678	$272	$226 to $2000
$ Unemployment	42	$552	$244	43	$574	$217	n.s.	85	$563	$230	$112 to $800
# Other Dependents	159	1.29	1.12	129	.26	.62	F=88.91 p=.00	288	.83	1.06	0 to 6
Months Gone	159	12.6	4.53	129	13.9	4.55	F=5.81 p=.02	288	13.16	4.58	3 to 30

on a 5-point scale showing the frequency (1 = never and 5 = all the time) of worrying that "total family income will not be enough to meet . . . expenses and bills."

Program Evaluations

In addition to these outcome measures, four evaluation measures are discussed; they focused on company organized programs for employees. These measures included the respondents' evaluation of the *preretirement* and *career continuation* programs, and of *the phase-out activities* as a whole. To indicate their opinions of the preretirement and career continuation programs, respondents used a 7-point scale (1 = not at all valuable and 7 = extremely valuable). For analyses purposes these scores were converted to a 3-point scale ranging from (−1) for negative responses to (+1) for positive ones. The respondents used a 5-point scale (1 = very poorly and 5 = very well) to indicate how well they felt "the management handled the phase-out." The fourth measure was the respondent's assessment of *the impact of the plant closing* on their lives. This measure was an open ended question, "What effects do you think the closing of the plant will have on your life in the long run?" The responses were late coded into either positive, negative, or neutral categories. The first response was reported in this research.

RESULTS

This section will present the research findings. The interpretation and discussion of these findings are presented in next section.[18]

Changes in the Outcome Measures

Economic Outcomes. In contrast to many reports of plant closings, the men and women in this study experienced a gain in both individual and family incomes between the two surveys. The increase for men, however, was greater than for women. The men's individual income was enhanced almost twice as much as that of the women; the income of men increased $7000, $4000 for women. This differential augmentation resulted in an even wider gap in the income of men and women at the point of the second survey. At the second survey point, men had an average income that was over $9000 greater than women's compared to one that was almost $7000 more at the first survey point. The family income also increased for both men and women. Although the workers' economic situation was enhanced, their subjective view of the existence of financial worries did not change; at both points it was in the "occasional" category. (See Table 4.3.)

Noneconomic Outcomes. The results indicate gender differences in both

Table 4.3
Means of Variables in Phase II and Phase III for Males and Females

| | Male | | | | | | Female | | | | | |
| | | Phase II | | Phase III | | | | Phase II | | Phase III | | |
Variables	N	Mean	S.D	Mean	S.D	t-stat	N	Mean	S.D	Mean	S.D	t-stat
Individual Income	159	$22971	$8226	$29670	$11806	8.81**	129	$16294	$5197	$20347	$8127	6.88**
Family Income	159	4.1	1.5	4.7	1.5	5.68**	129	3.3	1.6	3.8	1.7	3.4**
Financial Worries	159	2.2	1.1	2.2	1.1	0.69	129	2.4	1.2	2.2	1.0	-1.76
Present Health	159	3.2	0.8	3.0	0.8	-2.71**	129	3.0	0.8	3.1	0.8	1.39
Health Limitations	159	1.7	1.1	2.1	1.2	3.69**	129	2.0	1.2	2.2	1.3	1.43
Anxiety	159	8.2	2.1	8.3	2.2	0.78	129	9.0	2.3	8.9	2.5	-.66
Life Satisfaction	159	5.1	1.5	5.0	1.4	-.35	129	5.1	1.4	4.9	1.4	-1.06
Morale	159	7.2	1.9	7.3	2.2	0.15	129	7.0	2.1	7.3	2.3	1.85
Marital Happiness	135	4.4	1.0	4.3	1.0	-1.03	49	4.2	1.0	4.1	1.0	-2.42*

Family Income — 1 (<$15,000) to 6 (>$35,000)
Financial Worries — 1 (Never) to 5 (All the Time)
Present Health — 1 (Poor) to 4 (Very Good)
Health Limitations — 1 (None) to 5 (A Lot)
Anxiety — 5 (Low) to 20 (High)
Life Satisfaction — 1 (Completely Dissatisfied) to 7 (Completely Satisfied)
Morale — 1 (Low) to 10 (High)
Marital Happiness — 1 (Very Unhappy) to 5 (Very Happy)

* $p \leq .05$
** $p \leq .01$

the number and type of noneconomic variables that changed significantly. Women changed on one of the six noneconomic variables; it was a *psychological* health measure. They experienced a decrease in marital happiness. Males, on the other hand, had significant modification on two of the six measures; both were *physical* health outcomes. After leaving the plant, the men assessed their current health as poorer and indicated more health limitations than they had prior to the closing. We see, then, that the events during the plant phase out and closing had different noneconomic consequences for men and women. Women saw changes in a social relation: marriage. Men, however, perceived an influence on an individual characteristic: health. The noneconomic effect for both men and women was a negative one; they were worse after the plant closing.

Programs to Ease the Impact of the Closing

Preretirement Program. The study addressed two specific company-sponsored programs: the preretirement program available to salaried and unionized employees age 52 or over and their spouses and the career continuation program for only salaried workers. The preretirement program began in October 1980 and consisted of six weekly sessions. The meetings were held during worktime and covered topics such as adjustment to retirement, financial planning, relocation, and financial management. The program had strong involvement (80 percent) and was evaluated positively by a majority (62 percent) of participants. (Only one-tenth [11 percent] of the participants had negative comments and the remainder were neutral.) Many indicated they would have preferred the program had been offered much earlier in their careers. There were no gender differences in these responses.

Career Continuation Program. The career continuation program (summer of 1981) covered job search activities and organized employment fairs in which workers were interviewed by potential employers. These events were held at the plant. Of the salaried workers eligible for this program, almost half (47 percent) participated. Women were more than twice as likely to participate as men (64 percent versus 25 percent). Yet, men and women did not differ in their evaluation of the programs; about half of the females (48 percent) and males (46 percent) rated it as valuable. Many nonparticipants indicated the program should have been scheduled earlier.

Phase-out Activities. In terms of the respondents' overall evaluations of the plant's phase-out activities, two-fifths (42 percent) indicated that the plant phase-out was handled well. One-fifth (18 percent) thought the activities were managed poorly; and the remainder (40 percent) were neutral.

Impact of Closing. The most revealing indicator of the overall effect of the plant closing on workers' lives was their response to the item, "What effects do you think the closing of the Washington Plant will have on your life in the long run?" Two-thirds (67 percent) felt it would have a neutral effect; one-quarter (26 percent) thought it would be negative; and less than one-tenth (7 percent) expected positive consequences. Women more often than men anticipated a negative long-run effect (32 percent versus 21 percent) and less often expected a positive consequence (3 percent versus 9 percent).

DISCUSSION

In discussing the findings, one might be optimistic and see the glass as mostly (two-thirds) filled. From this perspective, one could say that on only three of the nine outcome measures were there negative changes. On the other hand, one might take a more pessimistic view and observe the glass as partly (one-third) empty. Here, one might say that in spite of the advanced notice and numerous programs, there were negative consequences of the plant closing. This author takes a middle of the road perspective and interprets the activities during the plant phase-out as at best buffering, and at least forestalling, the usual extensive problems displaced workers face.

Overall, the findings indicate the Washington Plant closing had few deleterious effects on workers one year after they left the plant. These results stand in contrast to much of the existing plant closing literature. Instead of having extensive problems, these mature workers were fairly healthy, satisfied, and content. At neither survey point were the scores in the poor or unsatisfactory range, relative to norms established in the studies that originally developed these measures.[19] Even though the significant noneconomic changes reflected a decrease in physical and psychological health, the magnitude of the change was relatively small. There were, however, some differences by gender.

Gender Differences

Why did the plant closing have differential outcomes for these men and women? While the data does not allow one to determine definitive causes, they and the literature suggest some plausible explanations. That women, and not men, reported a decrease in marital happiness likely reflects other variations between men and women in such things as the importance of relationships, expectations of the spouse, and employment status.

These data suggest social relationships at the plant were more important for women than for men. In the first survey, the female workers were more likely than the males to indicate they anticipated that following the closing, they would miss co-workers "a lot" (44 percent versus 32 percent). In addition, co-workers constituted a larger part of the social network of women compared to men; women were twice as likely as men (20 percent versus 11 percent) to indicate that over half of their social network was composed of women they worked with at the plant. It seems, then, that women may have been more sensitive to the loss of relationships the work place had provided.

It is probable that these women turned to their spouses for emotional support, possibly expecting the spouse to fill the void created by a loss of social relationships. Since a larger portion of women than men were displaced by the closing, it is likely that more women than men turned to the spouse for financial support as well; only 26 percent of the women compared to 42 percent of the men were working at the time of the second survey. The women who were disappointed in their spouses' reactions may have felt less happy about the marital relationship.

The varied noneconomic results for men and women may also reflect a gender difference in labeling and reporting problems. It may be that men were more reluctant than women to acknowledge and report interpersonal problems and were more comfortable in admitting health concerns. The process of adaptation to the closing may also be important. Women had been away from the plant for a longer period than men (13 months versus 12 months). It is possible that the women had experienced health problems which had abated by the time of the second survey.

The fact that women were more likely than men to be unemployed a year after leaving the plant may also have been related to gender discrimination in the marketplace. Literature indicates mature *women are more likely than similarly aged men to face age discrimination*. They are also more likely to encounter these prejudices at an earlier age than men.[20] Although we cannot delimit the causes, the data clearly indicate that this plant closing influenced men and women in a different way.

Level of Functioning

There were several possible explanations for the generally positive findings for both men and women. First, selection bias may have resulted in a differential response rate that was correlated with the outcome measures. In other words, the less well functioning workers may not have participated in the second survey. Second, it was possible that the most physically and psychologically distressed workers had left the plant prior to the first survey and were not included in the study at all. Similarly, the times of data collections may not have coincided with the most stressful period of adjustment. Another plausible explanation and the one which the data support was that the respondents' favorable socioeconomic situation and the company sponsored phase-out programs ameliorated, or at least forestalled, the usual negative effects.

Since one of the links between job loss and physical/mental health symptoms is economic deprivation, it is not surprising that these respondents had few deleterious consequences. In fact, a substantial number (35 percent) of the workers were employed following the plant closing. Almost all of these persons (90 percent) were reemployed at a plant located in the same geographical area and owned by the same corporation. Some workers transferred directly to the sister plant without sacrificing any work days. (The company organized van pools so that workers could more easily commute to the new work site which was about 30 miles from the Washington Plant). Thus, because of the transfer rights, over one-third of the workers were not permanently displaced from the labor market even though they lived in an area with a very high unemployment rate. Furthermore, a majority (80 percent) of all the respondents worked at least a part of 1981, the year for which the Phase III individual income was recorded; many worked the entire year. In addition, many respondents worked overtime in order to keep pace with the production needs and some terminated individuals were recalled to work at various times during the phase-out.

Among the 33 percent who were unemployed and the 32 percent who had retired at the second survey point, almost all received income from sources such as pension, severance, social security, and unemployment benefits. For example, the company had a relatively generous severance policy; all salaried workers, regardless of tenure, and all hourly workers, with at least two years of service who did not transfer to a sister plant, were eligible for severance benefits. Consequently, two-thirds (68 percent) of the nonworking respondents received severance payments averaging $18,000. A similar proportion (64 percent) of the unemployed and retired subsample were collecting pension benefits averaging almost $500 a month. Another 30 percent anticipated receiving pension benefits. Because of eligibility revisions, additional employees were eligible to receive pensions, and fewer were penalized for early retirement.

The 1981 income from the plant and these supplementary benefits were high enough to allow some unemployed respondents to postpone the job search. Among the 41 percent of the unemployed who had delayed looking for another job, the reason most frequently given was the adequacy of other sources of income. These positive income outcomes are tempered by the fact that often they were the calm before the storm of drastic income reductions. As time-limited resources such as overtime, severance, and unemployment benefits terminated, many respondents would have to cope with a substantially smaller annual income. Therefore, while the elevated income probably was a buffer, it also may have given the displaced workers a false sense of security.

Income issues aside, it appears that the plant closing was not currently perceived as a major disruption to the lives of a majority of workers. After leaving the plant, over half (53 percent) of the respondents appeared unchanged from pre-plant-closing career plans (e.g., to work or retire). The early notice, the completion of impact bargaining, the revision of pension eligibility, and the delineation of rules for severance benefits allowed most respondents to realistically plan for the change. The other side of the coin is that almost half (47 percent) had changed their work plans within a year after leaving the plant.

The greatest disruption occurred among those (33 percent) who continued to be unemployed a year following the closing. All of these displaced workers had indicated in the first survey they planned to work after the plant closed. Most, however, had assumed that employment at another local company-owned plant would not be available. Thus, they had indicated a plan to work for some other company after the shutdown. No doubt the areas' high unemployment rate was reflected in their unemployment status. So despite the availability of unanticipated employment at a sister plant, one third of the respondents had not found other employment a year after leaving the Washington Plant.

Overall, we see some negative consequences of the plant closing among these mature workers. Though the specific contributions of the advance notice and company programs cannot be demonstrated, there is evidence that the concerned responses of the company cushioned the immediate economic consequences of the shutdown and were well received. Generally, levels of all outcome measures remained in a satisfactory range.

SUMMARY OF FINDINGS

This chapter reports findings from a plant closing study involving workers 52 years and older with a long history of employment stability. These individuals were employed in a company which provided several programs during a two-year plant phase-out. The paper addressed the question, "Are there significant changes in economic, physical health, and mental health circumstances of men and women between the pre- and post-plant closing surveys, a period of at least one year?" The first survey was completed in fall 1980, a year after the announcement of the closing and a year prior to the scheduled plant shutdown; and the second survey was concluded on average a year after workers left the plant.

Results suggest that women and men were affected differentially by the plant phase-out and closing. Though both groups experienced an increase in income, the plant shutdown negatively influenced women's psychological health (e.g., marital happiness) and men's physical health (e.g., health evaluation and health limitations). The other measures remained stable for both groups. Under such relatively positive economic circumstances, the closing still had negative impacts, however. It is likely that these negative changes reflected job loss and related events such as changes in the social network, the challenge of restructuring one's time, and creating new opportunities to feel useful, productive, and needed. This plant had special significance to the employees, most of whom had worked there for more than half their

lives. Some had never worked anywhere else; others marked the third generation family member employed at the plant. It is also likely that, in addition
to these losses, workers who transferred to the neighboring plant or found
other employment faced concerns associated with that transition and with
the new work environment.

Despite the potentially bleak scenario, the women's and men's functioning
on each measure was in the normal range at the time of both surveys.
Increased income and the availability of various company programs, (e.g.,
up to a two-year advanced notice of the closing, transfer rights resulting in
alternative employment for one-third of the respondents, and pension and
severance benefits for most employees who permanently lost their jobs)
probably cushioned the workers against more negative consequences. Furthermore, the most senior workers were fortunate and actually enhanced
outcomes for their younger co-workers; that is, all workers (age 58 and
over) were eligible for pension benefits; this opportunity encouraged many
to forego their transfer rights. This gave transfer opportunities to the workers under age 58 and avoided their permanent dislocation, a job search in
a depressed economy, and/or relocation to geographical areas with greater
employment opportunities.

Consequences of this plant closing differed from many case studies which
describe severe negative outcomes for workers. The findings corroborated
results of selective and limited negative effects from the quasi-experimental,
longitudinal research of Buss and Redburn.[21] The context, sample, and
methodology in this study help illuminate these similarities and disparities.
Previous research has tended to focus on plant closings that have little or
no closing notice. Their samples were often comprised of white, male, blue-
collar workers whose average age ranged from 40 to 54, and who were
employed in declining heavy industrial settings located in areas with low
unemployment. This study had a more mature sample (X age = 58 years)
of occupationally diverse workers who were relatively highly educated. This
sample received a higher than average wage and included a large portion
of women in what had historically been a relatively secure and expanding
pharmaceutical industry located in an area of high unemployment. Moreover, the reported findings were from survey data which the literature indicated are usually more positive than those from interviews.

IMPLICATIONS

The plant closing literature and the findings of this study suggest the value
of distinguishing types of unemployment, the complexity of this form of
unemployment, steps for further research, and the development of social
policy.

Research

In relation to research, because there are distinctions in the context, sample, and methodology across studies, one cannot easily compare findings. In addition, without control groups we are not able to distinguish the effects of a closing from other concomitant events. Further research should be designed so as to allow comparisons between studies. This requires the selection of plants for study from a random sample of facilities, the inclusion of control groups in the research design, and the use of identical measures in several studies. Furthermore, longitudinal research initiated before the shutdown, in order to include the usual industrial contraction before a closing, and following the displaced workers for several years will: (1) increase our knowledge on how the process of closing affects the outcome; (2) further delineate the adjustment and coping processes of displaced workers; and (3) provide observations of respondents' situations after they exhaust their temporary financial resources (e.g., severance and unemployment benefits). This quasi-experimental, longitudinal research design requires both the cooperation of plant management, an uncommon occurrence, and a national listing of plants closing or likely to close.

In addition to a sampling frame for more sophisticated research, such a listing will also furnish national data on the extensiveness of plant closings. Current estimates of the incidence of plant closings rely heavily upon such data as that provided by Dun and Bradstreet. Often these data are not comprehensive.

Policy

The development of the list of plant closings would likely necessitate new national public policy. The policy should address at least two areas: (1) the requirement that closing facilities provide certain minimal data to a governmental agency; and (2) the availability of these data to researchers.

Another policy consideration is the feasibility of requesting that all companies give employees some minimal advance notice of a shutdown. This study showed that contrary to plant management's concern about employee retaliation and sabotage, the advance notice did not result in such behavior. This finding was remarkable considering that the plant was in a strategic industry where subversion may have resulted in deaths and expensive law suits. The policy should also encourage facilities that are closing to take more responsibility for the displaced workers by providing them programs and severance payments and by extending their medical benefits for at least a year following closing.

Other Steps

Even before such a policy is implemented, several steps can be taken. Longitudinal research such as the Panel Study of Income Dynamics, the

Current Population Survey and the Census can include questions about employment due to plant closings. Government agencies such as the Bureau of Labor Statistics which already collect unemployment data can begin to differentiate types of unemployment. These sources would then supply comprehensive information on the prevalence of plant closings and provide opportunities to study the long-term consequences and adaptations following plant closings. Data analyses should include attention to subgroups such as women, minorities, and older workers.

Unions and professional organizations should give increased attention to job security in their bargaining sessions. For example, unions need to include provisions in their contracts for phase-out programs, severance and mass lay-off benefits, and extension of medical benefits. As shown here, such interventions can result in a closing with minimal, short-term negative effects on the displaced workers. There is a need for more systematic attention to the development, utilization, evaluation, and cost effectiveness of such services. The findings of this study support the view that the company's forethought, phase-out schedule, and programs were beneficial. Should further research support these positive findings, varied methods to disseminate this information must be developed.

Regional task forces composed of community service agency administrators, researchers, union representatives, and other interested persons could advocate the use of intervention programs. They could provide consultation regarding phase-out strategies to the management of closing plants. The task forces could also insure the coordination of company, union, and community services and resources. Furthermore, they could help develop adequate outreach services to workers. For example, representatives from local family service, unemployment, physical health, and mental health agencies might be located in the union hall or at the closing company site during the phaseout.

In conclusion, unemployment due to mass layoffs and plant closings is likely to increase even in times of economic recovery because of the deindustrialization in America. No longer is this unemployment problem confined to certain segments of the labor market such as unskilled, blue-collar men usually employed in heavy industrial settings. Instead, it is affecting women and men of all ages in white-collar and skilled blue-collar positions. This phenomenon deserves additional research and social policy attention.

NOTES

This is a revised version of a paper presented at the Gerontological Society of America Conference in San Antonio, Texas in 1984. This research was supported by the American Association of Retired Persons, the National Institute of Mental Health Grant #MH09090–01, and the Ford Foundation through the National Research Council.

1. Robert W. Bednarzik, "Layoffs and Permanent Job Losses: Workers' Traits and Cyclical Patterns," *Monthly Labor Review* (September 1983): 3–12.

2. P. O. Flaim and E. Sehgal, "Displaced Workers of 1979–83: How Well Have They Fared?" *Monthly Labor Review*, 108 (June 1985): 3–16.

3. *Daily Labor Report* (Washington, D.C.: Bureau of National Affairs, April 20, 1982), pp. 1–2.

4. U.S. Bureau of Labor Statistics, *Permanent Mass Layoffs and Plant Closings, 1987.* Washington, D.C.: U.S. Government Printing Office, 1988.

5. See Jeanne Prial Gordus, Paul Jarley, and Louis A. Ferman, *Plant Closings and Economic Dislocation* (Kalamazoo, Mich.: W. E. Upjohn Institute for Employment Research, 1981), for a review of more recent plant closing studies; and William Harber, Louis Ferman and James Hudson, *The Impact of Technological Change: The American Experience.* (New York: W. E. Upjohn Institute for Employment Research, 1963) for a review of earlier studies.

6. A. Baum, R. Fleming, and D. Reddy, "Unemployment Stress: Loss of Control, Reactance and Learned Helplessness," *Social Science and Medicine* 22 (1986): 509–516; Katherine Hooper Briar, *The Effect of Long-Term Unemployment on Workers and Their Families* (San Francisco: R & E Research Associate, 1978); Katherine Hooper Briar, "The Impact of Long-term Unemployment on Workers and Their Families," in *The Forum*, ed. National Conference on Social Work (New York: Columbia University Press, 1978), pp. 102–112; Harvey M. Brenner, *Mental Illness and the Economy* (Boston: Harvard University Press, 1973); Harvey M. Brenner, *Estimating the Social Costs of National Economic Policy. The Social Costs of National Economic Policy: Implications for Mental and Physical Health and Criminal Aggression* (Washington, D.C.: U.S. Government Printing Office, October 26, 1976); M. Frese and G. Mohr, "Prolonged Unemployment and Depression in Older Workers: A Longitudinal Study of Intervening Variables," *Social Science and Medicine* 25 (1987): 173–178; Sidney Cobb and Stanislav V. Kasl, "Save Youngstown," *Termination: The Consequences of Job Loss* (Washington, D.C.: U.S. Government Printing Office, 1977), pp. 175–180; Sidney Cobb and Stanislav V. Kasl, "Some Mental Health Consequences of Plant Closing and Job Loss," in *Mental Health and the Economy*, Louis Ferman and Jeanne Gordus, eds. (Kalamazoo, Mich.: W. E. Upjohn Institute, 1979); Jeanne Gordus, Paul Jarley, and Louis Ferman, *Plant Closings and Economic Dislocation*; Illinois Advisory Committee to the United States Commission on Civil Rights, *Shutdown: Economic Dislocation and Equal Opportunity* (Washington, D.C.: U.S. Government Printing Office, 1981); Stanislav Kasl, Susan Gore, and Sidney Cobb, "The Experience of Losing a Job," *Psychosomatic Medicine* (1975): 106–122; R. Kessler, J. House, J. Turner, "Unemployment and Health in a Community Sample," *Journal of Health and Social Behavior* 28 (1987): 51–59; Ramsey Liem, "Beyond Economics: The Health Cost of Unemployment," *Health and Medicine* (Fall 1983): 3–9; Ramsay Liem, and Paula Rayman, "Health and the Social Cost of Unemployment," *American Psychologist* (1982): 1116–1123; Bernard Portis, and Michael Suys, *The Effect of Advanced Notice in a Plant Shutdown: A Case of the Kelvinator Plant in London, Ontario* (London, Ontario: School of Business Administration, University of Western Ontario, 1970); A. Shostak, "The Human Cost of Plant Closing," *Job Loss: A Psychosocial Study of Worker Reactions to a Plant-Closing in a Company Town in Southern Appalachia*, Ph.D. dissertation, (Washington, D.C.: U.S. Department of Labor, 1977).

7. Michael Aiken, Louis A. Ferman, and Harold L. Sheppard, *Economic Failure Alienation and Extremism* (Ann Arbor: University of Michigan Press, 1968); John W. Dorsey, "The Mack Case: A Study in Unemployment," in *Studies in the Economics of Income Maintenance*, Otto Eckstein, ed. (Washington, D.C.: Brookings Institution, 1967); Herbert Hammerman, "Five Case Studies of Displaced Workers," *Monthly Labor Review* (1964): 663–690; Illinois Advisory Committee to the United States Commission on Civil Rights, *Shutdown: Economic Dislocation and Equal Opportunity*; Joan M. McCrea, *The Reemployment Experience of Workers Displaced in the Closing of the American Viscose Plant at Roanoke* (Charlottseville: University of Virginia, 1968); Herbert Parnes, Mary G. Gagen, and Randall H. King, "Job Loss among Long Service Workers", in *Work and Retirement: A Longitudinal Survey of Men*, Herbert Parnes, ed. (Cambridge, Mass.: MIT Press, 1981); Bernard Portis, and Michael Say, *The Effect of Advanced Notice in a Plant Shutdown: A Case Study of the Closing of the Kelvinator Plant in London, Ontario*; Philip Rones, "The Labor Market Problems of Older Workers," *Monthly Labor Review* (May 1983): 3–12; George P. Schultz and Arnold P. Weber, *Strategies for the Displaced Worker* (New York: Harper and Row, 1969); James L. Stern, "Consequences of a Plant Closure," *Journal of Human Resources* (1971): 2–21; Robert G. Turner and William Whitaker, "The Impact of Mass Layoffs on Older Workers," *Industrial Gerontology* (1973): 14–21.

8. Terry F. Buss and Stevens Redburn, "How to Shut Down a Plant," *Industrial Management* (1981): 4–10; idem, *Mass Unemployment, Plant Closings and Community Mental Health* (Beverly Hills: Sage Publications, 1983); idem, *Shutdown at Youngstown* (New York: SUNY Press, 1983); Barry Bluestone and Bennett Harrison, *Capital and Communities: The Causes and Consequences of Private Disinvestment* (Washington, D.C.: Progressive Alliance, 1980); Shostak, "The Human Cost of Plant Closing"; Gordus et al., *Plant Closings and Economic Dislocation*; L. Ferman and J. Gordus, eds., *Mental Health and the Economy* (Kalamazoo, Michigan: The Upjohn Institute, 1979).

9. Buss and Redburn, "How to Shut Down a Plant"; idem, *Mass Unemployment, Plant Closings and Community Mental Health; Shutdown at Youngstown*; Kasl et al., "The Experience of Losing a Job"; Susan Gore, "The Effect of Social Support in Moderating the Health Consequences of Unemployment," *Journal of Health and Social Behavior* (1978): 157–165; "The Influence of Social Support and Related Variables in Ameliorating the Consequences of Job Loss," dissertation, University of Pennsylvania, 1973; Cobb and Kasl, "Some Mental Health Consequences of Plant Closing and Job Loss."

10. All names have been changed.

11. Joyce Beckett and Carol Hollingshead, *Older Workers, Retirement and Social Supports* (Ann Arbor: Institute of Gerontology, University of Michigan, 1982).

12. Angus Campbell, *Sense of Well Being in America: Recent Patterns and Trends* (New York: McGraw-Hill, 1980); Gerald Gurin, Joseph Veroff, and Shield Feld, *Americans View Their Mental Health* (New York: Basic Books, 1960); J. Veroff, E. Douvan, and R. Kulka, *Inner American: A Self Portrait from 1975–1976* (New York: Basic Books, 1981); idem, *Mental Health in America* (New York: Basic Books, 1981).

13. N. M. Bradburn, and D. Caplovitz, *Reports on Happiness* (Chicago: Aldine, 1965).

14. Standardized alphas for the positive and negative items in Phase II were .67 and .59, respectively; in Phase III, they were .73 and .67.

15. Gurin et al., *Americans View Their Mental Health*; Veroff et al., *Inner American: A Self Portrait from 1957–1976; Mental Health in America.*

16. These symptoms are similar to the criteria for the generalized anxiety disorder defined by the Schedule for Affective Disorders and Schizophrenia (SADS), an instrument prominent in clinical research and service delivery, and one for which detailed diagnostic criteria have been developed.

17. The standardized alphas in Phase II and Phase III were .71 and .74, respectively.

18. There are several statistical techniques appropriate for the analysis of change. These include bivariate methods, such as change scores and correlations between the scores at points of data collection, and multivariate analyses, such as regression and analysis of covariance. Since this research was exploratory, paired t-tests were used to assess reliable differences in means.

19. Veroff et al., *Inner American: A Self Portrait from 1957–1976; Mental Health in America.*

20. Jeanne Gordus, "The Human Resource Implications of Plant Shutdown", *Annals of the American Academy of Political and Social Science* (September 1984): 66–79; Herbert Hammerman, "Five Case Studies of Displaced Workers."

21. Buss and Redburn, "How to Shut Down a Plant"; idem, *Mass Unemployment, Plant Closing and Community Mental Health.*

5

Sex Differentials in Unemployment Rates in Male-Dominated Occupations and Industries during Periods of Economic Downturn

Elizabeth Monk-Turner

This chapter is concerned with the manner in which unemployment affects women differently than men, especially during depressed economic times, in male-dominated occupations and industries. Unemployment rates for women do generally exceed those for men. Women also tend to carry more of the burden of an increase in unemployment during a recession. Similarly, Monk-Turner found that women, who were the last employed in male-dominated industries, were affected more than men by cyclical changes in the economy. Women who are among the last hired in hard economic times are the first to be let go. This undermines gains women have made in entering nontraditional fields. Monk-Turner also points to the importance of legislation in softening the impact of market forces tendencies to create greater inequalities.

Increasing research interest has been devoted in recent years to analyzing sex differentials in unemployment rates. It is well known that unemployment rates for women exceed those for men and that this gap varies procyclically, being greatest at business cycle peaks. Many suggest that the unemployment situation of men deteriorates more than that of women during a recession because men are concentrated in jobs in the "industry sector." Business

Table 5.1
Timing of Business Cycle Peak and Trough Quarters since 1969

Peak	11/1969	11/1973	2/1980	7/1981
Trough	11/1970	3/1975	7/1980	11/1982

Source: Drawn from U.S. Bureau of Labor Statistics data, Employment and Earnings, 1969-1982.

downturns tend to be more severe in this sector, particularly in manufacturing and construction industries, than in the female-dominated "service industries" where employees are believed to be protected from the harshest effects of a recession.[1] While there may be merit to this analysis, it does not address how unemployment rates vary by sex over the business cycle in male-dominated occupations and industries.

An argument is made that the burden of increase in unemployment in male-dominated occupations and industries, during periods of economic downturn, is borne more by female than male workers. Female workers, in these male-dominated jobs, are likely to be among the first to be let go during bad economic times, because they are not perceived by employers and others as primary family workers. Women continue to be viewed as secondary workers, who are working for "pin money," and who are not committed to the labor force. Therefore, during periods of economic downturn, employers may act on these perceptions and, in making a decision between firing a male or female worker, will choose to fire the latter as this seems to them the most "fair" decision.

This study investigates sex differentials in unemployment rates during peaks and troughs of the business cycle since 1969. Data indicate that unemployment rates for women exceed those for men and that this gap varies countercyclically in many male-dominated occupations and industries, being greatest at business cycle troughs. The periods examined are outlined in Table 5.1.

A cyclical peak is defined as the last quarter before a recession (a decline, for at least two quarters, in real GNP) begins. A recession begins in the first quarter real GNP declines; it ends in the quarter when real GNP hits bottom, which is termed the cyclical trough. Once the economy has passed the trough quarter, it is in recovery.[2] A recession is distinguished from a depression in that a recession is a small downturn in GNP and employment, whereas a depression is a large downturn.

Much is written today implying that the women's labor market situation is vastly different than it was years ago. Yet the percentage of women who are professional workers has declined over time. Further, over three-fourths of women professional workers are secondary school teachers or nurses, both low-paying, low-status occupations.[3] Nevertheless, women have made some gains in entering male-dominated fields. My concern centers on how unemployment affects women compared to men, especially during depressed economic times, in male-dominated occupations and industries, as this may indicate how long-term such gains may be.

DEFINING A MALE-DOMINATED OCCUPATION/ INDUSTRY

Reubens and Reubens defined nontraditional jobs as those in which women constitute "a considerably smaller proportion of the work force than their current share of the total employed population."[4] In 1987, women constituted 42 percent of the civilian labor force 20 years of age and over. Occupations and industries where the proportion of women employed is less than 30 percent of the total will be defined here as male-dominated. See Table 5.2 for a breakdown of the percentage of women employed in selected occupations and industries in 1979. These figures are utilized in defining male-dominated occupations and industries for the time period of my investigation.

There has been little change in the proportion of women employed in male-dominated occupations since 1900.[5] Occupational segregation by sex is more extreme than that by race. Harriet Zellner found that 47 percent of all women worked in occupations which are female-dominated (where females constitute 80–100 percent of the total employed), whereas most men (87 percent) worked in occupations where women are underrepresented (where females comprise between 0 and 33 percent of the total employed). Few men or women work in occupations where females comprise between 33 and 49 percent of the total employed.[6] Based on small changes in occupational segregation by sex since 1960, some suggest a trend toward greater sex integration of occupations may currently exist.[7] My research suggests that any gains women have made may be short-term in nature.

WHY WOMEN WORK

Before analyzing sex differences in unemployment rates, it is important to review why women work. Most women work because of economic need. The majority of employed females are single, widowed, divorced or separated, or working to supplement the low income of their spouse.[8] Men are still generally perceived by employers and others as primary family breadwinners, and the myth persists that women work for "pin money."[9] The social consequences of such perception, for example, the problem of the feminization of poverty, are just beginning to be realized.[10]

Female labor force participation is on the rise. In 1948, less than a third

Table 5.2
Women as a Percentage of Total Employment in Selected Occupations and
Industries, 1979

Occupation*	% Female
White-collar workers	52.8
Professional and technical	43.3
Managers and administrators, except farm	24.6
Sales workers	45.1
Clerical workers	80.3
Blue-collar workers	18.5
Operatives, except transport	40.1
Transport equipment operatives	8.0
Nonfarm laborers	11.6
Service workers	62.0
Farm workers	18.0

Industry*	% Female
Mining	11.8
Construction	7.4
Manufacturing	30.9
Durable goods	25.1
Lumber and wood products	12.1
Furniture and fixtures	34.0
Stone, clay, and glass products	19.4
Primary metal industries	11.7
Fabricated metal products	19.9
Machinery, except electrical equipment	19.8
Electrical equipment	43.0
Transportation equipment	16.6
Automobiles	17.4
Nondurable goods	39.9
Food and kindred products	29.2
Textile mill products	46.6
Apparel and other textile products	79.1
Paper and allied products	22.2
Printing and publishing	38.8
Chemicals and allied products	25.4
Rubber and plastics products	34.2
Transportation and public utilities	24.4
Communication and other public utilities	47.3
Wholesale and retail trade	46.0
Finance, insurance, and real estate	57.6
Service industries	61.2
Professional services	65.6

*Male-dominated occupations and industries and underlined.
Source: U.S. Bureau of Labor Statistics, Employment and Earnings, January, 1980.

of all females worked outside the home. Female labor force participation has steadily increased, and, since May 1978, over half (50.1 percent) of all females 16 years of age and over were in the labor force.[11] This rate is, however, deceptively low because of the relatively large proportion of the female population which is over the retirement age, as a result of low female mortality rates. Thus, in 1978, 58.5 percent of women between the ages of 20 and 64 were in the labor force.[12]

Today women and men tend to be employed continuously over the life cycle. In the past, the peak participation periods for women were among women aged 18–19 and those aged 45–64. Younger women worked before entering their child bearing and rearing years, while older women returned to work after rearing children, to help pay for additional family expenses, such as children's college tuition. Since 1963, the most dramatic growth in female labor force participation has been among women aged 20–34.[13] Thus, by 1978, the familiar double peak in female labor force participation virtually disappeared.

Females are entering the labor force in increasing numbers, and, more importantly, they are not dropping out of the labor force during their child bearing and rearing years. This indicates that labor continuity, as well as participation, is increasing among women.[14] One would expect that as female labor force participation and commitment to work increased, then wage and unemployment inequalities by sex would diminish. On the contrary, the reverse situation appears to be the case. Women are in a worse relative position to men today, in terms of income and unemployment, than they were 20 years ago.[15]

MEASURING UNEMPLOYMENT

The unemployment rate is derived by dividing the number of unemployed by the total labor force.[16] The total labor force is defined as the sum of the employed and unemployed who are actively looking for work. Therefore, persons sixteen years of age and over are classified as (1) employed, (2) unemployed, or (3) not in the labor force. The employed includes all those who work for pay or profit at least one hour or more a week (or at least 15 hours a week on a farm or in a family business). Thus, part-time workers, even those actively looking for more work, are counted as employed.

The unemployed includes all those who do not work *and* who are actively looking and available for work, plus individuals on temporary layoff from a job.[17] The following activities qualify an individual as looking for work: registration at an employment agency, being on call at a personnel office, placing or answering ads, writing letters of application, and being interviewed by prospective employers.[18]

Two significant problems exist in measuring unemployment. First, part-time workers are categorized as employed even if they want and are actively seeking full-time employment. Secondly, unemployment statistics do not include "discouraged workers," individuals who would participate in the labor force if economic conditions, even in normal years, were better.[19] Significant numbers of women fall in the discouraged worker category.[20] These are women who desire to work; however, they believe that the likelihood of their finding employment is so negligible that they do not even look. Thus, comparison of unemployment rates may understate the impact of a recession on women relatively more than on men.[21]

CYCLICAL VARIATION IN UNEMPLOYMENT RATES BY OCCUPATION

Table 5.3 shows the level and differences in unemployment rates by occupation for both men and women. Male-dominated occupations are underlined. They include managers, blue-collar workers, transport equipment operatives, nonfarm laborers, and farm workers. Occupations where female employment is over 50 percent of the total, or female-dominated occupations, include white-collar workers, clerical workers, and service workers.

After reviewing the literature, I expected that differences in total unemployment rates by sex could be greater during business cycle peaks, not troughs. This holds true for two of the four periods examined. The unemployment gap is greatest in 1973 and 1981 during business cycle peaks; in 1970 and 1980, it is greatest during business cycle troughs.[22] (It should be noted that the unemployment rate for both men and women between 1969–1982 is greatest during the 1975 and 1982 downturns. In other words, the recession during these periods was greater than for the other two downturns examined). It is interesting to note that in the last downturn examined (1982 trough), the total unemployment rate is higher for men than women. This latest downturn hit manufacturing industries especially hard while service sectors of the economy continued to expand.

Differences in unemployment rates by sex are generally higher for female blue-collar and farm workers during business cycle downturns, not peaks. This pattern holds for three of the four periods examined. The unemployment gap is higher during business cycle troughs, in two of the four periods examined, for transport equipment operatives. It is only in the most recent 1982 trough, however, that the unemployment gap for female managers is greater than in peak periods.

The unemployment gap for nonfarm laborers, which includes construction workers, is greatest during business cycle peaks, not troughs, for three of the four periods examined. Further, the unemployment rate is higher for men than women in this occupational category for the past three business cycle troughs. It must be noted that Title VII of the 1964 Civil Rights Act amended prohibits discrimination on the basis of sex by federal contractors and subcontractors. Many suggest that the effects of this legislation were

Table 5.3
Level and Differences in Unemployment Rates by Sex and Occupation at Business Cycle Peaks and Troughs

Occupation	Unemployment Rate Nov. 1969 Peak			Unemployment Rate Nov. 1970 Trough			Unemployment Rate Nov. 1973 Peak			Unemployment Rate March 1975 Trough		
	Male (1)	Female (2)	Difference (2)-(1)	Male (1)	Female (2)	Difference (2)-(1)	Male (1)	Female (2)	Difference (2)-(1)	Male (1)	Female (2)	Difference (2)-(1)
White-collar	1.1	3.0	1.9	2.4	4.5	2.1	1.5	3.9	2.4	3.3	5.8	2.5
Professional	.9	1.3	.4	2.1	2.3	.2	1.3	2.4	1.1	2.2	3.1	.9
Managers	.7	1.9	1.2	1.5	2.3	.8	1.0	2.8	1.8	2.8	2.9	.1
Sales	1.2	3.6	2.4	3.5	6.0	2.5	1.8	5.0	3.2	4.7	8.7	4.0
Clerical	2.4	3.7	1.3	4.1	5.4	1.3	2.8	4.5	1.4	5.2	6.8	1.6
Blue-collar	3.4	6.2	2.8	6.1	10.0	3.9	4.5	7.3	2.8	13.2	20.0	6.8
Operatives	3.5	6.4	2.9	6.7	10.4	3.7	4.6	7.2	2.6	15.2	22.2	7.0
Transport							3.8	4.3	.5	9.8	4.6	-5.2
Nonfarm	6.8	9.2	2.4	9.9	13.4	3.5	8.1	12.5	4.4	19.1	15.0	-4.1
Service	3.7	4.0	.3	5.2	6.1	.9	5.9	5.8	-.1	8.7	8.5	-.2
Farm	1.7	2.3	.6	2.3	4.2	1.9	2.5	5.2	2.7	4.3	5.0	.7

$T_d = 1.32$

Occupation	Feb. 1980 Peak			July 1980 Trough			July 1981 Peak			Nov. 1982 Trough		
	Male (1)	Female (2)	Difference (2)-(1)	Male (1)	Female (2)	Difference (2)-(1)	Male (1)	Female (2)	Difference (2)-(1)	Male (1)	Female (2)	Difference (2)-(1)
White-collar	2.3	4.6	2.3	2.8	4.8	2.0	2.6	5.5	2.9	4.1	6.4	2.3
Professional	1.8	2.4	.6	2.2	3.6	1.4	2.2	4.5	2.3	3.2	3.9	.7
Managers	1.8	3.9	2.1	2.3	3.1	.8	1.9	4.5	2.6	3.2	6.1	2.9
Sales	3.8	7.0	3.2	3.3	5.0	1.7	2.9	7.0	4.1	5.2	7.3	2.1
Clerical	2.9	5.3	2.4	5.0	5.6	.6	5.2	5.9	.7	7.4	7.5	.1
Blue-collar	9.3	11.3	2.0	9.9	14.1	4.2	8.1	11.8	3.7	15.1	17.6	2.5
Operatives	9.3	12.8	3.5	13.5	15.8	2.3	10.1	12.5	2.4	19.9	20.6	.7
Transport	8.9	4.9	-4.0	10.0	16.0	6.0	6.8	11.8	5.0	12.2	13.0	.8
Nonfarm	16.5	11.6	-4.9	14.0	11.0	-3.0	12.2	13.7	1.5	20.2	16.2	-4.0
Service	13.4	10.0	-3.4	9.4	8.0	-1.4	8.9	7.9	-1.0	11.6	10.5	-1.1
Farm	4.3	12.4	8.1	3.3	2.6	2.6	2.9	7.2	4.3	7.7	13.2	5.5

$T_d = 1.46$

not realized until the early 1970s. The relative employment advantage women enjoy in this occupation may reflect, in part, the impact of this legislation. Thus, legislation may soften market forces.

In analyzing matched-pair comparisons of the means for male-dominated occupations, I found significant differences in unemployment rates by sex between peak and trough quarters for the first periods examined (at the .05 level), and for the third and fourth period (at the .3 level). The sign of the difference is negative, not positive as would have been expected if one accepted traditional theory, for the first two periods analyzed.[23]

A pattern begins to appear, in analyzing sex differences in unemployment rates in male-dominated occupations, that indicates the unemployment gap in these occupations is greatest at business cycle troughs, not peaks. This holds true for the major male-dominated occupation examined, blue-collar workers. One the other hand, in female-dominated occupations, the unemployment gap is generally greatest during business cycle peaks, not troughs. In fact, for service workers, the unemployment rate for men has been higher than that for women since 1973.

This impact of a recession on the employment status of women, however, does not appear as clearly in analyzing unemployment rates by occupation as by industry. The effects of a recession hit some industries harder than others, particularly durable manufactured goods, and these industries include various occupational categories.[24] Therefore, in order to analyze in more detail how downturns in the business cycle affect the employment status of women, the unemployment gap is now examined by industry.

CYCLICAL VARIATION IN UNEMPLOYMENT RATES BY INDUSTRY

Table 5.4 shows the level and differences in unemployment rates by industry for both men and women. Male-dominated industries include mining, construction, manufacturing (durable goods), lumber products, stone products, primary metal industries, fabricated metal products, machinery (except electrical equipment), transportation equipment, automobiles, and paper products. Female-dominated industries include apparel products, finance and real estate, service, and professional services.

Analyzing sex differences in unemployment rates by industry, the data show that women, not men, tend to carry more of the burden of an increase in unemployment during a recession. In reviewing these unemployment rates, one finds that women, who were last employed in male-dominated industries, were affected more than men by cyclical changes in the economy. In addition, the unemployment gap in these industries is greatest at business cycle troughs, not peaks. The unemployment gap in six industries—durable manufactured goods, stone products, machinery (except electrical equipment), transportation equipment, automobiles, and paper products—shows

Table 5.4
Level and Differences in Unemployment Rates by Sex and Industry

Industry	Unemployment Rate Nov. 1969 Peak			Unemployment Rate Nov. 1970 Trough			Unemployment Rate Nov. 1973 Peak			Unemployment Rate March 1975 Trough		
	Male (1)	Female (2)	Difference (2)-(1)	Male (1)	Female (2)	Difference (2)-(1)	Male (1)	Female (2)	Difference (2)-(1)	Male (1)	Female (2)	Difference (2)-(1)
Mining	3.2			.9			3.1			4.9		
Construction	5.2	5.1	-.1	8.8	6.0	2.8	7.7	7.4	-.3	24.6	9.0	-15.6
Manufacture	2.6	5.6	3.0	5.7	9.6	3.9	3.0	6.6	3.6	10.7	18.0	7.3
Durable	2.6	5.9	3.3	6.5	11.5	5.0	2.7	6.4	3.7	11.2	19.5	8.3
Lumber												
Furniture												
Stone												
Primary	1.9	5.1	3.2	5.6	12.9	7.3	3.5	10.0	6.5	10.1	15.6	5.5
Fabricated	2.1	5.5	3.4	6.5	17.0	10.5	4.4	3.7	-.7	12.6	20.5	7.9
Machinery	2.4	3.9	1.5	6.5	10.8	4.3	1.7	4.6	2.9	6.7	15.2	8.5
Electrical	2.3	6.0	3.7	5.5	11.0	5.5	1.5	7.3	5.8	9.0	19.8	10.8
Transport							3.0	6.4	3.4	15.3	22.3	7.0
Auto.							1.3	3.1	1.8	21.8	24.5	2.7
Nondurable	2.6	5.4	2.8	4.2	8.2	4.0	3.5	6.8	3.3	9.8	16.6	6.8
Food	3.5	6.1	2.6	4.6	6.9	2.3	4.6	9.2	4.6	9.3	16.5	7.2
Textile	3.5	5.9	2.4	3.9	7.4	3.5	4.0	3.6	-.4	10.3	20.9	10.4
Apparel	9.0	5.4	-3.6	10.7	9.5	-1.2	4.4	7.0	2.6	20.8	19.9	-.9
Paper												
Printing												
Chemicals												
Rubber												
Transport	2.1	2.7	.6	3.2	4.4	1.2	2.9	3.8	.9	6.6	5.1	-1.5
Comm.	1.4	2.1	.7	1.4	4.3	2.9	1.6	3.6	2.0	2.5	4.9	2.4
Trade	2.8	4.9	2.1	4.5	7.6	3.1	3.7	7.1	3.4	8.3	10.5	2.2
Finance	1.4	2.3	.9	3.1	3.1	—	2.2	4.4	2.2	4.7	6.1	1.4
Service	2.8	3.8	1.0	4.9	5.7	.8	4.8	4.3	-.5	7.1	7.2	.1
Prof.	1.3	2.2	.9	2.5	3.6	1.1	2.9	3.0	.1	4.1	5.6	1.5

$T_d = 4.04$

$T_d = -.38$

Table 5.4 (Continued)

Industry	Unemployment Rate Feb. 1980 Peak			Unemployment Rate July 1980 Trough			Unemployment Rate July 1981 Peak			Unemployment Rate Nov. 1982 Trough		
	Male (1)	Female (2)	Difference (2)-(1)	Male (1)	Female (2)	Difference (2)-(1)	Male (1)	Female (2)	Difference (2)-(1)	Male (1)	Female (2)	Difference (2)-(1)
Mining	7.0	1.3	-5.7	6.2	7.2	1.0	6.1	4.4	-1.7	18.2	1.9	-16.3
Construction	17.9	6.5	-11.4	13.1	5.9	-7.2	12.4	8.8	-3.6	19.9	13.5	-6.4
Manufacture	6.3	9.8	3.5	9.0	11.8	2.8	6.2	10.0	3.8	13.3	16.0	2.7
Durable	6.6	9.0	2.4	10.2	12.8	2.6	6.7	9.9	3.2	15.8	17.9	2.1
Lumber	13.1	6.1	-7.0	13.4	9.6	-3.8	8.2	18.8	10.6	17.9	17.1	-.8
Furniture	5.8	8.6	2.8	11.1	11.8	.7	5.2	14.0	8.8	13.5	19.3	5.8
Stone	8.4	13.5	5.1	7.5	12.9	5.4	5.1	3.6	-1.5	16.1	19.0	3.1
Primary	7.8	12.4	4.6	15.1	12.8	-2.3	8.5	6.8	-1.7	26.3	29.9	3.6
Fabricated	6.7	14.2	7.5	10.8	15.6	4.8	8.3	11.6	3.3	18.1	18.3	.2
Machinery	3.7	3.2	-.5	6.8	8.5	1.7	5.1	8.2	3.1	15.8	17.3	1.5
Electrical	2.7	6.4	3.7	7.5	11.3	3.8	4.1	8.8	4.7	10.7	16.0	5.3
Transport	10.8	16.3	5.5	14.7	22.1	7.4	9.4	13.0	3.6	16.3	22.2	5.9
Auto.	15.7	24.2	8.5	23.4	37.4	14.0	12.1	24.5	12.4	20.4	34.9	14.5
Nondurable	5.7	10.5	4.8	6.6	10.9	4.3	5.3	10.1	4.8	8.8	14.1	5.3
Food	7.0	16.2	9.2	7.2	8.4	1.2	6.5	8.4	1.9	11.0	17.3	6.3
Textile	4.5	10.5	6.0	8.0	11.3	3.3	6.8	10.4	3.6	10.2	11.2	1.0
Apparel	10.3	10.3	—	10.3	14.8	4.5	12.9	10.6	7.7	14.5	16.4	1.9
Paper	6.2	7.6	1.4	5.6	12.6	7.0	2.3	4.6	2.3	6.9	9.2	2.3
Printing	5.6	8.2	2.6	4.8	7.0	3.8	3.7	6.3	2.6	6.5	6.7	.2
Chemicals	4.1	7.0	2.9	4.7	3.7	-1.0	3.4	7.1	3.7	6.0	12.1	6.1
Rubber	4.7	9.9	5.2	10.5	17.7	7.2	5.3	15.5	10.2	10.4	17.5	7.1
Transport	5.4	4.1	-1.3	5.9	5.4	-.5	4.4	3.6	-.8	8.2	6.9	-1.3
Comm.	2.5	3.4	.9	1.8	3.4	1.6	1.6	2.8	1.2	2.6	3.6	1.0
Trade	6.2	8.9	2.7	7.0	7.9	.9	6.5	9.0	2.5	9.5	11.4	1.9
Finance	3.0	4.0	1.0	3.3	3.1	-.2	3.1	3.8	.7	5.7	5.5	-.2
Service	5.4	5.0	-.4	6.4	6.2	-.2	5.9	6.3	.4	9.0	7.5	-1.5
Prof.	2.6	3.7	1.1	3.9	4.8	.9	4.1	5.1	1.0	5.0	5.3	.3

$T_d = -1.52$

a consistent pattern of higher female unemployment during business cycle troughs. Seniority rules within some of these industries may help explain why the unemployment gap is higher for women than men in business cycle troughs, not peaks. Women are likely to be among the last hired in these industries, and in hard economic times also among the first to be let go.[25]

The evidence is mixed in analyzing the unemployment gap in other male-dominated industries, including mining, primary metal industries, and fabricated metal products. In mining and lumber industries, differences in unemployment rates by sex can be analyzed only for the last two periods examined. (Prior to 1980, the numbers of women employed in these industries was so small that unemployment rates by sex are not available). The unemployment gap in mining is positive, for one of the periods examined, during the business cycle trough, not the peak. In the primary metal industries and fabricated metal products, the unemployment gap by sex is higher for two of the four periods examined during business cycle troughs, not peaks. In other male-dominated industries, including lumber, mining, and construction, the unemployment rate for men is oftentimes higher than it is for women.[26] Once again, the relative advantage women experience, in terms of incidence of unemployment, may reflect the effects of protective legislation in these areas. Executive Order 11246, as amended by Executive Order 11375 (effective October 1968), and Title VII of the Civil Rights Act of 1964, as amended by the Equal Employment Opportunity Act of 1972, prohibit discrimination based on sex in hiring or firing; training; promoting; and layoff or termination. The provisions cover federal contracts and employers of 15 or more employees, employment agencies, labor organizations with 15 or more members, and labor-management apprenticeship programs. Nevertheless, an argument can be made that a pattern exists in a number of male-dominated industries that, during business cycle downturns, the increase in unemployment is borne more by women than men.

Computing matched-pair comparisons of the means for male-dominated industries, one finds a statistically significant negative difference in unemployment rates by sex between the 1969 peak and 1970 trough (at the .01 level, for a one-tailed test), and between the 1981 peak and 1982 trough (at the .2 level). And the sign of the difference is negative, not positive for three of the four periods examined. This supports my hypothesis that the mean difference in unemployment rates in male-dominated industries is generally greater for women than men during business cycle troughs, not peaks.

Industry analysis indicates that the unemployment situation of women is affected by cyclical changes in the economy. To argue that women are less adversely affected by a recession than men because they are concentrated in sectors that are not as sensitive to cyclical variation (apparel, finance, service, and professional service) ignores the fact that the unemployment gap by sex in a majority of male-dominated industries is higher during business cycle troughs, not peaks. Unemployment rates for women do generally exceed those of men. This gap varies countercyclically, being greatest at business cycle troughs, not peaks, for women last employed in male-dominated industries.

Generally women employed in male-dominated occupations and industries are the first to be let go during business cycle downturns. This undermines gains women have made in entering nontraditional fields. Notably, the unemployment rate is higher for men than women among nonfarm laborers (including construction workers). The relative employment advantage women enjoy in this occupation may reflect the impact of Title VII legislation that prohibits discrimination by federal contractors and subcontractors on the basis of sex. Still, in the majority of male-dominated occupations and industries examined, unemployment is borne more by female than male workers. Any gains women have made in integrating occupations may well be short lived.

NOTES

1. W. P. Bridges, "Industry Marginality and Female Employment: A New Appraisal," *American Sociological Review* 45 (February 1980): 58–75; Cynthia B. Lloyd and Beth T. Niemi, *The Economics of Sex Differentials* (New York: Columbia University Press, 1979), pp. 177–185; Phyllis A. Wallace, *Black Women in the Labor Force* (Cambridge, Mass.: MIT Press, 1982).

2. Robert J. Gordon, *Macroeconomics* (Boston: Little, Brown and Company, 1978), p. 232.

3. Barbara Sinclair Deckard, *The Women's Movement* (New York: Harper and Row, 1983).

4. Beatrice G. Reubens and Edwin P. Reubens, "Women Workers, Nontraditional Occupations and Full Employment," in *Women in the Labor Force*, A. Cahn, ed. (New York: Praeger Publishers, 1979), p. 106.

5. Reubens and Reubens, "Women Workers," p. 107.

6. Harriet Zellner, "Discrimination Against Women, Occupational Segregation and Relative Wage," *American Economic Review* 62 (May 1972): 157–160.

7. Reubens and Reubens, "Women Workers," p. 107; R. D. Roderick and J. M. Davis, *Correlates of Atypical Job Assignment* (Columbus: Center for Human Resource Research, 1972).

8. U.S. Department of Labor, Bureau of Labor Statistics (Washington: Government Printing Office, 1980).

9. Jean Tepperman, *Not Servants, Not Machines* (Boston: Beacon Press, 1976).

10. Approximately a third of all female-headed households in the United States are officially defined as poor. Half of all black and Hispanic female-headed households live in poverty.

11. U.S. Department of Labor, Employment and Training Report of the President (Washington: Government Printing Office, 1978).

12. Lloyd and Niemi, *Economics of Sex Differentials*, pp. 8, 37.

13. Lloyd and Niemi, *Economics of Sex Differentials*, p. 17.

14. Lloyd and Niemi, *Economics of Sex Differentials*, pp. 70, 73.

15. Lloyd and Niemi, *Economics of Sex Differentials*.

16. Prior to 1983, the base population consisted of the civilian noninstitution-alized population 16 years of age and over. (Prior to 1967, 14- and 15-year-olds were also included.) Since January 1983, this figure also includes military employees.

17. Lloyd and Niemi, *Economics of Sex Differentials*, p. 31.

18. Eleanor G. Gilpatrick, *Structural Unemployment and Aggregate Demand* (Baltimore: Johns Hopkins Press, 1966), p. 16.

19. Everett Johnson Burtt, *Labor in the American Economy* (New York: St. Martin's Press, 1979), pp. 17, 19.

20. Alice H. Amsden, ed., *The Economics of Women and Work* (New York: St. Martin's Press, 1980).

21. Amsden, *Economics of Women and Work*, p. 360; Howard J. Sherman, *Stagflation* (New York: Harper and Row, 1983), pp. 11–15.

22. The "unemployment gap" is the differential between the unemployment rate for men versus that for women. The term "unemployment gap" is used only in reference to the difference in unemployment rates between men and women. If the gap is positive, this means that the unemployment rate for women is higher than it is for men. And if the gap is negative, this means that the unemployment rate for men is higher than it is for women.

23. Matched pair comparisons of the means for occupations and industries were calculated as follows:

$$Td = d - O/sd$$
$$(Uf - Um)\, pi - (Uf - Um)ti = di$$
$$d = 1/n\, di$$
$$sd = (di - d)\, /n - 1$$
$$sd = sd/\, n$$

where

Td = standard error of the mean

sd = standard deviation

$(Uf)pi$ = unemployment for women in peak year

$(Um)pi$ = unemployment for men in peak year

$(Uf)ti$ = unemployment for women in trough year

$(Um)ti$ = unemployment for men in trough year

di = mean difference in unemployment rates by sex between peak and trough year.

24. James N. Baron and William T. Bielby, "Bringing the Firms Back In: Strat-ification, Segmentation, and the Organization of Work," *American Sociological Review* 45 (October 1980): 737–765; Seymour Spilerman, "Careers, Labor Market Structure, and Socioeconomic Achievement," *American Journal of Sociology* 83 (1977): 551–593; Charles M. Tobbert II, Patrick M. Horan, and E. M. Beck, "The Structure of Economic Segregation: A Dual Economy Approach," *American Journal*

of Sociology 83 (1980): 1095–1116. As Baron and Bielby note, many researchers assume industries to be relatively homogeneous with regard to technical and administrative arrangements.

25. Amsden, *The Economics of Women and Work*, p. 377.

26. The unemployment gap is higher for female construction workers during the trough, not peak, quarter in the first period examined. After 1970, however, women experience a lower instance of unemployment in this industry than do men.

6

GET A JOB: WOMEN AND EMPLOYMENT AND TRAINING PROGRAMS DURING THE REAGAN YEARS

PATRICIA BAYER RICHARD

Richard's analysis of employment and training programs begins by establishing how, despite the growing similarity in women's and men's life patterns, significant variations remain in the sexes' respective amounts of home and child care responsibilities, employment patterns, occupations, and earnings. Richard then focuses on how well, in light of these gender differences, employment and training programs serve women. She examines the principal employment and training program of the Reagan administration, the Job Training Partnership Act, and related welfare work programs. Revising data from a local service delivery area as well as from national reports, Richard finds sex differences in a number of areas, including placement in on-the-job and classroom training, willingness to relocate, and wages. She shows that policy design matters by drawing comparisons with JTPA's predecessor, the Comprehensive Employment and Training Act, and current programs in Massachusetts and New Jersey. Programs that take gender differences into account serve women better; those whose principal criterion is cost effectiveness will serve the most job-ready who tend to be disproportionately male.

Work and welfare have been called the Middle East of American politics. Despite decades of governmental activity in these areas, debate about what is needed and what is effective continues essentially unabated. This chapter enters into this controversy by inquiring into the gender differences in the adequacy of programs aimed at addressing economic insufficiency. More specifically it addresses how well employment and training programs serve women.

Like most public policy arenas, employment and training (e and t) is not explicitly gender-related as, for example, abortion policy is. Yet, e and t programs, again like most public policies, even when facially gender-neutral, have differential impacts on the sexes. This results from the dissimilar life situations of women and men and from institutionalized sexism which structures choices such that gender barriers or opportunities become imbedded in common standards. As a consequence, e and t programs which fail to confront the sexes' divergent positions will advantage one sex over the other.

THE ECONOMIC POSITION OF WOMEN

In recent decades, the life patterns of women and men have grown more alike. The sexual division of labor has eroded. But significant variations remain in the sexes' respective amounts of home and child care responsibilities or unpaid work, employment patterns, occupations, and earnings.

Unpaid Work

Women do an enormous amount of unpaid work, especially with regard to home and family, whether or not they participate in the paid labor force. In her review of the literature as well as her own research, Coverman (1989, 1985) found that wives devote two to four times as many hours as husbands to domestic labor. They perform about three quarters of all household chores, regardless of their employment status or the couples' level of education, income, or sex-role ideology. This disparity in time spent on home and family critically influences women's paid work force participation, employment status, occupational choice, earnings, and benefits.

Labor Force Participation

Women's dramatic increase in the paid labor market has been one of the most significant changes in the postwar period. The sex composition of the workforce has moved to near parity. With the added numbers, the modal woman worker metamorphosed from a young single woman to an older married one.[1] Female workers are also likely to be mothers. More than seven of ten women with children ages six through seventeen were in the labor force in 1988, as were 57 percent of women with children under six

(U.S. Bureau of the Census 1989, p. 386). Indeed 48 percent of the women who gave birth between June 1984 and June 1985 entered or reentered the workforce within a year of the birth ("The American Family" 1986, p. 1804); by 1986, the proportion grew to over one-half.

Yet women continue to face employment barriers based on structures in the work place as well as on social patterns and outside expectations. These influence un- and underemployment as well as status, pay, and promotion.

Unemployment and Underemployment

Women as a group suffer disproportionately from both unemployment and underemployment. Women's rates of unemployment exceeded men's all through the 1950s, 1960s, 1970s, and 1980s, according to Bureau of Labor Statistics data. In addition, women make up approximately two-thirds of "discouraged workers," those unemployed persons who have ceased looking actively for work and are therefore not counted in official unemployment statistics (U.S. Senate 1986, p. 644).

Despite this, programs geared toward the unemployed have focused on men. For example, women, whose labor force participation tends more than men's to part-time work, work interruptions, and low wages, find the unemployment insurance program (UI) structurally biased against them in a number of ways. Many part-time workers do not earn enough to qualify for UI. Others, who do, are ineligible if they are not available for full-time work. In addition, while workers can refuse jobs which are too far from home, they cannot refuse jobs which are too far from child care (Pearce 1985, pp. 455–456). Finally, UI labels homemakers, unpaid workers, low-paid and seasonal workers as new or reentrant workers, disqualifying them from job placement services and benefits accorded "regular" workers.

Women with jobs are often underemployed: they involuntarily work part-time or in marginal jobs (U.S. Commission on Civil Rights 1982, Table 5-4) and are relegated primarily to the secondary labor market (Orfield and Slessarev 1986, p. 14). Again, this reflects an institutionalized sexism which programs will mirror as well unless their design counters it.

The Earnings Gap

For these reasons, among others, working women find their earnings depressed relative to men's. Full-time female workers continue to earn less than two-thirds of what full-time male workers earn (U.S. Bureau of the Census 1989, p. 448).

Many analysts have investigated the causes of the wage gap, considering such factors as discrimination, level of job-related skills, and women's sacrifice of career advancement for home responsibilities. A study using regression analysis revealed that differences in education, work experience, work continuity, worker-imposed job restrictions (distance from home, for example), and absenteeism account for little of the wage gap (29 percent of that between white men and white women and 17 percent between white men and black women) (Corcoran et al. 1984, p. 238). Corcoran and Duncan advocate abandoning a "skills" explanation for the wage gap and looking toward socialization and institutionalized sex discrimination instead. In these areas, they find men favored ("Why Do Women Earn Less?" 1983, pp. 5, 8).

Occupational Distribution

The earnings gap arises in some measure because men and women tend to work at different jobs. Overall, women's occupational array is narrower than men's, with about half of all employed women working in fewer than thirty of the more than 400 detailed census occupations (Rytina 1981, p. 49). A high degree of occupational segregation by sex exists, with men working primarily in predominantly "male jobs" and women working in predominantly "female jobs." This segregated pattern has remained intact despite other transformations in the labor market. In fact, the index of sex segregation, based on the percentage of women (or men) in the labor force who would have to change jobs in order for the occupational distribution of female workers to match that of male workers, remained about 66 percent from 1900 to 1980 (Hartman and Reskin 1983).

Women's occupational distribution results in an economic status inferior to men's. As the National Research Council of the National Academy of Sciences put it: "Not only do women do different work than men but the work women do is paid less, and the more an occupation is dominated by women the less it pays" (Treiman and Hartman 1981, p. 28).

Poverty

These characteristics of women's position contribute to their poverty. Over their life cycle women are two times as likely to be poor as are men; currently they constitute two-thirds of impoverished adults in the United States (Shortridge 1984).

Women's poverty frequently produces children's poverty as well; almost half of all poor families in 1982 were single-parent, female-headed (Kamerman 1984, p. 250). While median family income in 1984 reached $26,433, that for female-headed families was only $12,883, the lowest median income of all groups, lower than Hispanic ($18,883) or black ($15,452) families (U.S. Bureau of the Census 1985).

Long-term poverty is also associated with women. Corcoran and her colleagues discovered that one in four families was poor at some time during a 10-year period, but only 10 percent of these were poor for eight or more years. Of this group, one-third were elderly, a group which over-represents women, while the remainder were families headed by women (1984, pp. 243–244). Such families include about one-fifth of the population but more than three-fifths of the persistently poor (Duncan 1984, p. 50).

In a recent study Duncan found that on all three important dimensions of economic status, average level of income, trend in income level, and stability of income level, as well as on the incidence of short-term and longer-run poverty, adult women fare substantially less well than their male counterparts (1987, p. 28).

These aspects of women's position suggest why public policies can differ in their impact by sex. Women and men are dissimilarly situated. To treat women and men equally, programs aimed at moving people toward economic self-sufficiency need to take into account and address their differences.

EMPLOYMENT AND TRAINING PROGRAMS

Employment and training (e and t) is a broad policy area containing a wide range of programs,[2] the two general rubrics being job creation, specifically public service and public works jobs and tax credits for businesses hiring targeted workers, and training, both classroom and on-the-job. The scope and range of these programs has varied considerably in different political and economic environments.

Since the 1960s, the bulk of spending and attention has been directed toward structural problems, including those based in the workers (lack of skills, training, or education) and those based in industries (lack of demand or competitiveness). Examples include the Manpower Development and Training Act (1962–1974), the Comprehensive Employment and Training Act (CETA) (1973–1983), and the Job Training Partnership Act (JTPA) (1983 to the present).

In the 1980s, the Reagan administration, with its stresses on a smaller federal role in social spending and on the private sector, radically constrained the federal role in e and t. Reductions in expenditures were dramatic: in constant dollars, spending dropped from $7.8 billion in 1978 to $2.6 billion in 1984 (Peirce and Guskind 1985, p. 2198). Orfield reported in 1986 that real dollars per unemployed worker had declined by 80 percent since 1978 (U.S. House 1986, p. 102). Overall, total public expenditures for e and t fell from .85 percent of the GNP at the end of the 1970s (Breneman and Nelson 1980, p. 205), to .45 percent in 1984 (Danziger and Weinberg 1986, p. 4).

JTPA

The Reagan administration's principal e and t program, the Job Training Partnership Act, went into effect in fiscal year (fy) 1984. Although it had only belated administration endorsement, President Reagan singled out

JTPA as a model program in his 1985 state of the union address. JTPA reflected the administration's philosophy and values in its elimination of funding for public service jobs, its structural inclusion of the private sector in planning and design, its devolution of some federal responsibility to the states, and its emphasis on cost-effectiveness.

Section 2 of the law, PL 97–300, states that the JTPA intends "to prepare youth and unskilled adults for entry into the labor force and to afford job training to those economically disadvantaged individuals facing serious barriers to employment, who are in special need of such training to obtain productive employment." It has several major components. The largest program, Title IIA, primarily serves disadvantaged adults. It provides job search assistance and classroom and on-the-job training (ojt). Title IIB is the youth program, for those 14 to 21. Unlike IIA, it includes paid work experience. Title III funds special programs for displaced workers.

Program Characteristics and Their Impact on Women

Several program characteristics influence the program's adequacy for women, including its targeting of the poor, its emphasis on performance standards, its requirement that 70 percent of program funds be used for training, its limits on supportive services, and its prohibition of public service employment.

Targeting of the Poor. One of JTPA's most promising features from the perspective of women is that it targets the poor, a group, as we have already noted, that is disproportionately female. Only 10 percent of participants may be noneconomically disadvantaged and they must experience some other barrier to employment.[3] While these program definitions should benefit women, other features undercut their efficacy.

Underfunding, Selection Criteria, and Performance Standards. First, the program is drastically underfunded. It cannot serve all or even most of those eligible. Studies estimate that between one in ten and one in twenty eligibles are served (Baumer and Van Horn 1985, p. 185; Corrigan and Stanfield 1984, p. 264).

Second, the program permits considerable leeway in setting criteria and choosing participants. A Westat study noted, "JTPA provides more latitude in setting criteria and choosing participants than any other federal training program in the last two decades" (U.S. Senate 1986, p. 49).

Third, JTPA's emphasis on performance standards leads to an emphasis on cost-effectiveness. Since funding depends on meeting these standards, service delivery areas or SDAs, the administrative units within which the job training programs operate, have incentives to select those most "job-ready" from among the eligibles. The very poor and those without recent or any job experience, who are more likely to be women, fare less well (Orfield and Slessarev 1986).

Creaming. Together, these features induce "creaming" or selecting from among the eligibles those who are most job-ready, who require the least training, and who are easiest to place. Only one in five of the SDAs emphasize those most in need, the very poor, and those without recent—or any—job experience, who are likely to be women (U.S. House 1985, p. 76). Moreover, the performance standards, especially in combination with the limits on stipends and supportive services discussed below, generally produce short-ened training programs which may be inadequate for those with low job skills and little experience:

While JTPA's intent to afford job training opportunities to the disadvantaged is clearly stated in the legislation, high unemployment rates, a growing working-age poverty population, an unprecedented emphasis on performance standards, and extremely low levels of funding have created a job training system that serves pri-marily the most advantaged segment of the vast eligible population. People most in need of training and from the kinds of backgrounds which have shown the greatest gains from training in the past can be served at only minimal levels. (Orfield and Slessarev 1986, p. 181)

Funding Limits on Supportive Services. JTPA's requirement that 70 per-cent of program funds be spent on training suggests a program high on muscle and low on fat. But this leanness means that program components particularly crucial for women to be served are limited or eliminated. JTPA mandates that supportive services such as subsistence payments, child care, and transportation, together with administrative costs, account for no more than 30 percent of funds, administration alone for no more than 15 percent. Since reporting requirements push the administrative portion toward the 15 percent ceiling, only a small share of funds remains for services or stipends. For example, Orfield and Slessarev found that in Illinois in 1985 fewer than five percent of those eligible for child care received it (1986, p. 222).

These limits curtail the participation of the hard-core unemployed, in-cluding those with minimal education and skills, discouraged workers, and the poor, again, most of them women. While JTPA channels a high pro-portion of funds toward training, those in greatest need may be unable to access the training. At a House oversight hearing, a San Diego Private Industry Council member, involved in implementing JTPA, observed that reliance on motivation alone was "at best naive and at worst smacks of 'let them eat cake' " (U.S. House 1985, p. 87).

Prohibition of Public Service Employment (PSE). JTPA forbids pse. It does not view unemployment as demand-deficient, or the result of an econ-omy that produces too few jobs. President Reagan opposed direct job cre-ation, despite the fact that unemployment had reached the double digits when JTPA was passed, based on the belief that federal responsibility reaches only to providing training to disadvantaged individuals (Bassi and Ashenfelter 1986, p. 134). Many local JTPA and welfare officials disagree, asserting that pse is an essential element of e and t policy in high unemployment and high poverty communities (Stadelman and Frech interviews; Orfield and Slessarev 1986, p. 8).

JTPA's prohibition of public service employment disproportionately disadvantages women. Studies of previous e and t programs show pse overall more effective in increasing women's earnings than men's (Saks 1983; Bassi 1983; Bassi and Ashenfelter 1986). In their review, Bassi and Ashenfelter found that pse, along with ojt and classroom training, resulted in significant post-program employment and earnings gains for women, although none of the programs had a consistently significant effect on men (1986, p. 142).

This evidence suggests that barriers to employment may differ for men and women, requiring dissimilar programmatic solutions. Here, public service employment, a strategy which produced positive results for women, has been abandoned because it is cost-ineffective for men.

Participants

Westat and Illinois JTPA studies found men overrepresented among participants (U.S. Senate 1986, p. 49; Orfield and Slessarev 1986, pp. 6, 228). Nevertheless, women, because of their predominance in the poverty population, were a majority of those enrolled in Title IIA, 52 percent during program year 1984 (July 1984 to June 1985). They constituted a smaller number, 48 percent, of terminees who entered employment in the same period (data from User Services of the Labor Department Information Division of the Ohio Bureau of Employment Services).

Those receiving public assistance at the time of application comprised 42 percent of enrollees during program year 1984. Half of them were recipients of Aid to Families with Dependent Children (AFDC), the major welfare program, serving primarily poor women and their children. Of terminees who entered employment in the same period, 38 percent had been receiving public assistance at the time of application, 18 percent AFDC (data from User Services of the Labor Department Information Division of the Ohio Bureau of Employment Services.) The public assistance statistics make clear that participants came lopsidedly from recipients of General Relief (GR) (a state and local program providing minimal cash and medical assistance to individuals and families not eligible for AFDC), a group far more male than AFDC. Most people on GR are single people or married couples without children. The absence of supportive services like day care creates no obstacle to JTPA participation or employment for them.

AFDC recipients, like women as a group, did less well in exiting JTPA into employment than other participants. In Illinois, women receiving AFDC made up one quarter of enrollees but only 19 percent of those getting jobs (Orfield and Slessarev 1986, p. 6).

WELFARE EMPLOYMENT PROGRAMS

Since the 1960s, welfare policy has been closely tied to e and t programs (Wiscombe 1986, p. 23). In 1967, Congress established the Work Incentive Program (WIN), the federal work program for those receiving AFDC. Unless exempted because of caretaking responsibility for children under age six or for other reasons, recipients are obliged to enroll in the WIN program which provides job search, job club, preemployment training, and work experience lasting a maximum of 13 weeks. For a variety of reasons, underfunding prominent among them, WIN has done little to reduce welfare rolls (*From Welfare to Work*, 1987).

Other work programs now coexist with WIN. The 1981 Omnibus Budget Reconciliation Act included provisions allowing states to establish workfare under Community Work Experience Programs (CWEP). Workfare requires that recipients work in exchange for their cash assistance. At least 25 states require aid recipients to work off their welfare checks (Wiscombe 1986, p. 23). The welfare work programs have connections with JTPA, for example, using its services for assessment.

The welfare employment programs in effect provide what JTPA prohibits: public service employment. While opposing pse in JTPA, the Reagan administration advocated a sort of mandatory pse, or workforce, for those on welfare. Local administrators implementing workfare and work experience programs report that jobs are similar to former CETA pse jobs (Frech interview).

Since, with natural turnover, just over half of all recipients move off the welfare rolls within two years (Wiscombe 1986, p. 23), measuring the effect of a work requirement is difficult. A Manpower Demonstration Research Corporation study showed these programs to have a modest but positive impact. On the other hand, Bradley Schiller, whose Potomac Institute for Economic Research evaluated Ohio's welfare program, maintains that work programs have little potential for decreasing welfare caseloads and even less for reducing welfare costs (Wiscombe 1986, p. 25). Workfare critics, like Jack Frech, director of the Athens, Ohio Department of Human Services, argue that because welfare recipients want to work, mandatory programs are unnecessary and divert needed resources from the poor.

A CASE STUDY

To view the impact of JTPA and work programs on women in practice, the author interviewed program principals and reviewed data in an Ohio service delivery area in 1986. JTPA requires SDAs to have a minimum

Figure 6.1
**The JTPA Administrative Structure, Showing Tri-County Community Action
Agency's Position**

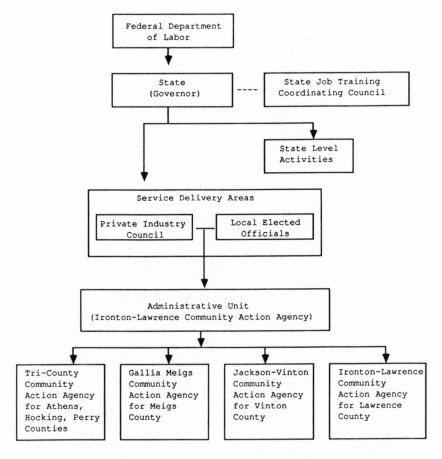

population base of 200,000. Ohio has 31. The interviews took place in SDA
24, a district covering seven rural counties in the southeastern part of the
state. The administrative unit for SDA 24 is the Ironton-Lawrence Community Action Organization. Tri-County Community Action Agency
(TCCAA) works as a subcontractor for three counties, Athens, Hocking,
and Perry, which together have a population of 113,000, over half in Athens
county. Research focused here. Figure 6.1 shows TCCAA's place in the
organizational structure.

Both Ohio and SDA 24 had unemployment rates above the national
average for the period studied. In 1985, according to the Labor Market
Information Division, Ohio's rate fell below 8.5 percent for only one month

and reached as high as 9.7 percent. In SDA 24, unemployment remained over 10 percent all year, averaging almost 12 percent. Athens was the healthiest of the counties on this index, close to the state average in unemployment. Yet almost 22 percent of Athens' population lived below the poverty line, more than twice the state rate of 10.3 percent. More than 9200 of Athens' 58,000 residents received food stamps and 4600 got AFDC payments (data from the Athens Department of Human Services). JTPA and WIN faced significant tests in this area.

Since both the administrative agency and its subcontractors are community action agencies, organizations that maintain a commitment to helping those most in need, if women do poorly here, they are unlikely to fare better with JTPA generally.[4]

TCCAA offers the following JTPA services: classroom and skills training, on-the-job training, job club (a three week activity involving intensive job search), basic education, adult literacy, occupation skill training (several week training for specific jobs), youth competencies, including the acquisition of job readiness skills, work experience for youth 16 to 21, and placement services.

By far, the largest numbers take part in job club. Here, costs associated with job search, for example, phone calls, xerox copying, resumes, and postage, are assumed by JTPA. In addition, participants get a $5 per day stipend, near the national average of $30 per week (U.S. House 1985, p. 22). Everyone participating in the JTPA program goes through job club either immediately or after training, unless she or he has found a job.

As is the case nationally, programs have waiting lists. TCCAA uses a set of "priority point selection criteria" to determine access to classroom training. The points attached to various characteristics are found in Table 6.1. Certain categories enhance the likelihood of women having high point scores (public assistance, single parent head of household), although others do not (veteran).

Program Participants

Year end reports for July 1985 to June 1986 from TCCAA reveal the following characteristics of program participants:

Age. Male participants tended to be younger, more than half under 22 and more than three-quarters less than 30, while 42 percent and 65 percent of the women were in these age groups.

Women. Women made up a bare majority of participants in Title IIA; in earlier years they constituted less than half.

Single Heads of Households. Single heads of households with dependent children, a category exclusively female according to local JTPA personnel, made up about 17 percent of participants.

Displaced Homemakers. The participation of displaced homemakers[5] var-

Table 6.1
JTPA Classroom Training: Priority Point Selection Criteria (used by Tri-County
Community Action Agency, Hocking, Athens, and Perry Counties, Ohio)

POSITIVE POINTS

Knows school and technology, would like to attend	10
High school graduate or GED	8
Presently working toward GED	4
Currently in school	10
Would accept a job after training, either local or relocate	5
Agrees to attend Job Club after training if not employed	7
Black, Hispanic, or Other	4
Public Assistance	10
Single Parent, Head of Household	10
Parent in a two-parent family	2
Handicap	6
Veteran	10
Offender	5
Registered at Ohio Bureau of Employment Services	10
Has own transportation	10
Currently has a full-time or a part-time job	1
Working and earning minimum wage	1
Working and earning less than minimum wage	7

DEDUCTIONS

Previous skill training with a diploma	-20
Previous skill training but dropped out	-5
Previous JTPA	-10
Refused employment	-10

ied widely across the counties, from only two percent in Hocking County the first quarter to 19 percent in Athens County the last. The numbers and percentages of displaced homemakers went up in all three counties during the year. The increases resulted not from a new program thrust but rather from the existence of a sex equity grant for training displaced homemakers. The grant, held by Tri-County Joint Vocational School, paid for tuition and books, as well as transportation and other supportive services, including child care. These benefits far exceed those available from JTPA, but extended for only two academic quarters. Since programs tend to be three quarters in length, in the latter part of the year, women in the displaced homemaker

Table 6.2
Male-Female Differences in On-the-Job Training Placements: JTPA Title IIA
(Athens, Hocking, and Perry Counties, Ohio, July 1, 1985 through March 31,
1986)

Percentage of	Athens	Hocking	Perry
Females	20	20	11
Male	26	30	28

Data provided by Tri-County Community Action Agency, subcontractor
SDA 24.

program moved into JTPA. This exemplifies the way this JTPA program
leveraged its money through cooperation with other human development
programs in the area: JTPA personnel insured that anyone qualifying for
the displaced homemaker program would use its resources first, thus getting
the client better benefits, at least temporarily, and at the same time stretching
scarce JTPA dollars.

Findings

A more detailed analysis of JTPA participants through March 1986 carried out by the author revealed sex differences in placements for on-the-job
and classroom training, in willingness to relocate, and in outcomes and
wages.

On-the-Job-Training Placements. Women entered ojt placements less
often than men. Table 6.2 shows data for one sample period of time.

Ojt is the most desirable placement because it provides income during
training and usually leads to a job. Individuals get ojt placement through
two routes. TCCAA job developers contact employers to inform them about
JTPA generally and about ojt specifically. Interested employers may request
referrals from the JTPA office. Alternately, participants solicit jobs for themselves from employers using an ojt contract as an incentive. Thus, the sex
difference in ojt may issue from employers' preferences, variations in participants' pursuit of OJT placements, access to transportation and child
care, among possible sources.

The phenomenon of fewer women in ojt may be common. It occurred
also in the Illinois JTPA program (U.S. House 1986, p. 106). Orfield and
Slessarev report that men obtained placement in ojt programs twice as often
as women (1986, p. 6).

These local studies signal that women have not shared equally in these relatively attractive JTPA placements. Equality of outcome may require modifications in program design which take into account barriers to women.

Classroom Training. The classroom training tended to be sex-stereotyped, for instance, men in programs for auto body repair and processing occupations with women in cosmetology and clerical training programs. Kris Stadelman, the director of e and t programs for TCCAA, suggested that few clients had an interest in reaching beyond traditional boundaries, noting, however, that those who received nontraditional training (men in nursing, a woman in ceramic engineering) were in demand. She said, "we grab those who have this attitude," yet this behavior was not clearly fostered. For example, the brochure put out by TCCAA under a "JTPA Ohio" cover used five sex-stereotypic photographs as illustrations (two showing women cooking, one a woman typing, another a man repairing a typewriter, and the last a man about to enter a truck); the stories of those who entered occupations primarily filled by those of the opposite sex do not appear.

Such gender routing in training, like the differential placement in ojt, is not unusual. With equal standards and no particular encouragement, women for the most part will opt for female-associated jobs, with the obverse holding for men.

In Indianapolis, JTPA funded two programs, one in occupations considered traditional for men, such as the construction trades preapprenticeship training and telephone installation repair, and another in "female" occupations, such as nurse-assistant, word processor, and general office worker. Besides the average wage discrepancy between the two groups of jobs, the "male" set of training programs included preparation for the GED, the high school equivalency diploma, while the "female" set required that applicants have either a high school diploma or a GED already in hand for acceptance into training (U.S. Senate 1986, p. 86). Here more is offered to those enrolling in the male-associated occupations. Unless the program facilitates women's choice of the "male" track, the Indiana JTPA program both reproduces the economic gender structuring of the society and explicitly advantages men.

Relocation. Women and men differ in their willingness to relocate. One job club activity involves drawing concentric circles on a map, one representing the greatest distance a participant is willing to drive to get to work, the other the distance she or he is willing to relocate in order to gain employment. With the exception of young, single women, women are more averse to relocating. Since many women with children rely on informal arrangements for child care, usually on family, a move away from this support structure can remove the conditions which make working possible and financially viable.[6]

Outcomes. Participants exit the program for many reasons. Successful outcomes include placement in jobs and "local PIC recognized youth competencies" or the accomplishment of some defined skill, often related to schooling. Of the terminees, 59 percent of the males found jobs as did 63 percent of the females. Another 16 percent of the male youth and 13 percent of the female youth achieved some youth competency. Thus, three-quarters of both sexes attained desired outcomes.

Wages. Male average wage at placement exceeded female average wage, $4.81 per hour compared to $4.26. This reflects occupational placement differences, with women tending to find employment in low-paying service jobs.

Discussion

Interviews with local e and t principals revealed agreement on several points: that the absence of support services, stipends, and paid work experience restricts some needy persons, many of them women, from becoming participants; that, in their view, public service employment should be a component of JTPA; and that the Comprehensive Employment and Training Act or CETA, JTPA's predecessor program, served women more adequately.

On the other hand, overall evaluations of JTPA varied. The JTPA director said he had become a partial convert "much to my surprise." She found that people who made a decision to participate in JTPA located the means to do so. The gaps in what the program supplies compelled would-be participants to come up with the missing pieces. In Stadelman's experience, this enhances commitment. "I've discovered that it is correct that a personal investment contributes to success."

On the other hand, Jack Frech, Athens Department of Human Services director, focussed on JTPA's omissions. He contended that JTPA fails to address the needs of those further from being "job-ready" and leaves most of the poor still poor. He further observed that the demand-deficient component of unemployment, too few jobs, cannot be addressed by training alone.

Both views acknowledge that JTPA works for some and not for others. TCCAA personnel concurred with Frech that welfare people cannot compete with the well-trained unemployed. CETA's pse, in their view, served some of these people. At both TCCAA and the DHS, as at other local sites, CETA "successes" hold regular jobs. Many are former AFDC mothers. JTPA eliminated the option of full-time, longer-term paid work program, which worked for these less "job-ready" people.

Since many JTPA personnel also worked with CETA, other comparisons arose. Program personnel agreed that CETA benefitted women more. In part this is because JTPA performance standards can be met without women. JTPA has no equal employment opportunity unit. Women with children and without day care, for example, can be screened out.

In the present, TCCAA worries about meeting performance standards while serving low-income people. Those involved in JTPA are concerned that TCCAA is out on a limb in its attempt to live up to the community action agency's mission and philosophy. Stadelman attributes the agency's success thus far to TCCAA's good reputation for performance, to the fact that it is established and known in the community, and to its efforts in the business sector.

E AND T WITH WOMEN IN MIND

JTPA has many defects as far as meeting women's distinctive needs. Not only does it exclude specific program components of particular benefit to women, but it operates in an environment skeptical of women's claims for training and jobs. For example, George Gilder, whose *Wealth and Poverty* (1981) was distributed to Reagan administration cabinet members, champions the position that "the first priority of any serious program against poverty [be] to strengthen the male role in poor families." Nonetheless, e and t programs which speak to women already exist. One example is Massachusetts' ET (Employment and Training) Choices.

ET Choices takes a different tack than JTPA or workfare programs in moving people off welfare and into jobs. Since it focuses on welfare recipients, its eligibles tend to be harder to place, with less employment background and job skills than the JTPA eligibles. To accomplish its task, ET provides options, such as education, training, supported work, and job search, from which the client chooses, as well as supportive services, both during the time in the program and after a job has been secured, the latter to enable the transition off welfare.

ET has produced positive results. In less than three years after the program began in October 1983, more than 25,000 AFDC recipients, equivalent to almost 30 percent of the current caseload, have obtained full- or part-time jobs through ET (in addition to 500 clients per month who got jobs on their own). Eighty-eight percent of the ET job finders are women (Atkins 1986, p. 21), as are a similar percentage of adult AFDC recipients. Of the people who moved off welfare through ET, 86 percent remained off a year later (data from the Employment and Training Choices as of May 1986). From January 1983 to July 1985, the welfare caseload declined nine percent despite benefits being increased 16 percent and eligibility being extended to pregnant women. During the same period, six of the 12 largest welfare caseload states experience increases of 4.6 to 16.6 percent, while the five others had reductions ranging from 4.2 to 8.5 percent, none as high as Massachusetts' 9.4 percent (Department of Public Welfare of Massachusetts 1986, p. 6). While Massachusetts' economy has performed strongly, unemployment rates fell in all the states during this period, five more steeply than in Massachusetts.

Program Characteristics

Emphasis on Education and Training. ET replaced an earlier WIN demonstration project which emphasized job search and deemphasized education and training. ET stresses education and training as preparation for long-term, self-sustaining employment. For the first nine months of fy 1986 (July 1985 to March 1986), more than half of ET participants chose an education program or some kind of training, 7 percent selected supported work, and 36 percent chose job development and placement (data from ET Choices).

Participants. Women make up more than three-quarters of participants. Although women with children under age six are not required to participate, they made up 18, 35, and 44 percent of participants in fy 1984, 1985, and 1986 (data from ET Choices).

Yet men are overrepresented and ET has benefitted two-parent families qualifying for AFDC through the Unemployed Parent program (UP) far in excess of their numbers. UP cases "are often headed by men with recent employment histories" (Department of Public Welfare 1986, p. 7) and, as such, make easier placements, another instance of the phenomenon of creaming. In the first quarter of fy 1985, men comprised 38 percent of those placed into employment, although men represented just 4.7 percent of the AFDC caseload at that time. The proportion of male AFDC clients dropped a year later to 29 percent and was expected to continue its decline (Department of Public Welfare 1986, p. 8) as this more job-ready strata of AFDC recipients moves into employment.

Massachusetts anticipated that the AFDC clients in ET in fy 1987 would be less job-ready. In response, ET expanded educational options to include remedial and tutorial programs, basic education, and English as a second language. It also implemented a youth services program including drop-out prevention (most high school drop-outs are girls who usually leave because of pregnancy) and services for pregnant and parenting teens (Department of Public Welfare 1986, pp. 14–15).

Supportive Services. ET's design acknowledges the needs of disadvantaged unemployed women in ways JTPA and many welfare work programs do not. ET pays for child care and transportation costs. The state attributes a substantial part of ET's success to this (Department of Public Welfare 1986, p. 4). Massachusetts planned to spend $22 million in fy 1987 for a voucher day care system that allows the client to choose the child care provider (Department of Public Welfare 1986, p. 39). Clients also receive up to $10 per day for transportation, public or private, including transportation to and from child care (data from ET Choices).

In addition, the program provides support services for a transition period. With day care costs averaging $2800 per year, and considerably more for infant care, many recently employed ET "graduates" would be forced to return to public assistance if subsidized day care were not available in their first year of employment. Similarly, when jobs include no health insurance, ET graduates often find it impossible to remain employed due to high health care costs. In 1987, a health choices program was to be established, granting ET graduates who do not receive coverage in their jobs, approximately one in four, health coverage during the first year of employment (Department of Public Welfare, 1986, p. 15).

Through these supportive services, extending into the first year in a job, the Massachusetts program enhances the likelihood that long-term employment will be a real alternative to welfare. Through this and other program components, ET Choices takes into account the needs of women in employment and training.

Massachusetts is not the only state to offer e and t programs more sensitive to women's needs than JTPA. New Jersey, for example, negotiated with the federal government in 1987 for regulatory changes to enable it to begin an experimental program for AFDC recipients. Its plan, Reach, for Realizing Economic Achievement, requires all able-bodied welfare recipients with children over age two to take part in either job training or education and to try to find full-time employment. In return, the state will provide the training, child care, transportation and Medicaid coverage, the last, like in Massachusetts, available for up to 12 months after finding a job ("Jersey Is Given Waivers in Welfare Overhaul Bid" 1987, p. 17). Wisconsin also received waivers from regulations; its program stresses education and is aimed at keeping young welfare recipients with children in school. Both these programs' designs take into account women's particular situations.

CONCLUSIONS

Programs geared toward enabling the poor, the unemployed, and underemployed to gain economic viability through jobs should direct their attention to women. Women are the "majority minority" in this case as in others. The problems of economic insufficiency belong disproportionately to women. Solutions must involve them to as great an extent.

JTPA and workfare fail to meet this test. They direct limited resources at a vast group of eligibles, offer little training on the average, and place people in generally sex-stereotyped jobs, which for women are low-paying, dead-end jobs. Some are helped, but many more are left behind.

Employment and training programs must be designed for needs arising from women's home and family commitments, their unemployment and underemployment, their relatively low wages, their occupational distribution, and their poverty if those programs are to achieve success in improving women's economic status. Elements such as provision of child care, training in a wide range of non-sex-stereotyped areas, and transitional benefits for women moving off public assistance enhance the employment and training programs' ability to serve women.

The Massachusetts program, ET Choices, demonstrates how resources can be applied to women's needs. Paying the costs of child care, transportation, and health care, not only during training, but for a subsequent transition period, marks a significant step forward in facilitating disadvantaged women's movement to self-sufficiency. The supported work program, like pse, may produce real dividends for women as similar programs have. While sex-stereotyped training and the number, kind, and wage rates of jobs available remain major concerns, ET and the New Jersey and Wisconsin programs reveal that e and t programs can take women into account. To do so, they must be framed in ways that recognize the sexes' dissimilar situations, and proceed toward equality by addressing these differences.

NOTES

An earlier version of this chapter was presented at the annual American Political Science Association meeting, Washington, D.C., August 28–31, 1986.

1. In 1940, almost one-half of the female labor force was single, 36 percent married, with the remainder widowed or divorced. In 1988, one-quarter was single, 59 percent married, the remainder divorced or widowed (U.S. Bureau of the Census, 2989, p. 385).

2. Ripley and Franklin categorize six types of government initiatives in e and t based on the location of the jobs (in the public or private sector) and the part of the work force (the cyclically unemployed, the structurally unemployed, or both) that they target (1983, p. 698). All six types have been tried.

3. The economically disadvantaged include those receiving welfare or food stamps, foster children, or families with incomes below either the Office of Management and Budget poverty level or 70 percent of the Bureau of Labor Statistics lower living standard, whichever is higher. Those facing barriers to employment include the handicapped, non-English speakers, and teenage parents.

4. TCCAA describes itself in its current brochure ad as a "unique Agency specifically designed to help low-income people help themselves," serving not only by providing "programs to meet the needs of economically disadvantaged community residents [but also serving] as an advocate for the rights of low-income people."

5. Defined as persons, usually women, whose primary occupation has been providing unpaid services to family members in their homes, who have lost the support of the person upon whom they have been financially dependent through separation, divorce, death, or disablement of that person.

6. Reluctance to move is widespread among all JTPA participants. Even in the most economically depressed areas, few wish to relocate, according to David Ford, associate director of Rutgers University's Center for Human Resources (Corrigan and Stanfield 1984, p. 260). Human capital resources are far from perfectly mobile.

REFERENCES

"The American Family: A Period of Transition." 1986. *National Journal* (July 19): 1804.

Atkins, Charles M. 1986. "20,000 Choose Paycheck over Welfare Check." *Public Welfare* 44, no. 1 (Winter): 20–22.

Bassi, Laurie J. 1983. "CETA—Did It Work?" *Policy Studies Journal* 12, no. 1 (September): 106–118.

Bassi, Laurie J., and Orley Ashenfelter. 1986. "The Effect of Direct Job Creation and Training Programs on Low-Skilled Workers." In *Fighting Poverty*, ed. Sheldon H. Danziger and Daniel H. Weinberg, pp. 133–151. Cambridge, Mass.: Harvard University Press.

Baumer, Donald C., and Carl E. Van Horn. 1985. *The Politics of Unemployment.* Washington, D.C.: Congressional Quarterly.

Breneman, David W., and Susan C. Nelson. 1980. "Education and Training." In *Setting National Priorities: Agenda for the 1980s*, ed. Joseph A. Pechman, pp. 205–245. Washington, D.C.: Brookings Institution.

Corcoran, Mary, Greg J. Duncan, and Martha S. Hill. 1984. "The Economic Fortunes of Women and Children: Lessons from the Panel Study of Income Dynamics." *Signs* 10, no. 2 (Winter): 232–248.

Corrigan, Richard, and Rochelle L. Stanfield. 1984. "Casualties of Change." *National Journal* (February 2): 252–264.

Coverman, Shelley. 1985. "Explaining Husbands' Participation in Domestic Labor." *Sociological Quarterly* 26: 81–97.

———. 1989. "Women's Work Is Never Done: The Division of Domestic Labor." In *Women: A Feminist Perspective* ed. Jo Freeman, 4th ed. pp. 356–368. Mountain View, Calif.: Mayfield.

Danziger, Sheldon H., and Daniel H. Weinberg. 1986. "Introduction," *Fighting Poverty*, ed. Sheldon H. Danziger and Daniel H. Weinberg, pp. 1–7. Cambridge, Mass.: Harvard University Press.

Department of Public Welfare of Massachusetts. 1986. *The Massachusetts Employment and Training Choices Program: Program Plan and Budget Request FY87.*

Duncan, Greg, et al. 1984. *Years of Poverty, Years of Plenty.* Ann Arbor, Mich.: The Institute for Social Research.

———. 1987. *The Volatility of Family Income Over the Life Cycle.* Ann Arbor, Mich.: Survey Research Center.

From Welfare to Work: Minority Female to Single Parent Program. 1987. N.Y.: The Rockefeller Foundation.

Gilder, George. 1981. *Wealth and Poverty.* N.Y.: Basic Books.

Hartman, Heidi I., and Barbara Reskin. 1983. "Job Segregation: Trends and Prospectus." *Occupational Segregation and Its Impact on Working Women.*, ed. Cynthia H. Chertos, Lois V. Haignerc, and Ronnie J. Steinberg, pp. 52–78. Albany, N.Y.: Center for Women in Government.

"Jersey Is Given Waivers in Welfare Overhaul Bid." 1987. *New York Times* (October 25): 1, 17.

Kamerman, Sheila B. 1984. "Women, Children, and Poverty: Female-Headed Families in Industrialized Countries." *Signs* 10, no. 2 (Winter): 249–271.

Labor Market Information Division, Ohio Bureau of Employment Services. 1985. *Civilian Labor Force Estimates.* (December).

Orfield, Gary, and Helene Slessarev. 1986. *Job Training Under the New Federalism.* (Chicago: University of Illinois).

Pearce, Diana M. 1985. "Toil and Trouble: Women Workers and Unemployment Compensation." *Signs* 10, no. 3 (Spring): 439–460.

Peirce, Neal R., and Robert Guskind. 1985. "Job Training for Hard-Core Unemployed Continues to Elude the Government." *National Journal* (September 28): 2197–2201.

Ripley, Randall A., and Grace A. Franklin. 1983. "The Private Sector in Public Employment and Training Programs." *Policy Studies Review* 2, no. 4 (May): 695–714.

Rytina, N. 1981. "Occupational Segregation and Earnings Differences by Sex." *Monthly Labor Review* (January): 49.

Saks, Daniel H. 1983. "Jobs and Training." In *Setting National Priorities: the 1984 Budget*, ed. Joseph A. Pechman, pp. 145–177. Washington, D.C.: Brookings Institution.

Shortridge, Kathleen. 1984. "Poverty Is a Woman's Problem." In *Women*, ed. Jo Freeman, pp. 492–50. Palo Alto, Calif.: Mayfield.

Treiman, Donald J., and Heidi I. Hartman. 1981. *Women, Work and Wages: Equal Pay for Jobs of Equal Value*. Washington, D.C.: National Academy Press.

U.S. Bureau of the Census. 1985. *Money Income of Households, Families and Persons in the U.S.: 1984*, Series p-60, no. 151. Washington, D.C.: U.S. Government Printing Office.

———. 1989. *Statistical Abstract of the U.S. 1989*. Washington, D.C.: U.S. Government Printing Office.

U.S. Bureau of Labor Statistics. 1986. *Employment and Earnings*. Washington, D.C.: U.S. Government Printing Office.

U.S. Commission on Civil Rights. 1982. *Unemployment and Underemployment among Blacks, Hispanics and Women*. Washington, D.C.: U.S. Commission on Civil Rights.

———. 1983. *A Growing Crisis: Disadvantaged Women and Their Children*. Washington, D.C.: U.S. Government Printing Office.

U.S. House. 1985. *Oversight Hearing on the Job Training Partnership Act*, Hearing of the Employment Opportunities Subcommittee of the Committee on Education and Labor, 99th Congress, 1st session. Washington, D.C.: U.S. Government Printing Office.

———. 1986. *Income and Jobs Action Act of 1985*, Hearing of the Committee on Education and Labor, 99th Congress, 1st session. Washington, D.C.: U.S. Government Printing Office.

U.S. Senate. 1986. *Oversight on the Job Training Partnership Act, 1985*, Hearing of the Subcommittee on Employment and Productivity of the Committee on Labor and Human Resources, 99th Congress, 1st session. Washington, D.C.: U.S. Government Printing Office.

"Why Do Women Earn Less?" 1983. *ISR Newsletter* 11, no. 1 (Spring/Summer): 4–5, 8.

Wiscombe, Janet. 1986. "Workfare Might Work," *State Legislatures* 12, no. 7 (August): 22–25.

1986 INTERVIEWS

Jack Frech, Director, Department of Human Services, Athens, Ohio.
Karen Harvey, County Commissioner, Athens, Ohio.

JTPA clients, Athens, Ohio.

Kris Stadelman, Director, Employment and Training Programs, Tri-County Community Action Agency, Sugar Creek, Ohio.

Linda Swift, former director of My Sister's Place, a shelter for battered women, Athens, Ohio.

7

WOMEN AND TAX POLICY

RUTH RUTTENBERG AND
AMY A. MCCARTHY

This chapter explores many of the major types of federal, state, and local taxes paid in the United States. It examines the differential impact of these taxes on women as spouses, single parents, divorcees, women of color, survivors, and retirees, as well as on poor, working poor, and wealthy women. It also considers women owners of small businesses, women workers, and homemakers. In addition to gender differences, the authors identify differences among classes, between single and married persons, and between the elderly and the non-elderly. They argue that there is no such thing as a neutral tax and therefore no such thing as a gender neutral tax.

INTRODUCTION

The complex system of federal, state, and local taxation we know today has been many years in evolving. The original intent of taxation was simply to raise revenue as efficiently as possible. But since the early 1960s, taxation has taken on an added dimension, that of furthering social, political, or economic goals. There are those who argue that tax policy properly has no policy goals as such, but that any revision should aim at making the tax system more "fair and simple." Others would suggest that federal, state, and local taxes can and should be used to promote specific social goals, to ameliorate many of the problems in our economic system, and that in combination with other types of government programs, tax policy could facilitate the full integration of women into the economy.

Taxation involves two dimensions, one the payment of taxes, the other the exemption from payment of taxes. Some taxes or tax exemptions are targeted at specific individuals, as in the federal income tax's extra deduction for the elderly and the blind. Other taxes, though not explicitly directed at any particular group, when put into practice affect one type of individual more than another. For example, the mortgage interest deduction in the federal income tax provides no benefit to non-homeowners.

President Reagan directed federal agencies to review all of their regulations to find, and in most cases, change rules that are overtly sex-biased, that is rules which afford special treatment to men or women based solely on sex. The president also encouraged the fifty states and the District of Columbia to conduct similar examinations of their own legislation and regulations. While this process is commendable in itself, it does not address the second problem that faces our society, that men and women play different roles in our economy and in our culture.

Differential Impact

These differences affect women and men in a variety of social, political, and economic ways. A few demographic observations should make clear just how different these situations are:

Table 7.1 shows women with a lower labor force participation rate than men, comprising 40 percent of those employed. Families headed by women presently have a median family income of $14,560 compared to married couple families, where the husband as the only worker has a median income of $21,164, and two-earner families where the median income is $33,436. Nearly 46 percent of all poor families are headed by women; 23 percent of all children under the age of 15 are poor. Women are also more likely than men to be elderly or to be employed only part time. These differences are only a sampling of the many ways in which men and women vary in the way they fit into society and the labor market. These differences have a large impact on the effect of taxation on men and women, as will be seen below.

The social security system provides a clear example of the impact of women's separate role in the economy. Social security benefits are calculated based upon an individual's earnings and the number of years of employment during which social security taxes were paid. Dependent spouses without work records sufficient to pay substantial benefits receive a benefit equal to half of the working spouse's retirement benefit. Divorced spouses also re-

Table 7.1
Selected Characteristics by Sex

Percentages	Women	Men
Percentage of those employed	40.0	60.0
Managers	4.2	14.9
Clerical/Sales workers	38.6	8.2
Skilled blue-collar workers	2.5	23.2
Percent in labor force	52.4	75.3
Head of household	15.4	84.6
Head of poor household	45.7	54.3
Black head of household	42.0	58.0
Black head of poor household	57.0	43.0
Claimed child care credit as single head of household	79.0	21.0
(Numbers in 1000's)		
Keeping house	32,276	479
Age 65 and over	15,492	10,699
Employed part time	10,879	5,165

Source: Employment and Earnings, May 1984; Stephen J. Rose, Social Stratification in the U.S., 3rd edition, Social Graphics Company, Baltimore: 1983.

ceive the same benefit as the current spouse. This arrangement leaves women with relatively low social security benefits because, by and large, women's work experience has been at lower pay and for fewer years than that of men. In addition, women are more likely than men to have worked in employment not covered by social security at all. Many women find that the benefits they earn by working are lower than the benefits they would receive by accepting half of their husband's earned benefit, as a dependent spouse.

The federal income tax code is also written as a gender-neutral system, but it affects individuals with different types and levels of income and different types and levels of expenses in different ways. Since men and women differ systematically in the way they earn and spend income, they are necessarily treated differently within the tax system. For example, women have lower levels of income, on average, than men, and therefore, pay taxes at a lower absolute rate than men. For this very reason, women benefit less from tax cuts than men do. Women are also far more likely to be single parents than are men, are more likely to pay for child care, and therefore are more likely to receive the child care credit than are men. On the other hand, women cannot take advantage of such tax deductions as the deduction for credit card interest to the same extent that this deduction is available to men, if women experience discrimination in applying for and receiving credit.

Most states have a state income tax system, which is fraught with the same types of problems faced by women in the federal system. But states also have sales tax provisions which are thoroughly regressive. Low income earners pay a much higher proportion of their incomes in sales tax than high income individuals. In many states, even food is taxed. Property tax is also a regressive tax in many states. Homeowners often pay at a higher rate than the owners of large commercial buildings. Renters often pay a high premium within their rent bill, which covers the owner's property tax.

Even corporate taxation tends to affect women differently than it does men. Women are more likely than men to be employed in low-paying jobs in competitive industries which benefit less from tax credits, accelerated depreciation allowances, and the tax benefits of multinational operations. Corporations which are able to benefit from favorable tax treatment are also those best able to pay relatively high wages, and they hire relatively fewer women.

The conception popular decades ago that the typical family consisted of a breadwinning husband, a housewife, and several children is certainly not the typical case today, if it ever was. In 1981, 66 percent of all working women were either not married (single, widowed, divorced, or separated) or were married to husbands earning less than $15,000 per year. These women are considered to be working for "economic reasons," and not for pin money.[1]

This chapter explores many of the major types of federal, state, and local taxes paid in the United States, and examines the differential impact of those taxes on women as spouses, single parents, divorcees, women of color, survivors, retirees, the poor, the working poor, and the wealthy. It also considers women owners of small businesses, women workers, and home-makers. Each of these groups is affected in some particular way by the various elements of our system of taxation. Reform aims at "fairness" but this is probably an illusory goal. At best the system might strive toward establishing specific objectives and modifying tax codes and regulations to attain those goals. What policy makers must understand, and what this chapter addresses, is the fact that there is no such thing as a neutral tax, and therefore no such thing as a "gender-neutral" tax. Every tax discussed here has a differential effect on men and women, rich and poor, old and young, employed and not employed, parent and nonparent.

The role of policy makers is to be conscious of the direct and indirect aspects of all taxation, and to develop tax policy with a clear understanding of who will be affected and whether or not the effect is desirable. This is certainly no easy task, and the design of policy itself is beyond the scope of this chapter. This chapter simply suggests a way of looking at tax issues that recognizes that, for example, an across the board tax cut does not actually benefit all taxpayers equally.

Goals of Tax Policy

Before assessing the specific issues and policy considerations affecting women, it is useful to step back and determine the actual goals of tax policy. There are several principles on which we can probably all agree:

1. The tax should be a good raiser of revenue.
2. The costs of collecting the tax and enforcing compliance should be kept to a minimum.
3. The tax should have only those impacts on the overall economy that are considered favorable. Early economists believed that taxes should be neutral—affecting neither the behavior of the individual taxpayer nor the behavior of the economy as a whole. Since Keynes, however, fiscal policy has become a major part of economic policy. Whether or not there is agreement with a given economic policy, there is general agreement that tax policy should be consistent with economic policy goals. Questions of consumer choice, incentives for work vs. leisure, quantity of production, methods of production, relative output of consumer vs. capital goods, etc. are all areas where tax policy can affect planned economic programs.
4. The distribution of the tax burden should conform with the patterns of income and wealth distribution regarded as the optimum for our society. Taxes must be seen as fair and equitable, based on social values. Two major types of equity are the focus of public finance experts: horizontal equity and vertical equity. Horizontal equity is the rule of "equal treatment of equals;" that is, that persons in the same circumstances should be taxed to the same extent. Vertical equity is the rule that persons who are in some sense better off than others should pay more taxes. There are long-standing debates on how to determine which persons are in the same circumstances, what constitutes "better-off", and on the appropriate relative burdens on persons in different circumstances.

The first two goals—good revenue-raising ability and minimum cost—are easy to measure. The second two goals, consistency with economic goals and with equity in society, are far more difficult. They involve issues of redistribution of income, as well as altering society's incentives—to work or not to work, to start a new business or not, to save or to spend. The issues are every bit as much political as they are economic. Each local, state, and federal administration influences economic policy and social equity through its actions in the tax arena.

This chapter examines the social security tax, the federal income tax, federal gift and estate taxes, and other federal, state, and local taxes, to evaluate in a general way their impact on income distribution, incentives, and the well-being of women in our society.

SOCIAL SECURITY

Social Security tax is paid by 92 percent of all American workers and their employers. Benefits are received by the workers themselves, when they retire or become disabled, by spouses, ex-spouses, and their dependents. Social security benefits were never intended to provide a person's full support in retirement, but merely to supplement other pensions and savings. Nevertheless, a large number of the 36 million adult social security recipients depend upon social security as their sole source of retirement income. Of all beneficiaries 54 percent are women.

The future solvency of the social security system has been a matter of concern or at least a matter of debate in recent years. But the health of the system is not the issue that concerns us here. Rather, we will analyze two other aspects of the social security system: its tax burden and the payment of benefits based upon taxes paid.

As a tax, social security is regressive. It currently taxes only the first $37,800 of earned income and does not tax property income such as interest, dividends, and capital gains. Therefore, the higher a person's wages or salary above the taxable limit and the more unearned income a person receives, the lower that person's effective social security tax rate will be. Firms must pay a share of the tax as well, and the more highly paid employees a firm has, the lower effective tax rate it will face.

What began as a small burden (in 1937 the combined employee and employer contribution was 2 percent of payroll up to $3000 of earnings) has taken a progressively greater share of GNP growing from 0.7 percent to nearly 6 percent.

As the payment of taxes raises questions of equity for the social security system, so too does the distribution of benefits. Benefits may be paid to the former wage earner and to a spouse, a former spouse, and dependent children. Benefits are paid to workers who qualify based on their contributions over 25 to 35 years worked. The rate at which benefits are paid is based upon an average of those years' earnings adjusted for inflation, the individual's "average indexed earnings." Benefits are calculated progressively, that is, they are paid at higher rate to those whose earnings were lower. Retired workers receive benefits based on their contributions to the social security system and their average earnings at the age of retirement. Spouses may choose to receive either half of the retirees' benefits or benefits based on their own work experience. Ex-spouses, to whom the beneficiary had been married for at least ten years and who have not remarried, are entitled to the same spousal benefit as the current spouse. Table 7.2 shows the complexity of the system and illustrates the disproportionality between taxes

Table 7.2

Social Security Average Indexed Earnings and Benefits Paid, Selected Cases

	Average Indexed Earnings	Retirement Benefits	Survivor's Benefits
Sam	12,000	5.698	-0-
Sara (current spouse)	-0-	2,849	5,698
Ethel (ex-spouse)	-0-	2,849	5,698
		11,396	11,396
Single, childless person	12,000	5,698	-0-
George	6,000	3,778	
Phyllis (current spouse)	6,000	3,778	3,778
Sue (ex-spouse)	-0-	1,889	3,778
		9,445	7,556
Frank	22,523	8,525	
Betty (as income earner)	6,000	3,778	8,525
Betty (as dependent)	-0-	4,260	8,525

Based on the formula [(.90 x $267) + (.32 x $1,345) + (.15 x remainder)] calculations by authors.

paid and benefits received by the different families and individuals high-lighted in the scenarios that follow.

Consider the following case. Sara and Sam have been married for 25 years, during which time Sam worked in covered employment while Sara raised their children and occasionally worked part-time. Sara did not ac-cumulate enough credits to qualify for social security benefits on her own. Sam was also previously married to Ethel for ten years. Ethel never remarried and worked for the local government in noncovered employment. When Sam retired at age 62 in 1984 he was receiving average indexed earnings of $12,000 per year, or $1000 per month. His retirement benefit would be $5698 per year. His wife, Sara, would receive half of Sam's benefit, or $2849 per year, for a total yearly benefit of $8547. Sam's former wife, Ethel, would also receive half of Sam's benefit, $2849. If Sam should die before Sara and Ethel, both women would be entitled to survivor's benefits, $5698 each, for a total of $11,396, the same total benefit paid while Sam was alive.

A single worker, who had an earnings record identical to Sam's would receive a benefit of $5698 until his or her death, and there would be no survivor's benefit paid.

In the case of a two-earner couple, George and Phyllis, who each qualify for benefits based on their work experience, the total benefit can be computed two ways. George's average indexed earnings of $6,000 entitle him to benefits of $3,778 per year. As his dependent, Phyllis would get $1,889, as would George's former wife of ten years, Sue. This gives George and Phyllis a total benefit of $5,667. But in this case, Phyllis qualifies for benefits in her own right. If Phyllis's average indexed earnings were also $6,000 per year, she would also qualify for a benefit of $3,778. The couple would receive a total of $7,556. Clearly in this case, Phyllis would take her own earned benefit rather than the spousal benefit, which is lower. If George were to predecease both Phyllis and Sue, Phyllis would get either George's survivor benefit or her own benefit, both of which are $3,778. For Sue, the divorced wife, the benefit would double upon George's death, to $3,778.

A third case is that of Frank and Betty. Frank has worked for 45 years in covered employment and retires with the maximum allowable average indexed earnings of $22,523. His wife, Betty, has also worked for 45 years and retires with $6,000 average indexed earnings. In this case, Frank would receive annual benefits of $8,525. Betty's earnings would entitle her to benefits of $3,778 but this is 11 percent less than the $4,262 she would be entitled to as Frank's dependent. As a widow, Betty would receive Frank's benefit $8,525.

These few examples demonstrate some of the problems inherent in the social security system as it presently exists. First, vastly different benefits may be paid to families with equal contributions. The one-earner couple, Sara and Sam, received benefits of $8,547, while the two-earner couple with the same income, George and Phyllis, received only $7,632, 11 percent less. When Sam's former wife Ethel's benefit and George's former wife Sue are included, those totals rise to $11,396; and $9,445, a difference of 21 percent. In addition to the higher retirement benefits received by the family with a full-time homemaker, Sara and Sam's family has also had the tax-free benefit of Sara's work within the home, affording her family a higher standard of living than would be possible for a two-earner family with the same income.

On the other hand, the benefit paid divorced wives in general is quite low and does not consider "years of service." A wife divorced at age 28 after ten years of marriage would be entitled to the same credits as a wife divorced at age 58, after forty years of marriage. The older woman would have only a limited opportunity to begin accumulating employment credits on her own account following her divorce.

The issue for tax policy that arises from an examination of the social security system is to establish a reasonable relationship between taxes paid and benefits received. To pay benefits solely to the wage earner (as was planned in the earliest days of the system in the 1930s) ignores the real although unpaid contribution of those who do housework. This contribution often enhances the ability of the employed spouse to earn income, but any extra income is credited to the employee's account, thus ignoring the real monetary value of the housewife's contribution. Some have suggested adding credits to the social security system for housework, so that the housewife would receive benefits based on her own work, rather than as a dependent of her husband. Suggestions for funding such a system range from having the family pay tax at the self-employed rate (which is lower than the combined employer-employee rate, but higher than the amount employees pay), to the argument that no contribution should be needed, since housewives currently receive benefits anyway. Providing for housewives to earn credits could reduce the inequity between wives with different numbers of years on the job and it could give housewives the status of having earned their benefits rather than being dependents.

Secondly, policy makers are continually examining the question of the level of benefits the system should pay. Presently, more than three million single retired women live on less than $6,000 per year in income. Another nearly three million live on less than $12,000 per year.

Part of the problem of low benefits comes from the system's express goal of supplementing other retirement income and from the great expense that would come from trying to provide more complete support. But the greater problem with the system is its policy of calculating benefits based on lifetime earnings, when women's employment has traditionally been less continuous and at lower pay than men's. The system of taxation and benefits that presently exists does very little to encourage married women to work outside the home.

THE FEDERAL INCOME TAX SYSTEM

President Reagan is fond of stating that the graduated income tax was the idea of Karl Marx. In reality, Abraham Lincoln signed the first progressive income tax into law, and a similar tax was enacted in the Confederacy, long before most people in the United States had ever heard of communism. The Civil War tax was repealed in 1871, and the federal government reverted to raising revenues through sales taxes and tariffs. Considerable dissent over the regressive nature of these taxes raged for the next forty years, until the sixteenth Constitutional Amendment was ratified, clearing the way for a progressive income tax.

Since that time, the nature of the tax system has changed considerably, most notably in three ways. First, the rate of income taxation has risen substantially from 1.3 percent of personal income in 1940 to an average of more than 13 percent today. Second, the proportion of total income tax paid by corporations and individuals has shifted dramatically, from nearly equal in 1945, to the present situation in which individuals pay more than four times as much as corporations pay. The third major change has been an enormous increase in loopholes. On the corporate side, $1.67 is lost through loopholes for every dollar collected. On the personal side, $0.83 is lost for every tax dollar collected.

Almost everyone agrees that the current tax system is in need of reform. Hardly anyone agrees on what should be done about it. The growing perception that the tax system is unfair has led to increased attempts by individuals to avoid taxes, as well as numerous proposals to make the system more equitable.

The macroeconomic figures—the growth in tax rates, the changing distribution of the burden—suggest that something might have gone awry. But to understand exactly where the problems lie, one must examine the microeconomics of the tax system, that is, who is affected by taxes and in what way?

The federal income tax system has evolved into a gender-neutral system with regard to the tax code. Even the concept that the male is automatically the head of the household is on its way out. The impact of the tax system, however, is still felt very differently by women than by men due to women's separate place in the economy and women's specific role within society.

The income tax system is based on the concept that those with higher incomes should pay higher rates of income tax. But at the same time, the tax code allows various types of income to be taxed at different rates, and it allows some income to escape taxation because of deductions, tax credits, and tax shelters. The nature of these tax rates and of the untaxable portions of income creates incentives and disincentives which help to direct individual behavior in ways considered socially desirable by policy makers. If men and women fit differently into the economy or respond differently to incentives and disincentives, then they will automatically be taxed differently. Our research shows that this is exactly what happens: the tax code is gender-neutral; the effect of the tax code is not.

This section of the chapter examines the differential effect of the federal income tax system, focusing on the earned income, the credit, the income tax threshold, the spousal IRA, and the dependent care credit.

The Earned Income Credit

The earned income credit is designed to help low-income working taxpayers with dependent children. For 1987, if the individual's or couples' earned income and adjusted gross income are each less than $15,432 (slightly above the poverty rate for a family of four), the taxpayer can get a refund of up to $851. The amount of the credit is determined according to an

Table 7.3
The Earned Income Credit

Earned Income	Tax Due	Credit	Net Due Refund
$3,000	-0-	422	(422)
6,924	65	851	(786)
10,000	451	542	(91)
15,431	11261	1	(1260)

1) Assumes head of household with one child (standard deduction + two personal exemptions).
Source: 1987 Federal Income Tax Tables, computations by authors.

earned income credit schedule. Examples of the amounts of credit available at different levels of earnings are shown in Table 7.3.

As the table shows, the amount of credit increases as earnings rise to $6,924 per year; then the credit decreases to zero at $15,432. The credit is not available to those who have no earned income (but it does include wages, strike benefits, net self-employment earnings, and disability pensions). It is available to those who have earned and unearned income (interest, dividends, workers compensation, unemployment compensation, social security payments, veterans benefits, pensions, or annuities) as long as the total adjusted gross income does not exceed $15,432. The credit is available even if the taxpayer is not otherwise required to file and refunds exceeding tax liability are returned. Individuals who believe they qualify can receive advance payments of the earned income credit through their employer. The credit will be indexed for inflation and increase with the cost of living in the future enabling more women to qualify. Some states like Maryland are now accepting at least a portion of the federal earned income credit as an adjustment to state tax owed.

Since women disproportionately earn less than $15,432 and have disproportionate responsibilities for dependent children, women will be disproportionately benefitted by this credit.

The Dependent Care Tax Credit

Another tax credit which disproportionately benefits women is the credit for child and dependent care. This care is often described as the one which "allows women to work." What the credit actually does is to subsidize child and dependent care costs, thus helping a caretaker afford those costs. Since the overwhelming majority of the time, the mother is charged with child care, this is viewed as a women's benefit. But it is only because women bear the disproportionate share of the responsibility that they receive the disproportionate share of the tax credit. In 1979, the last year for which these data were compiled, nearly four times as many female as male non-joint filers claimed the child and dependent care credit.

Although the tax credit for child care is certainly to be applauded, it comes nowhere near alleviating the problem of costly child care. Many would argue that tax policy alone cannot or should not solve this entire problem. Table 7.4 illustrates the magnitude of the costs involved. Women who earn the least reap the smallest benefit from this tax credit because it is not a refundable credit like the earned income credit.

A minimum wage worker earns $3.35 per hour, which is $134 per week or $6,968 per year. If child care costs an average of $40 per week, or $2,080 per year, this worker receives an income tax credit of $624. However, this credit only applies to total tax liability. Since this worker would owe only $70 in federal income taxes in the absence of the credit, $554 of the tax credit cannot be used by the taxpayer. Child care costs, even after the tax credit claim 30 percent of this minimum wage worker's pay, leaving her with less than $5,000 for all other expenses.

The minimum wage worker who places two children in relatively inexpensive child care at $40 per week can take advantage of none of the $1,248 tax credit to which she is entitled. Her child care costs take 60 percent of her budget. In this situation, the mother faces basically two choices. First, she could take her children out of paid day care to join the estimated one child in six under the age of 13 who has no organized care at all.[2] Second, she could quit her job to care for her children herself, supported by various social programs. Neither of these choices can be considered optimal from a long-range social perspective. The problem could be attacked in a number of ways, from providing child care insurance similar to medical insurance, to providing federally or state-funded child care services as public education is now provided. The federal government uses tax policy in two ways to subsidize child care, first through the dependent care tax credit, which costs $1.5 billion per year, and second through allowing employers to provide child care services or vouchers as tax-free benefits. The problem with both of these approaches is that they benefit upper income families more than the poor.

This is not a problem solely for poor women, however. Child care costs can be a serious drain on the budgets of women with higher incomes as well. The median income for a female head of household is $13,500. If she places two children in a moderately priced day care center, she would pay $4,160 per year, or 31 percent of her income. The tax credit to which she would be entitled would be $1,164, $473 more than her tax liability. She

Table 7.4
Effect of Dependent Care Tax Credit on Female Heads of Household

	Gross Income	Child Care Cost ($40/wk.)	Tax	Tax Credit	Net*	Child Care Costs as % of After Tax Budget
Minimum wage worker 1 child	$6,968	$2,080	$70	$624	($554)	30%
Minimum wage worker 2 children	$6,968	$4,160	$0	$1,248	($1,248)	60%
Median income for Female Head of Household 1 child	$13,500	$2,080	$976	$582	$394	16%
Median income for Female Head of Household 2 children	$13,500	$4,160	$691	$1,164	($473)	31%

*Under the current tax code, excess dependent care tax credits are not refunded. The taxpayer simply has no tax liability.
Source: Authors' computations based on 1987 Income Tax Code.

would be unable to take advantage of the maximum tax credit of $1,344 even if she paid more for child care.

The Income Tax Threshold

Included in the federal income tax tables is an "income tax threshold," an amount of income below which no income tax is paid. This threshold is justified on the basis that income tax should be based on the ability to pay. The government also computes various "poverty levels," amounts of income below which families of various sizes are considered poor. Single persons have the lowest poverty levels; large families the highest. The relationship between the income tax threshold and the poverty level has been quite variable over time, as Table 7.5 shows.

Table 7.6 shows the amount of taxes paid by families of different sizes at the poverty level for the years 1978 to 1985. In 1978, poor families, except for single people, paid no income tax and in some cases received refunds based on the earned income credit. This refund partially offset the tax for social security which is paid on all earned income and has no threshold. The combined tax as a percent of income shown in Table 7.6 for 1978 was no more than 6.1 percent for families of two or more.

The Spousal IRA

Under today's law, wage earners not covered by an employer retirement plan may establish Individual Retirement Accounts (IRAs) and contribute up to $2,000 in tax-deferred income per year. In addition, if a spouse has no earned income (alimony received may be considered earned income), the income earning spouse may establish a spousal IRA, so that the two IRAs total $2,250 or less and neither is greater than $2,000. Families with two wage earners, therefore, can shelter up to $4,000 per year from income tax, while one-earner families can shelter only $2,250. If one spouse in the two-earner family earns less than $2,000, that spouse's contribution is limited to his or her earnings. For workers covered by an employer retirement plan, IRA directions are further limited by adjusted gross income. Deductions start phasing out at $25,000 (single/head of household); $40,000 (married/qualifying widower); and $1 (married filing separately).

For nearly 70 percent of married couple families, $4,000 represents at least 11 percent of gross family income which is nearly double the average rate at which Americans save. For 75 percent of all nonretired single women, $2,000 is 11 percent or more of their gross income. This means that only relatively high-income families can comfortably spare $4,000 per year to shelter in IRA accounts, and with tax reforms, only workers not covered by their employers can take the full deduction as a tax credit.

Table 7.5
Relationship between Income Tax Threshold and Poverty Level for a Family of
Four, 1959–1986

Year	Income Tax Threshold	Poverty Level	Percentage Gap between Tax Threshold and Poverty Level
1959	2,667	2,973	-10.3
1960	2,667	8,022	-11.7
1965	3,000	3,223	-6.9
1966	3,000	3,223	-9.6
1968	3,000	3,553	-15.6
1969	3,000	3,743	-19.9
1970	3,600	3,968	-9.3
1971	3,750	4,137	-9.4
1972	4,300	4,275	+0.6
1973	4,300	4,540	-5.3
1974	4,300	5,038	-14.6
1975	6,692	5,500	+21.7
1976	6,892	5,815	+18.5
1977	7,533	6,191	+22.0
1978	7,533	6,662	+13.1
1979	8,626	7,412	+16.4
1980	8,626	8,414	+2.5
1981	8,634	9,287	-7.0
1982	8,727	9,862	-11.5
1983	8,783	10,166*	-13.6*
1984	8,783	10,613*	-17.2*
1985	8,936	11,101*	-19.5*
1986	9,102	11,601*	-21.5*

Note: Tax thresholds assume full use of the earned income tax credit.
*Estimated.
Source: Joint Committee on Taxation, "Federal Treatment of Families Below the Poverty Line," Washington, D.C.: U.S. Government Printing Office, 1984.

Summary on Federal Income Tax

The federal income tax system represents an amalgam of incentives and disincentives, some effective and some not, which both encourage and discourage marriage, homemaking, or work outside the home. The marriage tax discourages the marriage of two-earner singles but encourages the mar-

Table 7.6

Tax Thresholds, Poverty Levels, and Federal Tax Amounts for Different Family Sizes with Earnings Equal to the Poverty Level, 1976–1985

	Family Size					
	1	2	3	4	5	6
Income tax *threshold:*						
1978	$3,200	$5,200	$6,930	$7,520	$8,183	$9,167
1982	3,300	5,400	8,237	8,727	9,216	9,706
1983-84	3,300	5,400	8,315	8,783	9,251	9,719
1985	3,445	5,638	8,447	8,936	9,424	9,913
Poverty level:						
1978	3,311	4,249	5,201	6,662	7,880	8,891
1982	4,900	6,280	7,690	9,860	11,680	13,210
1983	5,052	6,475	7,928	10,166	12,042	13,620
1984	5,274	6,760	8,277	10,613	12,572	14,219
1985	5,517	7,071	8,658	11,101	13,150	14,873
Income tax at *poverty level:*						
1978	16	0	-280	-134	-12	0
1982	202	106	-134	285	417	491
1983	206	118	-91	318	431	507
1984	226	150	-9	365	480	570
1985	237	158	50	383	504	599
Payroll tax at *poverty level:*						
1978	200	257	315	403	477	538
1982	328	421	515	661	783	885
1983	338	434	531	681	807	913
1984	353	453	555	711	842	953
1985	389	499	610	783	927	1,049
Combined income *and payroll tax* *at poverty level:*						
1978	216	257	35	269	465	538
1982	530	527	381	946	1,200	1,376
1983	544	552	440	999	1,238	1,420
1984	579	603	546	1,076	1,322	1,523
1985	626	657	660	1,166	1,431	1,648
Combined tax as *percent of income* *at poverty level:*						
1978	6.5	6.1	0.7	4.0	5.9	6.1
1982	10.8	8.4	5.0	9.6	10.3	10.4
1983	10.8	8.5	5.5	9.8	10.3	10.4
1984	11.0	8.9	6.6	10.1	10.5	10.7
1985	11.3	9.3	7.6	10.5	10.9	11.1

Source: Joint Committee on Taxation, "Federal Treatment of Families Below the Poverty Line," Washington, D.C.; U.S. Government Printing Office, 1984.

riage of a single earner and a homemaker. The dependent care credit encourages parents to work outside the home, but its benefits fail to help many of the poor. The spousal IRA, particularly the current administration's proposed changes, discourage part-time work. Economists are unclear about exactly how strong an incentive most taxes create at low levels of earnings. At higher levels of income, incentives such as home mortgage interest deductions are thought to have a very strong effect on behavior. Whatever the true impact of these various tax incentives, the system needs to be scrutinized to remove the contradictory messages it sends the population and to ensure that it promotes socially desirable goals.

Gift and Estate Taxes

When individuals receive a gift or a bequest, that is, a gratuitous transfer through an estate, they experience a gain in economic well-being but a gain which U.S. tax laws treat differently from other gains in income or wealth. There are several reasons for this disparate treatment. First of all, many estates pass from decedent to a spouse or minor children and, as such, do not represent a real improvement in the economic well-being of the beneficiaries, since even without title to the estate they had already had full use of the property. (In fact, they are probably worse off because the death of the spouse or provider resulted in loss of family income.) Second, gratuitous transfers are highly irregular from year to year and, therefore, are not easily adaptable to income taxation. Third, many gifts are in small amounts or in kind and are very difficult to detect.

Because historically most women have been financially dependent on their husbands and because women usually survive their husbands, the impacts of gift and estate taxes have usually fallen on women. Women, especially those with minor children, found themselves no better off by holding title to property than they had been with full use of it, yet they owed tax—and at a time when the husband's income had disappeared. Small credits, high marginal tax rates, and limited marital deductions have been issues long resented by women facing the tax burdens on their husbands' estates. Federal estate taxes mean to exempt small- and moderate-sized estates, but inflation constantly pushes the value of estates and gifts into higher tax brackets and can thus force families to liquidate small farms, ranches, and businesses in order to pay the inheritance taxes. High marginal tax rates can force the sale of middle-sized family and closely held businesses, too. But the most difficult probably has been the so-called "widow's tax" which arose from limited marital deductions. Because the maximum estate tax marital deduction generally has been limited to a decedent's adjusted gross estate when an entire estate was bequeathed to the remaining spouse, half of the estate was usually subjected to a tax even though the property remained within the marital unit. When the property was later transferred, often to surviving children at the death of the surviving spouse, the entire estate was subject to taxes. The cumulative tax effect was one-half on the death of the first spouse and again fully on the death of the second spouse, thus subjecting the property to taxation one-and-a-half times, with the unfair burden usually falling on widows and their children.

Gift and estates taxes have had these consistent problems. They also have never been important raisers of revenue, partly because of high exemptions, partly because of numerous loopholes.[3] Since passage of the Economic Recovery Tax Act (ERTA) of 1981, some of the unfair burdens are being addressed, but they are causing gift and estate taxes to become even less important as revenue producers. This virtual elimination of the federal estate tax helps women especially, since women on average outlive men by eight years.[4] Three changes provided by ERTA estate and gift tax provisions are especially important:

1. ERTA provides for an increase in the unified credit, over a six-year period, to increase from $47,000 to $192,800, with no estate or gift tax on transfers aggregating $600,000 or less.

2. ERTA reduces the maximum estate and gift tax rate from 70 percent to 50 percent over a four-year period. This provision is meant especially to help prevent the forced sales of closely held and family businesses after the death of a spouse.[5]

3. ERTA eliminates the so-called "widow's tax" by providing for an unlimited marital deduction. Congress has provided for unlimited lifetime transfers between spouses without the imposition of any estate or gift tax.

Women, especially women whose household wealth is substantial, should applaud the reforms of ERTA. Women of limited means are virtually unaffected by any ERTA reforms on estate and gift taxes since they do not usually pay these taxes. Or are they? The revenue shortfall from these reforms must either be made up by other taxpayers or be reflected in reduced federal expenditures.

Other less obvious inequities exist. Single persons of means do not get nearly the advantages for their households that they could achieve if they were married. There is no estate tax if the total assets of husband and wife are $1.2 million or less, but if an individual is single, there is an estate tax for assets above $600,000. Whereas the annual gift tax exclusion under ERTA was increased from $3,000 to $10,000 per donee, if a household consists of both husband and wife, and they agree to split a gift of property, they are entitled to a maximum exclusion of $20,000 per donee. Households headed by females cannot pass on to their beneficiaries the same gifts and estates as households headed by both husband and wife.

One of the last major areas of overt sex discrimination in gift and estate taxes, that of gender-specific actuarial tables which are used to value reversionary interests, was reformed when a federal district court ruled in October 1983 that use by the Internal Revenue Service (IRS) of gender-based mortality tables was unconstitutional. The suit was filed by Manufacturers Hanover Trust Co. as executor of the estate of Charlotte Wallace. Ms. Wallace died in 1976, retaining a reversionary interest in a trust she established in 1923. Using the life tables in sections 20.2037-1, 20.2031-7, and 20.22031-10, the IRS determined that the present value of Ms. Wallace's reversionary interest in the trust should be included in her gross estate under section 2037. In response to this IRS decision, Manufacturers Hanover filed a refund suit, claiming that the life span tables in the regulations were gender-based, with the result that Ms. Wallace's reversionary interest exceeded five percent of the value of the trust corpus. If Ms. Wallace's reversionary interest had been calculated under gender-neutral life tables, according to Manufacturers Hanover it would not have exceeded the five percent threshold for inclusion in the gross estate. Hence, argued Manufacturers Hanover, the use of gender-based tables was unconstitutional. U.S. District Judge Steward agreed and held the use of gender-based mortality tables to value a decedent's reversionary interest constitutes impermissible discrimination under the Fifth Amendment.[6] The court found that the use of gender-based mortality tables "does not serve an important government interest and does not bear a substantial relationship to the objective of accurately valuing reversionary interests for federal estate tax purposes."[7]

The ruling struck down Treasury Department regulations that governed mortality tables used to value reversionary interests for purposes of section 2037. The responses of the federal government executive branch since that ruling have seemed less than consistent. The Internal Revenue Service, on October 31, 1983, published a proposal in the *Federal Register* to shift from gender-based to gender-neutral tables. But the solicitor general authorized an appeal in this case, and on February 10, 1984, an Assistant U.S. Attorney for the Southern District of New York filed an appeal, "based solely on the issue of the constitutionality of the IRS's use of its sex-based regulations and mortality tables in valuing reversionary interests to determine estate tax liability."[8] Subsequent to this appeal the IRS officially adopted these long-discussed unisex tables (published in the *Federal Register* of May 11, 1984) that do not differentiate between the life spans of men and women for valuation purposes.[9] These tables apply to annuities, life estates, terms of years, remainders, and reversions, and they overlap the income, estate, and gift tax fields.

These new gender-neutral tables do not, however, remove all gender differentiation from U.S. tax regulations. Five examples of gender differentiation that remain, even after some 30 paragraphs of the current regulations have been modified, were cited in a letter from Michigan Congressman John Dingell, Chair of the House Committee on Energy and Commerce, to Internal Revenue Service Commissioner Roscoe Egger, Jr.

The following five regulations either require or enable the use of gender-based tables:

—IRS Regulation 1.72-1 et seq., including Tables in 1.72-9, which sets the amount of employees' investment in an annuity which the annuitant can deduct before paying income tax on benefits received.

—IRS Regulation 1.101-2(e)(1)(iii)(b)(1) and (b)(2), which sets the value of employer-provided annuity death benefits payable to a retiree or beneficiary excludable from gross income.

—IRS Regulation 1.401(j)-4(a)(ii), which sets the cash surrender value of insurance or annuity under a fully insured defined-benefit Keogh plan.

—IRS Regulation 1.403(b)-1(d)(ii)(ii), which sets the amount of employer contribution to tax-sheltered annuity when the exact amount is not known, excludable from employee's gross income in determining the latter's taxable income.

—IRS Regulation 1.408-2(b)(6)(iv), which sets the amount of required withdrawals from an Individual Retirement Account beginning at the end of the taxable year in which the IRA owner becomes 70 1/2 years old.

Despite efforts by Dingell to have federal tax regulations complete the process of gender neutralization, IRS failed to eliminate these aspects of gender-based valuation. It is important to note that the use of sex-based tables has never been required by the Internal Revenue Code itself. It is not the code but rather IRS regulations adopted in January 1971 that established sex-based regulations as the method for determining tax obligations and liability.

Estate and gift taxes have always been and, today even more, are the domain of those with assets in U.S. society, especially the near wealthy and wealthy. Any liberalization of such taxes reduces revenue and therefore is against the interests of poor and working women. Any reforms which fail to equalize burden between men and women are against the interests of all women, rich and poor.

Federal Corporate Income Tax

U.S. tax laws that provide tax credits for profits earned overseas and that defer tax liabilities on unrepatriated earnings encourage U.S. businesses to expand outside of U.S. borders. The jobs lost through lack of domestic expansion, or directly through U.S. plant closings followed by foreign expansion, are often the lower and semiskilled jobs of trades dominated by women. The manufacture of textiles, apparel, electronic components and accessories, and radio and TV electrical receiving equipment are cases in point. Each of these product areas represents goods once largely produced in the United States but increasingly imported today. Each of these product areas has a greater share of women employees than the private work force

Table 7.7
Employment of Women by Industry

Industry	Percent Women of All Employees
Textiles	47.4
Apparel	80.7
Electronic Components and Accessories	71.3
Radio and TV Receiving Equipment	52.3
Total, private sector	43.4

Source: U.S. Department of Labor, Employment and Earnings.

generally. (See Table 7.7.) Those 20 industries whose employment was most negatively impacted by trade, according to a U.S. Labor Department study had a female work force of 41 percent.[10] These included such especially female-dominated industries as apparel, non-rubber footwear, other leather products, knit apparel mills, and fabricated textiles, all of which had work forces which were more than 57 percent female. The 20 industries that were most positively impacted by trade, on the other hand, had a female work force of only 21 percent.

U.S. tax laws are not, of course, the only factor influencing the location of industry, but they can be an important factor. According to the former chief economist for the AFL-CIO:

What government policy there is has tended to encourage rather than discourage the export of technology. The tax provisions of foreign income which make foreign investment more attractive than domestic investment are an example. Both the dollar tax credit on profits earned overseas, and the deferral tax liability on unrepatriated foreign income are a case in point.[11]

State and Local Taxes

Despite the $171.4 billion dollars collected in 1983 by state and local government, taxes are a declining share of the total revenues of these levels of government.[12] This is true even though the transfer of federal funds to state and local governments has declined. The nontax share of state revenues is made up from licenses, fees, borrowing, lotteries (in 13 states) liquor stores (operated in 17 states), plus the contributions and investment earnings received by employee-retirement, unemployment compensation, and other insurance trust systems of state government.[13]

Whereas taxes tend to be based in a philosophy of "ability to pay," fees and licenses are more often based in a public finance philosophy of benefits received. To the extent that the state and local tax systems are pledged to providing services in the public interest, services which in many cases exist specifically because of the inability of certain individuals to pay, the state and local tax systems of this nation are placing increasing burdens on the poor, who are disproportionately women.

In addition, the total U.S. system of collecting tax revenues is increasing at the state and local level, from 38.2 percent of the total revenues during the fourth quarter of 1981 to 43.3 percent in the fourth quarter of 1983.[14] In 1983, while state tax collections rose 9.7 percent and local government tax revenues climbed by 8.0 percent, federal tax collections actually fell by 1.1 percent, with corporation net income tax revenues falling by 2.7 percent. This has an important negative effect on the poor. Whereas federal taxes have tended to be progressive; that is, the less one's ability to pay, the lower one's relative tax burden; state and local taxes have traditionally been regressive; that is, the less one's ability to pay, the greater the relative tax burden.

The tax variations from state to state and within each state are substantial. While the largest tax revenue producer for 42 of the 50 states is still the sales tax (all but Alaska, Delaware, Massachusetts, Minnesota, Montana, New York, Oregon, Virginia and Wyoming), state income taxes are a growing source of revenue.[15] While property taxes are still the predominant source of revenue at the local level, their dominance has fallen in recent years. The so-called "tax revolt" of the 1970s led to substantial legislative and citizen-mandated changes in local and state tax programs. And, as a matter of course, changes are made each year that affect tax collection. Since one's state tax burden is different from state to state—both by type of tax and amount—the impact on women varies widely.

Because of the vast number of local governments within the United States, the variation of taxes, tax rates, and tax regulations is difficult to summarize. As local governments increasingly diversify their taxing sources beyond the property tax, they have moved both toward the more progressive income tax and toward the more regressive sales tax. Each jurisdiction must be evaluated individually to ascertain its impacts on the women within its taxing boundaries. In most localities, because of the predominance of women in lower income categories, a local jurisdiction (and the states and federal governments, as well) would require progressive taxes in order to prevent women from bearing a larger relative share of the tax burden.

The property tax, the major but declining source of local taxation, has always been difficult for public finance experts to analyze. The literature is replete with debates about whether the tax is neutral, progressive, or regressive; about the shifting and the incidence of the tax; and about the various impacts of market forces in the real estate market on the property

tax. While the majority of analysts probably agree that the tax is usually
regressive and especially so in tight rental housing markets and when shifting
to tenants occurs, there is less than full agreement. To the extent that
property taxes on rental properties are shifted to consumers for commercial
and industrial business and to tenants in residential markets, the tax will
be regressive—and the poor, who are disproportionately women, will bear
a greater relative burden.

The property tax can have an especially cruel effect on lower income
elderly homeowners. Elderly households are disproportionately made up of
women and women heads of household. Even though many elderly homeowners have paid off their mortgages, they are finding that their property
tax liabilities are so high that they can no longer afford the shelter they live
in, their home of perhaps 20, 30 or even 50 years.[16] Sometimes their current
monthly tax bill is higher than their monthly mortgage payment. Several
localities have struggled with policies to ameliorate the displacement effects
of the property tax, especially on elderly widows. Some have discussed
putting caps on the amount of one's income that can be obligated to property
taxes. Other cities have considered exempting some portion of the elderly
from some amount of their property tax obligation. Still others have considered accepting a lien on an individual's estate for unpaid tax revenues.
All are aimed at preventing the property tax from displacing elderly individuals of limited means from their homes.

Some cities have made efforts to make their tax systems more progressive.
Santa Monica, California, for example, has imposed new fees and obligations on builders and property owners in a conscious effort to increase the
purchasing power of tenants.[17] But most cities, counties, and states are doing
just the opposite under pressure and even under statutory obligation from
local tax-cutting referenda. Spurred in part by the success of Proposition
13 in California, the Jarvis-Gann initiative which called for a drastic across-
the-board property tax cut in California, states and localities across the
nation have chosen to cut taxes and public services. From Michigan to
Massachusetts to Tennessee, from Elgin, Illinois to Prince George's County,
Maryland measures to cut taxes and/or balance budgets have won at the bal-
lot box. The impact on women? Women heads of households are more likely
to be renters than homeowners and so property tax cuts benefit them only
indirectly and only in some housing markets and sometimes only partially.
Renters may face less of a rent increase from property tax cuts but are not
likely to receive rebates or reductions. To the extent that cuts in public services have been a result of tax-cutting initiatives, those who have suffered most
have tended to be the poor, and, therefore, disproportionately women.

EVALUATION

Tax policy has grown so complicated and is so decentralized that no
single philosophy or set of goals can be said to exist. Many taxes seem to

provide contradictory incentives, pushing individuals in opposing directions at once. (The income tax penalizes marriage, while social security encourages it through dependent and survivor's benefits, for example.) The distribution of income within the United States has shifted rather dramatically in recent years, while the tax burden has increased for the lowest half of the population. Wealthy income earners, making $200,000 per year, have experienced tax reductions of more than one-third.

Budget cuts have added to the burden of an increasingly regressive system, as has the shift from federal taxation toward lower levels of government and toward more user fees. We have seen an increase in the regressiveness of taxation, as states pick up some of the federal burden and also reduce social spending.

At the same time, the tax burden has shifted away from corporations and on to individuals. Thirty years ago, corporations paid 25 percent of all federal taxes. Now they pay around 6 percent. The difference has fallen to individual taxpayers. A recent congressional study shows 213 firms in the Fortune 500 paid income tax at the rate of 16 percent. Many profitable firms, including General Electric, Dupont, RCA and Texaco, paid no taxes at all or even received refunds.[18] These issues must be considered at a microeconomic level; policy makers must consider the policy implications of every tax change, every new regulation.

While significant changes in tax policy might be called for, it is important to remember that tax policy does not operate in a vacuum. Rather, taxes combine with many other types of public policy in trying to achieve specific goals. Often the interaction of various policies prevents tax policy from achieving its apparent objective. For example:

• The dependent care tax credit does little to offset the high cost of private day care. Federal and state programs to assist in child care have been cut drastically, reducing by thousands the number of children served as well as the level of aid per child. As a result, many mothers were forced to quit work to care for their children, supported by social programs such a AFDC.[19]

• In the face of rapidly rising medical costs, the loss of medical insurance by unemployed workers, and the refusal of Congress to legislate a rational national health care program, the amount of medical expenses necessary to earn an income tax deduction is increased, and the deduction for medical insurance is eliminated.

• The combined effect of tax and budget cuts has distributed after-tax income away from low-income families toward high-income families, as shown in Table 7.8.

• Services provided by homemakers prove especially troublesome to tax policy makers, probably because it is difficult to establish a monetary value for them. Treatment of homemakers is contradictory in several ways. First, they cannot establish IRA accounts if they have no earnings although their spouse may establish one for them. Second, they may receive social security benefits as a dependent without paying any payroll tax personally.

Table 7.8
Tax and Budget Cuts: The Impact on Household Incomes

	Gain from Tax Cuts	Loss in Cash Benefits	Loss in Noncash Benefits*	Net Gain or Loss
All households	$1090	$-170	$-100	$820
$10,000 or less	20	-250	-160	-390
$10,000-20,000	330	-210	-90	30
$20,000-40,000	1,200	-130	-60	1,010
$40,000-80,000	3,080	-90	-80	2,900
$80,000 or more	8,390	-90	-40	8,270

Note: Projections for the 1984 calendar year. Numbers have been rounded.
*Include food stamps, Medicaid, Medicare, and housing subsidies.
Source: Congressional Budget Office.

The real policy debate in the near future revolves around three key questions:

1. Who benefits from the federal, state, and local tax cuts and who bears the burden of the resulting program cuts?
2. As lower tax assessments yield smaller revenues and the public sector finds itself unable to meet its minimum levels of expenditures, how will the additional revenues be raised (tax increases, user fees, etc.) and who will bear the burden of these increases?
3. How can tax policy be used effectively to promote social goals and to complement other types of government policy?

We already have some data to answer the first question. Specific women's programs have been cut at the federal level. The tax cuts that accompanied the spending cuts could never help the very poor because those with low tax liabilities have little to gain from reductions in taxation. The programs cut have been targetted programs more than general population programs. Women have been disproportionately hurt by the federal tax-spending cut package.

At the state level, Proposition 13, for example, cut specific programs like school sports and introduced user fees for other previously state-provided programs such as parks and school books. Again, the poor bear a disproportionate burden of the tax and program cutting. At the local level, the impacts are similar.

There are now calls for tax increases. If the current trend toward a more regressive system continues, women—poor and elderly women—will bear a disproportionate burden. Before any further changes in the tax system are considered, there needs to be a thorough, comprehensive study of the macro- and microeconomic impact of taxation on the population in general and on specific demographic groups. The goals of tax policy must be clearly stated and policy must be designed to achieve those goals, working in concert and not in opposition to other government policy.

Generally, the tax system, both at the federal and state level, does not provide the benefit to women that would be possible if the system were designed with different goals in mind. If our national political consensus could reach the conclusion that providing care for our society's children while their parents worked was a legitimate national goal, then the tax system could be revised to affect the transfer of funds necessary to accomplish that goal, through the dependent care credit. If our society concluded that a certain minimum standard of living should be guaranteed to all families, the tax system could provide that, through a more substantial earned income credit. The tax system provides a tool to be used in conjunction with other types of government policy to affect necessary changes in our economic and political systems. What is needed now is conscious effort to reevaluate tax policy, not just with an eye toward making it "simpler" but with a genuine concern for the many other social goals tax policy could help us achieve.

NOTES

This chapter was first developed for presentation at the National Conference on Women, the Economy and Public Policy, Washington, D.C., 1984. We wish to thank Susan B. McMillan for updating material from the earlier paper.

1. The Women's Bureau, U.S. Department of Labor, taken from the Current Population Survey, 1981.

2. Testimony of Helen Blank, Children's Defense Fund before the Joint Economic Committee on Women in the Workforce, April 4, 1984.

3. John Due, *Government Finance*. (Homewood, Ill.: Richard D.Irwin, 1963), p. 327.

4. White House Office of Policy Information, "Issues Update," No. 15, September 19, 1983, p. 7.

5. U.S. Congress, Joint Committee on Taxation, *General Explanation of the Economic Recovery Act of 1981*, JCS-71-81, December 29, 1981, p. 229.

6. *Tax Notes* 23, no. 4, April 23, 1984, p. 378.

7. Ibid, 373.

8. *Federal Register*, October 31, 1983.

9. *Federal Tax Guide Reports: Tax Week* (Chicago: Commerce Clearing House, May 18, 1984), p. 1.

10. Ruth Ruttenberg and Iris Lav, *The Impact of Manufacturing Trade on Employment* (Washington, D.C.: Department of Labor, International Labor Affairs Bureau, 1978).

erg, President, Ruttenberg, Friedman, Kilgallon, Gutchess & Associates, Before a Joint Hearing of the Senate Subcommittee on Science, Technology and Space, and the House Subcommittee on Science, Research and Technology, February 14, 1978, pp. 8–9.

12. U.S. Department of Commerce, Bureau of the Census, *State Government Finances in 1983*, GF 83 no. 1, January 1984, p. 7.

13. U.S. Department of Commerce, Bureau of the Census, *State Government Finances in 1983*, GF 82, no. 3, October 1983, p. 1.

14. Ibid., p. 7.

15. U.S. Department of Commerce, Bureau of the Census, *Quarterly Summary of Federal, State and Local Tax Revenue*, GT 83 no. 4, April 1984, p. 1.

16. Experience of author Ruttenberg as member, Board of Equalization and Review (Hearing property tax appeals), Government of the District of Columbia, 1981–1982.

17. Richard Margolis, "Reagonomics Redux: A Municipal Report," *Working Papers*, June 1983, p. 47.

18. Democracy Project Reports, No. 7 "Less Taxing Alternatives," New York, 1984, pp. 6–7.

19. Statement of Helen Blank, Children's Defense Fund, Before the Joint Economic Committee on Women in the Workforce. Reprinted in *Daily Labor Report*, Washington: Bureau of National Affairs, no. 65, April 4, 1984.

8

THE IMPACT OF AMERICAN TOURISM POLICY ON WOMEN

LINDA K. RICHTER

Women have a relationship to American tourism policy that is decidedly distinct from that of men. There are four key areas in which gender differences appear to be important: (1) Women have much less control over the formation and direction of tourism policies at all levels than do men; (2) The tourism industry has been disproportionately receptive to the employment of women and minorities. While women are extremely active in tourism, their employment is almost exclusively at the most labor intensive, poorly paid, weakly organized part of the labor pyramid; (3) Women, as the more economically disadvantaged sex, may be the most affected by the type, level, and scale of tourism encouraged by government policies; (4) Despite their role in travel decisions, women as a group are trivialized, degraded, and exploited in advertising, in souvenirs, and in tourist activities. National monuments and historic sites have routinely ignored the cultural, artistic, scientific, and commercial achievements of women. Although the impact of tourism on women has been almost totally ignored, Richter writes that tourism is too important and too complex not to be taken seriously. Tourism needs to be carefully examined by women.

"The spending for tourism services in the U.S. directly generates about 16.7 million jobs, accounting for 14 percent of the total employed civilian labor force."[1] This translates into an estimated $562 billion in travel and tourism spending, making travel and tourism the fastest growing and the second largest industry in the United States.[2]

Still, American tourism policy is as important for what it is *not* as for what it *is*. It is not a high profile policy issue; it is not coordinated, integrated, or even highly regarded. Its impact on American society, values, families, and particularly women is largely unexamined. Yet it has immense potential for improving or degrading the lives of millions.

This chapter will focus on the impact of tourism by considering its multidimensional impact on American women. But that cannot be understood without at least some reference to the larger global issues surrounding travel and tourism. The article is, therefore, divided into three parts. The first part describes the importance of tourism and its unfortunate neglect as a subject of policy analysis. The second section summarizes American tourism policy by governmental level. The third part discusses four issue areas where gender differences appear to exist, and the final section focuses on these problem areas for women in terms of current American tourism policy.

INTERNATIONAL TOURISM: THE NEGLECTED GIANT

Travel or tourism has been defined in many ways, but the United Nations defines international tourism as travel more than 100 miles from home involving an overnight stay in another country. Thus, the millions of day trips across borders for shopping and touring are not included. The *purpose* of travel is also not a part of the definition. Domestic travel, defined as overnight stays more than 25 miles from home, also excludes the day trip.

Statistics then have a conservative bias in their measurement of the impact of travel and tourism. Few policy-makers, let alone the general public, are aware that tourism is the world's largest business involving over 12 percent of the global gross national product. In 1981, world spending on tourism surpassed that spent on the world's military. By 1984, tourism spending was two times that of global military expenditures.[3]

The impact of all this travel and the enormous sums of money involved have profound influence on nations and the lives of their citizens. It is also important to recognize that effects are neither uniform in type nor evenly distributed. Eighty-five percent of all international travel takes place in Europe and North America. A majority of developing nations are dependent on tourism from the industrialized countries, however. That relationship is also asymmetrical, with the citizens of the poor nations usually the host, rarely the guest. The relative powerlessness of the men and women serving the affluent guests may reinforce visitors' racist or sexist fantasies about those employed in the visitor industry. Relative deprivation, prostitution, begging, homelessness, venereal disease, inflation, juvenile delinquency, truancy, and ecological degradation are but a few of the possible negative side effects of tourism development. Host governments can exacerbate or reduce these effects by their policies, but they can seldom remove such dimensions from the impact of tourism, particularly in developing countries.[4]

On the other hand, tourism can be a means of educating one's citizens and visitors, conveying national pride, earning foreign exchange, serving national ethnic and regional integration, fostering employment, promoting wholesome leisure activities, and stimulating professional education, innovation, and business.[5] These effects too can be the result of government policies or of concerned nongovernmental groups.[6]

Many factors have encouraged global tourism. In the developed countries, demographics encourage tourism growth. Larger and larger percentages of the population are older. This means increasing numbers of men and even more women are reaching retirement with both the time and the health to travel. Growing affluence and lower birthrates also encourage travel. Women plan most of the family's discretionary travel, and surveys have shown their number one priority goal for using discretionary income is "travel abroad." Travel ranks second with men.[7]

The increase in leisure time is another factor. Sixty-five nations actually guarantee leisure in their constitutions while in many developed countries the work week has become shorter and vacation time has increased. West Germany, for example, has a higher percentage of vacationers than any other nation, in large part facilitated by the five to six weeks paid vacation provided most workers.[8] Travel and leisure time, as a consequence, are growth industries, stimulants to the very economies whose policies provide leisure.

The United States, on the other hand, despite its affluence and reputation for traveling citizens, has no leisure time policy, one of the longest work-weeks, and some of the shortest vacation periods in the industrialized world. Additionally, the United States is behind at least 100 other countries which provide some form of leave for new parents. In the United States sick leave or vacation time is often used to patch together some respite from outside work for the new mother.[9]

The worldwide acceleration of women into the work force over the last 15 years has stimulated travel in several ways. The increased education and income have encouraged more interest in travel—for its own sake and as a focus for competition and conspicuous consumption. Moreover, both men and women are traveling much more now in conjunction with their employment. U.S. statistics, for example, show that women account for over 31 percent of all business travelers, although they are only 10 percent of the "frequent flyers" (those making 10 or more business trips a year).[10]

Increased discretionary time and income, demographics, better education, and "upscale" leisure tastes, plus the growth of two career families, and more business and professional travel have combined to increase global travel dramatically. These trends are expected to continue through the middle of the twenty-first century.

Because of this, even nations without a base for large-scale domestic tourism are active in the development of tourism, hoping its growth will provide the foreign exchange that will finance other investment.[11] Often this does not happen, and towns, regions, and even nations are left with an enormous tourism infrastructure and a host of social problems.[12]

The policy mistakes are often a product of several factors. First, because tourism and travel seem like frivolous activities, it has been easy for social scientists to overlook the fact that their social consequences are anything but trivial. Those anthropologists, sociologists, and political scientists who are interested in charting the policy impacts of tourism promotion have until recently been accused of merely wanting a tax deductible way to cover their junkets.

Only economists and those in the business of monitoring international trade have kept pace with tourism's spectacular growth. As a result, even those governments that take travel and tourism seriously as a policy sector are often dependent on the scarcely impartial advice of the international travel industry. Not too surprisingly, that advice encourages tax holidays, large capital-intensive investment, and mass tourism of the very type the industry can organize easily. Thus, patterns of ownership; questions of scale; ways to maximize employment or use local products, particularly handicrafts; or methods for maximizing the benefits from tourism policy are seldom a part of the dialogue on tourism development.

Some of the most glaring tourism policy debacles have been in Third World countries where corrupt governments have often abused tourism development for the leadership's personal gain. An example is the Philippines when former President Marcos used the finances of the nation's retirement system to overbuild and underfinance luxury hotels at the expense of low-income housing or modest capital investment. Bankrupt hotels once owned by Marcos' cronies became the property of the government, sustained only by an enormous prostitution racket.[13] This situation has been improved since Marcos was replaced in 1986 by President Aquino, but it is very difficult to "de-sleaze" a destination or turn around elaborate infrastructure mistakes.[14]

In Thailand, the *absence* rather than the involvement of government has encouraged the blurring of tourism promotion with the selling of its women.[15] Over one million Thai women (2 percent of the female population) are currently estimated to be involved in prostitution, most in conjunction with well-organized sex tours to Thailand.[16] The only barrier to the expansion of sex tourism throughout Thailand and the Philippines is not government policy, but the epidemic proportions of an antibiotic-resistant strain of gonorrhea and the growing fear of AIDS.[17] Countries as varied as

Kenya, Sri Lanka, Jamaica, and West Germany are but a few of the destinations struggling with *massive*, organized tourism for sex.[18]

Other countries insist on direct control of the travel industry. Socialist countries represent perhaps the furthest departure from the laissez-faire approach to tourism policy of Thailand or the former Marcos government's intervention for the president's personal power and wealth. Eastern Europe and the USSR, for example, while until recently discouraging travel beyond the Warsaw Pact nations, have very broad tourism policies which not only guarantee vacation time but provide the resorts and other tourism infrastructure needed. These governments also own and control the promotion and marketing facilities for tourism thereby making certain that the image of the nation conveyed is supportive of the type of tourism targeted. The economic and political revolutions in Eastern Europe during 1989 and the plummeting number of tourist arrivals in China after its political crackdown in the same year make predictions about tourism policy in any of these regions unwise.

AMERICAN TOURISM POLICY

Public policies—by their presence, absence, or specific design—dramatically affect tourism's impact on society. In the United States, national policy is fragmented and piecemeal. Thus, while the federal government has over 100 programs in 50 agencies which deal with travel and tourism, no overall strategy exists despite efforts in that direction.[19] In 1981, the National Tourism Policy Act was passed which attempted to encourage coordination of the industry. It has been rendered largely irrelevant by the Reagan administration's disinterest. Though he signed the National Tourism Policy Act into law, and in 1984 proclaimed the first National Tourism Week, President Reagan sought each year of his presidency to kill the U.S. Travel and Tourism Administration by recommending no funding for it.[20] The Bush presidency thus far does not appear to be a departure from this course. In any case, the National Tourism Policy was never designed to do more than promote tourism and force travel industry interests to be considered in the shaping of energy, immigration, tax, and other related policies. Social impact studies or leisure policy were beyond its purview.

Diffusion of tourism across many subindustries like restaurants, accommodations, transportation, and recreation serves to mask the travel industry's collective impact on the nation.[21] Thus, though the Travel and Tourism Caucus is the largest of the congressional caucuses, its clout is minimal because many proposed policies divide caucus members.[22]

State governments are quite active as one might suspect when one considers that tourism is among the top three sources of income in 46 of 50 states and four U.S. territories, but their primary role has been in promo-

tional marketing, special tax exemptions, and industrial policies rather than
in research on the industry's impact beyond job creation.[23] The latter is, of
course, extremely important. Most tourism jobs are in the service sector
which is the most rapidly growing area of the national economy. The federal
government has been slow to recognize this, and it was only in the early
1980s that the service sector was organized as a separate part of the U.S.
Department of Commerce.[24] States, on the other hand, have seen tourism
development as central to their economic development efforts in recent years
and have increased financial support even during periods of recession.

City governments have been the most active with the hundred largest
cities, most major cities, and literally thousands of small towns actively
promoting tourism through a variety of municipal policies. These policies
range from creating and maintaining visitor information centers and advertising to establishing tax policies (especially the use of industrial revenue
bonds and hotel taxes), building convention centers, financing special fairs
and expositions, and legalizing casinos, race tracks, or—in the case of Nevada—prostitution.[25]

At *none* of these levels are impact data being gathered on the effect of
travel and tourism on quality of life in the area. Surveys of tourism directors
at state and local levels show they are extremely sanguine about that impact,
citing increased employment opportunities and city pride. They do, however,
note that among the *perceived disadvantages* of tourism that the public
senses are increases in litter, noise, inflation, and crime. But these are only
hunches. Research money, such as it is, goes almost exclusively into marketing. Measures of success are confined to (1) percentage increase in tourist
arrivals and receipts and (2) market share compared with comparable cities
and states.[26]

Tourism development is rarely on the public agenda until it becomes a
major component of the economic and political environment as in Cape
Cod or Hawaii. Critics of tourism are often overwhelmed because the available data—which is so limited and strictly economic—does not allow for a
genuine cost benefit analysis to take place.

In summary, even though the magnitude of the travel and tourism industry
is enormous and the public sector is deeply involved, neither those in the
industry nor policymakers recognize how flawed and lopsided is the empirical data on tourism.

WOMEN'S RELATIONSHIP TO AMERICAN TOURISM POLICY

As previously stated, women have a relationship to American tourism
policy that is decidedly distinct from that of men. The differences are often
difficult to measure and quantify, but that makes them no less important.
Research in tourism is still very crude and erratic; hence much of what can

be said about gender differences in tourism policy formation and impact must be inferred. Research on women is rarely if ever considered salient to data collection in the early stages of a policy analysis of a particular sector. Thus, it is disappointing but scarcely surprising that even with an industry as multifaceted, enormous, and intrusive as tourism, the experiences of women can only be indirectly approached.

Most policy research studies focused on women have generally concluded that gender differences usually are the result of women's relative political, economic, and social inequality to men. In some respects tourism policy research appears to be consistent with those studies. It is critical, however, to linking normative values validly to empirical data, that the gender differences found not automatically be assumed negative for women. Whether women are *always* or even *primarily* at a disadvantage in their relationship to tourism policy is still an unresolved issue.

There are four key areas in which gender differences appear to be important: (1) Women have much less control over the formation and direction of tourism policies at all levels than do men; (2) The tourism industry has been disproportionately receptive to the employment of women and minorities; (3) Women as the more economically disadvantaged sex may be the most affected by the type, level, and scale of tourism encouraged by government policies; (4) Despite their role in travel decisions, women as a group are trivialized, degraded and exploited in advertising, souvenirs, and tourist activities. These four gender differences in tourism policy are not presumed to be exhaustive but suggest areas in which gender differences occur and where future research may most profitably be directed.

Control over Policy

Women have very little control over tourism policies. This is consistent with other policy sectors, but is reinforced by the perception of tourism as a benign force for general economic development and business prosperity. Thus, it is seen as beyond traditional female areas of interest like health and human services by both the overwhelmingly male policymakers and economists but also by the general public. The tourism industry's organizations, lobbies, and major industry components are also male dominated. While women are extremely active in tourism, their involvement is almost exclusively at the most labor-intensive, poorly paid, weakly organized part of the occupational pyramid.

The role of women in the tourism industry and in the policy process is extremely slight at the national level. The major travel and tourism industry lobbies are male dominated, with their primary focus being on the large corporate supporters of the lobbies, which are in male hands. While annual testimony before congressional committees constantly reiterates that 98 percent of the tourism industry is composed of small businesses, actual policy proposals are primarily designed for the large firms which can afford full-time lobbyists. Like the family farm, the "Mom and Pop" motel, restaurant, or small resort exists as an endangered species largely *despite* government indifference. The small tourist establishment cannot even garner, however, the sentiment and nostalgia of the family farm, though the roots of American tourism go back before the Revolutionary War.[27] Then as now, the small inns, spas, and resorts were often primarily run by the labor of women. This is true overseas as well.[28]

Travel and tourism has always been a labor-intensive sector, disproportionately dependent on the labor of females for its actual maintenance. Only in the transportation sector has the actual *operation*, as opposed to capital investment and infrastructure development, been primarily in the hands of males.

The national government's fickle and uncoordinated interest in tourism has been concentrated in four areas: (1) international tourism's impact on the U.S. balance of trade; (2) tax concessions for business travel; (3) the safety and adequate supply of commercial transportation in the United States; and (4) the development and preservation of the national parks and historic monuments.

In each of these areas the primary beneficiaries have been male. International tourism has been structured primarily to facilitate convention and business travel, not the travel of families nor the reunions of relatives. Travel to the United States is encumbered with numerous restrictions designed to prevent illegal immigration or the attraction of permanent residents, but which encourage overwhelmingly male-dominated convention and visitor traffic. In 1983, 60 percent of overseas visitors to the United States were male adults.[29]

Tax concessions for business travel subsidize activities that remain primarily male. While the proportion of women involved in business travel continues to grow, historically and currently men are the chief and most direct beneficiaries of such policies.

Similarly, the government's involvement in the safety and regulation of commercial transport also primarily affects men. In recent years this has extended to the government's concern for protecting its traveling citizens at home or abroad from terrorist activity.

The fourth major area of national policy concerns the development and preservation of the national parks and historic monuments. Park franchises have emphasized large corporations, such as, for example, Old Faithful Inn in Yellowstone National Park, or restaurant chains on interstate highways. While large-scale, male-controlled enterprises have been favored, economics of scale, varieties of experience, and diffusion of income have not necessarily resulted. Commercial development in the parks has also assumed primacy in recent years over environmental and educational concerns.[30]

National monuments, museums, and historic sites have routinely ignored the cultural, artistic, scientific, and commercial achievements of women. So glaring have government omissions of the contributions of American women become that private philanthropic groups constructed in Washington D.C. a national museum dedicated to the achievements of women. Tax-supported funds, at all governmental levels, however, continue to support monuments and museums overwhelmingly devoted to the adulation of prominent males. As a result, tourism's important educational role is distorted, and the sexist unbalanced socialization of the traveling public continues at taxpayer expense.

The primary reason why U.S. tourism policy has not taken a more holistic approach to tourism is because of its fixation on tourism as a *revenue-producing activity* rather than as an important facet in improving the quality of life by reducing stress, enhancing education, instilling variety, and contributing to shared family experiences. While a concern for revenue is reasonable since tourism generates over billions in federal, state, and local taxes, such a perspective ignores the nonmonetary features of tourism policy and the not so easily quantified monetary *costs* of tourism development. Unlike much of the industrialized world, which also appreciates tourism's economic impact, the United States and its policy has not moved beyond the profit motive to a consideration of the role of leisure in the promotion of health, reduction of crime, reward of labor, or the importance of travel as an information medium.[31]

When President Ronald Reagan contended that trees are a major source of air pollution and that "when you've seen one redwood, you've seen them all," one could hardly expect from him a sensitive concern for the effects of acid rain on lakes and fishing, for the preservation of wildlife habitat, or for the need for family and student travel assured by the policies of many developed countries. The low priority tourism had at the federal level extended to President Reagan's appointments. James Watt's tenure as Secretary of the Interior has been chronicled elsewhere, but it suffices to say that his was considered the most aggressively commercial and most antienvironmental perspective to be in that post since the national park system began. President Reagan's appointment of Donna Tuttle to head the U.S. Travel and Tourism Administration also sent a signal to women's groups as well as travel and tourism groups as to the president's commitment to that sector. Ms. Tuttle's qualifications for the $70,000 tourism post rested less on her experience as a high school history teacher and a clothing retailer than on her being the daughter of one of the president's favorite California friends.[32] She was given the unenviable task of supporting the president's call for the dismantling of the USTTA, an agency with a budget smaller in size than those many major cities have for promoting tourism.[33] That she performed generally well and proved an effective spokesperson for U.S. policy was fortunate. President Bush's attitudes toward tourism policy are not yet apparent, but he has announced that he intends to be an "environmentalist president." It is a promise that will be closely monitored.

At the state and local level, tourism policy making is overwhelmingly under male direction. Only six states in 1984 had female tourism directors while state legislatures had an average of 14 percent female representation. Thus far, there have been no studies that have distinguished between men and women political leaders in their support for or level of interest in the travel and tourism industry. However, in my 1984 study of state sponsored tourism, no differences were found between the attitudes of the female and male state tourism directors.

Tourism policy continues to be seen almost exclusively as an economic development measure generating employment and taxes. Policy consists not only in facilitating private sector tourism development through tax holidays and public infrastructure commitments like airports and convention centers, but also in promotion of the state or community.

State tourism policy impacts on women in several ways. In terms of specific expenditures, the state determines both the priority tourism will assume relative to other sectors and what level of tax support will be demanded of the industry. Often in areas that have become dependent on tourism, the industry is able to assure a preferred tax status, despite the cost of the industry to the state. In the expensive state of Hawaii, for example, where low-cost housing is almost nonexistent and where pay in most of the tourism industry is at the minimum wage, there was no hotel tax until the late 1980s. Proposals to have such a tax were strongly resisted even though the industry was pushing for more infrastructure commitments from both the state and Honolulu governments.[34]

Employment

The tourism industry has been found unusually receptive to the recruitment of women and minorities. That may reflect the relative powerlessness of these groups, however. Since women and minorities have the highest unemployment and underemployment rates in the nation, their disproportionate presence in seasonal, part time, and low paid positions may be more an indication of their desperation than a lack of racist or sexist bias in the travel and tourism industry.

Tourism has been an important source of female employment since the beginning of the nation. Even by 1890, tourism was one of the ten major sources of paid female employment in the nation.[35] The majority of the women were employed, then as now, as chambermaids, waitresses, and cooks, leading many social critics to contend that tourism employment is vastly overrated as a source of meaningful, well-paid work. This problem is particularly acute in small, developing countries where control of the industry and top management jobs is in expatriate hands and where some nationalists contend large-scale tourism creates a citizenry of "maids and bellhops."[36]

Still, as one industry analyst noted, not only are travel-related jobs the fastest growing component of the skyrocketing service sector, but many employees appreciate the flexibility and working conditions in the travel industry. Professor Victor Fuchs, service-sector specialist and economist at Stanford University, acknowledges that many tourism jobs pay less than production of goods, but contends that service jobs "are more rewarding and interesting than assembly line jobs" and may be in less danger of losing out to foreign competition than other more lucrative jobs.[37]

While that may appear to many women in that sector as an apologia for their low wages, no one denies that the tourism sector is opening up more rewarding careers as well. Accounting, computing, real estate, banking, insurance, advertising, law, journalism, and public relations jobs are important components of tourism. Also, women are 40 percent of all restaurant managers, another career area closely involved with tourism.[38] Moreover, the surveys of state- and city-sponsored tourism development emphasized that computer specialists and public administration specialists are also career specialties being sought for public sector tourism development. Indeed, public sector tourism has been a real growth area in a generally retrenching public sector during the last 10 years.[39]

Travel agency growth is also indicative. A nearly 400 percent increase occurred in the number of such agencies between 1970 and 1984, despite two serious recessions. Moreover 70 percent of travel agency employees are women, and an astounding 48 percent of all these agencies in the United States are owned by women. Part of the explanation for such heavy involvement may reflect the female role in planning travel and tourism, the largely clerical nature of much of the work, and the fact that nearly a quarter of such jobs are part-time, accommodating most women's extra homemaking responsibilities. Full-time pay averaged between $275–375 a week, compared to a national average of $325 a week in wages. Ownership patterns may be a result of the relatively low start-up costs, the low risk of opening an agency, and the short training investment required.[40]

Unfortunately, not all female-dominated employment opportunities in tourism offer such pristine and low risk careers. As we shall see in the consideration of quality of life affected by tourism policy and in the government's own tourism marketing, the exploitation of women is a serious and largely unresolved problem.

Women's Economic Status

Women, as the most economically disadvantaged class, may be the most affected positively or negatively by the type of tourism government encourages, the scale of tourism sought, and the ways in which government spending *for* tourism is allocated and tourism revenues *from* tourism are spent. Research has shown that gradual development, diversification of tourism attractions, local control and local participation in tourism development, attention to scale, and the "carrying capacity" of a destination are critically important for solid tourism growth without controversy and backlash. That has not occurred in Atlantic City where low cost housing has disappeared, the crime rate has soared, the unemployment rate has remained constant, and the casinos have accelerated rather than halted the decline in other sectors of the city.[41]

Problems are particularly numerous in terms of special events tourism like world fairs and Olympics where there is a special temptation to waive rules and regulations for the temporary tourist spectacular. Unfortunately, as New Orleans and Knoxville discovered, promoters of such fairs have a way of vanishing after the big events, leaving cities to cope with the inflation, debt, and housing problems that they have created. While the problems faced are not unique to women, the pursuit of the tourist dollar often impacts on the more economically vulnerable, those more likely to be unemployed or underemployed. As a consequence, bad policies and budget shortages take their heaviest toll on women.[42]

Government Policy and the Status of Women

Despite their role in decision making, women are increasingly trivialized, patronized, and exploited in travel promotions financed by both the public and the private sector. American travel advertising is an enormous business ($1.01 billion in 1987) and its media impact can have a dramatic effect on both business and recreational tourism.[43] It can have an impact not only on who is attracted, but also on the destination's own perception of itself and its relative desirability.

State and local governments are also strongly involved in setting the tone and image of the state through both their laws and their advertising promotions. Decisions to legalize casinos as Nevada and New Jersey have, horse racing as Nebraska and Florida have, and prostitution as Nevada does—all effect the tourism milieu, the clientele, the behavior and status of women, and the resulting quality of life for full-time residents.

Consider the prostitution issue, for example. While women have no monopoly on careers as prostitutes, female prostitutes are far more numerous, and more likely to be the ones arrested, the ones controlled by pimps, or the ones subject to licensing and health checks in states and municipalities where prostitution is legal.[44] Without debating whether prostitution should or should not be legal, it is important to recognize that the type of tourism marketed and promoted by the state has a decided impact on the extent of prostitution, the expectations of tourists, and the ambience found.

For example, emphasis on family vacations, honeymoons, or special event sport tourism is likely to encourage an entirely different clientele and perhaps a visitor lifestyle less intrusive on communities than an emphasis on marketing conventions with casinos or other types of gambling would encourage. The experiences of Virginia and Hawaii are instructive. Both states have been extremely active in promoting tourism, but in recent years there has been a real backlash against tourism among some groups in Hawaii. The reasons are many: huge numbers of tourists, overcrowding, some ecological degradation, low wages in the industry, and a feeling that Hawaii has come to support tourism rather than vice versa.[45] Some argue that when infrastructure, water, sewers, roads, fire and police protection are factored in, Hawaii actually *subsidizes* tourism.[46]

However, more germane to this chapter is a growing concern that the haole (white) males and an increasing number of Japanese men who market Hawaiian tourism are really selling ethnicity and sex. Specifically, Polynesian women are featured in each of a series of sexually ambiguous advertising campaigns launched by the Hawaii Visitors Bureau. Since these promotions are financed substantially by the state in conjunction with the private sector, they represent state policy even if indirectly.

In each advertisement or poster, a beautiful, scantily clad young Polynesian woman is shown alone in a remote setting, for example, near an isolated waterfall. She is shown as sitting on her knees, a single lei at her side. The caption: "The Beauty Remains to be Seen." Does the ad mean that Hawaii is more than a pretty girl and a waterfall? If so, perhaps the marketing could be more direct. Does it mean *this* beauty remains to be seen? Certainly nothing in the dress or setting suggests reticence. Clearly, an expectation of romance with an exotic stranger in an idyllic setting is implied.

No men, children, or families are seen. There is no emphasis on the cosmopolitan nor on the flora and fauna, nothing except a lone woman, who bears not even an ethnically accurate resemblance to native Hawaiian women. She is a generic Polynesian, unattached and implicitly available.

Contrast the Hawaii state promotion of "The Beauty Remains to be Seen" with the "Virginia is for Lovers" campaign. Like Hawaii, Virginia hopes to lure visitors to spend time and money in the state. Unlike Hawaii, the emphasis is on all kinds of people having all kinds of fun in the state. The ad campaign shows Virginia's beauty and diversity in a wholesome rather than suggestive way.

While "Virginia is for Lovers" grabs one's attention, the "Lovers" are children playing on the beach, elderly couples holding hands, teenagers dancing, young couples horseback riding or exploring shops. The overall message is Virginia is for all types of people who love life. Virginia is a romantic place to visit but you bring your own love interest. You don't rent a mate at your destination!

"So what?" one might ask. Pretty girls have been used to sell everything.

Perhaps that's part of the reluctance to take women seriously, but in the tourist context it is especially troublesome. First, much tourism, even after-hours business tourism, is escapist. But in this case the escapism—mass tourism—is taking place in someone else's home town. There is an anonymity for the tourist that other types of escapist behavior don't involve. But for the residents there's no easy retreat. In 1988 there were over six times as many tourists visiting Hawaii as there are permanent residents.

Increasingly in Honolulu, there are unpleasant incidents of local women being accosted and propositioned by male tourists.[47] Non-Caucasians are assumed fair game in a setting where advertising assures the fulfillment of male fantasies. Already, teenage girls are warned not to shop or swim in certain tourist areas for fear they will be approached by strangers intent on renting some pleasure. Rape is also a threat to female tourists who discover that their own fleeting presence in the community emboldens rapists. To the state's credit it now flies tourist victims back to Hawaii and pays their expenses during trials.

There has also been an increase in the number of clubs with live sex shows and in the number of prostitutes soliciting in tourist areas. Efforts by local authorities to control the seamier by-products of tourism have met with resistance from some of the sleazier entrepreneurs.

Tourism-linked prostitution is particularly dangerous for both prostitute and client. The anonymity that tempts the tourist to sexual adventure may also be a threat to his security. He can disappear for days before anyone suspects foul play. Similarly, the prostitute is often the victim of rapists and drug dealers. Sometimes a runaway, she is rarely able to protect herself from those who might exploit her.

As prostitution increases, a general sleaziness seems to develop. This is reflected in some of the souvenirs of Hawaii. Nutcrackers in the shape of girl's legs and "scratch and sniff" cards are new items. In the case of the latter, postcards of nude women give off tropical flower scents if scratched in strategic places! Adult book stores, peep shows, and the like are also flourishing. One doesn't need to be a prude to point out that while individual entrepreneurs may prosper from the "selling of Hawaii," the state as a whole may be losing control over the very industry in which it has so lavishly invested.

Catering to the single male and increasingly to the Japanese sex tour where sex is included in the package price is likely to dilute the very market which has been the backbone of Hawaii tourism: retirees, young couples, college students, and small conventions (less than 1000). Thus, even if taste, the dignity of local women, and the quality of residents' life in Hawaii were not at issue, the current tax-financed advertising campaign is bad business because the exploitation of women attracts a market antithetical to Hawaiian lifestyles and one likely to heighten the controversy surrounding Hawaii's number one industry. Similarly, the campaign does nothing to attract the more wholesome tourists who are the bulk of Hawaii's tourist clientele. In fact, they may become repulsed by the growing tawdriness in the islands. Then, as a locale becomes more dependent on sex tourism, it faces the difficult dilemma of either expensively changing its image and suffering short term economic loss or succumbing to the tastes of an intrusive and often fickle clientele. Tourists coming for sex not only have shorter lengths of stay than other tourists but their presence is also more likely to be associated with crime and drugs.

Thailand and the Philippines, known as "the brothels of Asia," have discovered that de-sleazing a destination dependent on sex tourists is difficult. While an epidemic of venereal disease has persuaded many such tours to bypass these countries, other unspoiled "exotic" locales like Hawaii are now in additional jeopardy.

A particularly disturbing example of government complicity in the selling of sex with tourism is the U.S. government's promotion of its Caribbean territory, the Virgin Islands. With federal tax dollars, the Virgin Islands Tourism Office is distributing truly tacky and sexist buttons. They say "TRY A VIRGIN" in huge letters and in tiny letters is added "island." These have been also made by local entrepreneurs into T-shirts, including nightshirts labeled "SLEEPING ON A VIRGIN . . . island."[48]

These items manage to be not only sexist but racist and neocolonial. Since the United States owns the Virgin Islands and administers the territory, the local people have little control over the tourism industry. Moreover, the major tourism market is white North Americans to the predominately non-white islands. I'm certain the advertising is someone's not too bright attempt to be clever. But really how smart is it to promote inuendos linking sex and tourism in an age of AIDS in conservative nonwhite societies already under siege from leisure, sun-loving white Americans? Is it really then so surprising that in September, 1989, following Hurricane Hugo, many islanders went on the rampage, terrorizing tourists and shouting "Go Home Yankees." Maybe being insensitive to local values isn't good business!

Conclusion

Government policy must monitor its promotional advertising, regulate standards for its tourist labor force, and assure health, safety and overall quality of life not be held hostage to the rhetoric of "free enterprise."

Women have been found to make most of the *leisure* travel decisions within the family. Thus, they are an especially important focus for advertising and consumer education. As the "tastemakers" in tourism, it is important that their consciousness be raised as to the political and social impact of their spending decisions on quality of life for themselves and the communities in which they travel.[49]

Tourism needs to be carefully examined by women. Too few policymakers, male or female, recognize its impact goes far beyond the economic tallies of visitor spending, arrivals, and departures. Characteristically, women have been most politically active in those issue areas closest to home. However, I would argue that the economic dazzle of tourism promoters has been more salient to men. Thus, an issue of paramount importance to quality of life, community solidarity, and pride has been relatively ignored by many women activists.

Even at the national level, few congresswomen are members of the Travel and Tourism Caucus. Given that body's rather uncritical "boosterism" that may not be bad, if it means female representatives are more questioning of its motivations and directions as Congresswoman Pat Schroeder is.[50] However, if congresswomen have remained aloof out of ignorance or indifference, then their apathy is misplaced.

Travel and tourism can be a positive policy area for the creation of employment, for encouragement of the arts, for the environment, and for political integration. It can be a policy sector conducive to better health, more beautiful communities, more meaningful leisure, and more informed professional and business growth.

On the other hand, unplanned or myopic uncritical tourism development can be disastrous. Currently, academic research, economic studies, and state and public sector development are dangerously negligent in monitoring the impact of tourism policies on American quality of life.

Its impact on women has been almost totally ignored. This chapter has only suggested some of the key areas in which research is indicated. But such research will be pursued only when policymakers recognize that tourism is too important and too complex not to take seriously.

NOTES

1. Somerset Waters, *The Big Picture—The Travel Industry Yearbook* (New York: Child and Waters, 1989), p. 9.

2. Ibid., p. 11.

3. Ibid., p. 9.

4. Linda K. Richter, "The Political Uses of Tourism: A Philippine Case Study," *Journal of Developing Areas* 14 (January 1980): 137–157.

5. Linda K. Richter, "Tourism and Political Science: A Case of Not So Benign Neglect," *Annals of Tourism Research* 10, no. 4 (October-December 1983): 313–335.

6. Linda K. Richter, "The Political Dimensions of Tourism," in *Travel, Tourism and Hospitality Research*, ed. J. R. Brent Ritchie and Charles R. Goeldner, pp. 215–229. (New York: John Wiley and Sons, 1987).

7. Valene L. Smith, "Women: The Taste-Makers in Tourism," *Annals of Tourism Research* 6, no. 1 (1979): 49–60.

8. Cor Westland, "The Development of National Free Time Policies," in *Recreation and Leisure: Issues in an Era of Change*, ed. T. L. Goodale, pp. 357–358. (State College, Penn.: Venture Publications, 1982).

    9. "Expectant Moms, Office Dilemma," *U.S. News and World Report*, March 10, 1986: 52.
    10. Waters, *The Big Picture*, p. 21.
    11. Linda K. Richter, *Land Reform and Tourism Development: Policy-Making in the Philippines*, (Cambridge, Mass.: Schenkman Publishing Co., 1982).
    12. Linda K. Richter, "The Fragmented Politics of U.S. Tourism," *Tourism Management* (September 1985): 163–173.
    13. Linda K. Richter, "Tourism by Decree," *Southeast Asia Chronicle* 78 (1981): 37–42.
    14. Linda K. Richter, *The Politics of Tourism in Asia* (Honolulu: University of Hawaii Press, 1989), pp. 77–82.
    15. "Thailand, Sex as a Travel Motivator," *Asia Travel Trade* (June 1983): 49.
    16. Truong Thanh-Dam, "The Dynamics of Sex Tourism: The Case of Southeast Asia," *Development and Change* 14 (1983): 533–553.
    17. Tourism Authority of Thailand, *Annual Report* (1983).
    18. Benjamin Whitaker, *Slavery* (New York: United Nations, 1984), p. 13.
    19. Richter, "Fragmented Politics," *Tourism Management*: 166.
    20. Albert Borcover, "Funding Cuts Imperil U.S. Tourism Industry at Inopportune Time," *The Atlanta Constitution* (May 12, 1985): 3F.
    21. Charles Faust, Staff of the Senate Committee on Commerce, personal interview, (Washington, D.C.: March 1984).
    22. Tom Lloyd, Travel and Tourism Government Affairs Council, personal interview, (Washington, D.C.: March 1984).
    23. Richter, "Fragmented Politics," *Tourism Management*.
    24. David Edgell, Office of Policy Analysis, U.S. Travel and Tourism Administration," personal interview (Washington, D.C.: March 1984).
    25. Linda K. Richter, "State-Sponsored Tourism: A Growth Field for Public Administration," *Public Administration Review* (November-December 1985): 832–839.
    26. Ibid.
    27. Horace Sutton, *Travelers: The American Tourism from Stage Coach to Space Shuttle* (New York: William Morrow and Co., 1980).
    28. Peter Stringer, "Hosts and Guests: The Bed and Breakfast Phenomenon," *Annals of Tourism Research* 8, no. 3: 357–376.
    29. Somerset Waters, *The Big Picture—The Travel Industry Yearbook* (New York: Child and Waters, 1985).
    30. "Patches Showing up in National Parks," *U.S. News and World Report* (June 17, 1985): 69–70.
    31. Cord D. Hansen-Sturm, Speech before the Travel and Tourism Research Association, Philadelphia (June 1984).
    32. Confidential interview, March 1984.
    33. Borcover, "Funding Cuts," *Atlanta Constitution*: 3F.
    34. Personal notes as delegate to Hawaii Governor's Conference on Tourism, Honolulu, Hawaii (December 11, 1984).
    35. Virginia Sapiro, *Women in American Society* (Palo Alto, Calif.: Mayfield Publishing Company, 1986).
    36. Richter, *Land Reform and Tourism Development*.
    37. Waters, *The Big Picture* (1985), pp. 10, 25.

38. Sapiro, *Women in American Society*, p. 25.
39. Richter, "State-Sponsored Tourism."
40. Waters, *The Big Picture* (1985), pp. 10, 107.
41. George Sternlieb and James W. Hughes, *The Atlantic City Gamble* (Cambridge, Mass.: Harvard University Press, 1983).
42. Sapiro, *Women in American Society*, pp. 24–25.
43. Waters, *The Big Picture* (1989), p. 23.
44. Sapiro, *Women in American Society*, p. 27.
45. Viveca Novak, "Hawaii's Dirty Secret," *Common Cause* (November–December 1989): 11–27.
46. Noel Kent, *Hawaii: Islands Under the Influence* (New York: Monthly Review, 1983).
47. Juanita Liu, Associate Professor in the Travel Industry Management School, University of Hawaii, personal interview, (Honolulu: September 1984).
48. Linda K. Richter, "Action Alert," *Contours* 4, no. 4 (December 1989): 4.
49. Smith, "Taste-Makers."
50. Patricia Schroeder, U.S. Representative from Colorado, personal conversation, March 1983.

Bibliography

Borcover, Alfred. "Funding Cuts Imperil U.S. Tourism Industry at Inopportune Time." *The Atlanta Constitution* (May 12, 1985): 3F.

Edgell, David. Office of Policy Analysis. U.S. Travel and Tourism Administration, personal interview, Washington, D.C., March, 1984.

"Expectant Moms, Office Dilemma." *U.S. News and World Report*, March 10, 1986: 52.

Faust, Charles. Staff of the Senate Committee on Commerce, personal interview, Washington, D.C., March 1984.

Hansen-Sturm, Cord D. Speech before the Travel and Tourism Research Association. Philadelphia, June 1984.

Kent, Noel. *Hawaii: Islands under the Influence*. New York: Monthly Review, 1983.

Liu, Juanita. Associate Professor in the Travel Industry Management School, University of Hawaii, personal interview, Honolulu, September 1984.

Lloyd, Tom. Travel and Tourism Government Affairs Council, personal interview, Washington D.C., March 1984.

Novak, Viveca. "Hawaii's Dirty Secret". *Common Cause* (November–December 1989): 11–27.

"Patches Showing Up in National Parks." *U.S. News and World Report* (June 17, 1985): 69–70.

Richter, Linda K. "Action Alert." *Contours* 4, no. 4 (December 1989): 4.

———. "The Fragmented Politics of U.S. Tourism." *Tourism Management* (September 1985): 163–173.

———. *Land Reform and Tourism Development: Policy-Making in the Philippines*. Cambridge, Mass.: Schenkman Publishing Co., 1982.

———. "The Political Uses of Tourism: A Philippine Case Study." *Journal of Developing Areas* 14 (January 1980): 137–157.

———. *The Politics of Tourism in Asia*. Honolulu: University of Hawaii Press, 1989.

———. "State-Sponsored Tourism: A Growth Field for Public Administration." *Public Administration Review* (November-December 1985): 832–839.

———. "Tourism and Political Science: A Case of Not So Benign Neglect." *Annals of Tourism Research* 10, no. 4 (October-December 1983): 313–335.

———. "Tourism by Decree." *Southeast Asia Chronicle* 78 (1981): 37–42.

Sapiro, Virginia. *Women in American Society*. Palo Alto, Calif.: Mayfield Publishing Company, 1986.

Schroeder, Patricia. U.S. Representative from Colorado, personal conversation, March 1983.

Smith, Valene L. "Women: The Taste-Makers in Tourism." *Annals of Tourism Research* 6, no. 1 (1979): 49–60.

Sternlieb, George. *The Atlantic City Gamble*. (Cambridge, Mass.: Harvard University Press, 1983).

Stringer, Peter. "Hosts and Guests: The Bed and Breakfast Phenomenon." *Annals of Tourism Research* 8, no. 3: 357–376.

Sutton, Horace. *Travelers: The American Tourist from Stage Coach to Space Shuttle*. New York: William Morrow and Co., 1980.

"Thailand, Sex as a Travel Motivator." *Asia Travel Trade* (June 1983): 49.

Thanh-Dam, Truong. "The Dynamics of Sex Tourism: The Case of Southeast Asia." *Development and Change* 14 (1983): 533–553.

Tourism Authority of Thailand, *Annual Report* (1983).

Waters, Somerset. *The Big Picture—The Travel Industry Yearbook*. New York: Child and Waters, 1989.

———. *The Big Picture—The Travel Industry Yearbook*. New York: Child Waters, 1985, p. 17.

Westland, Cor. "The Development of National Free Time Policies." In *Recreation and Leisure: Issues in an Era of Change*, ed. T. L. Goodale, pp. 357–358. State College, Penn.: Venture Publications, 1982.

Whitaker, Benjamin. *Slavery*. New York: United Nations, 1984.

9

INVISIBLE SEGMENT OF A VETERANS POPULATION: WOMEN VETERANS, PAST OMISSIONS, AND CURRENT CORRECTIONS

JUNE A. WILLENZ

This chapter deals with women veterans at a time when the armed forces are increasing their utilization of women. Women make up the fastest growing segment of the veterans population. As of March 31, 1986, there were 1,177,900 women veterans, making up 4.2 percent of the veterans population. As Willenz explains, until recently women veterans have certainly been an invisible population. Women were not counted in statistics and were ignored in the studies that were conducted on the veterans population. All materials and outreach programs were aimed toward the male population. In addition, women deprecated their own contributions; they expected little, and they made few demands. Furthermore, in the past women veterans were treated differently than men, and those differences lead to greater inequality. VA hospitals were very good for male veterans but virtually irrelevant for female veterans. The VA system was designed by men for men. Male-biased attitudes prevailed throughout the VA health care system. However, Willenz shows clearly the reasons why the solution to that problem is not now to attempt to treat men and women the same. Biological differences between men and women call for different kinds of physical exams, expertise, equipment, and facilities in veterans hospitals. To make up for historical omissions, women veterans need differential treatment in order to achieve greater equality.

A striking instance of how gender differences impact on public policy has been the long-benign neglect of the women's segment of the veterans population. While there were some instances of legal discrimination on the basis of gender in several of the veterans benefits programs, on the whole the legal situation was nondiscriminatory. Except for these instances, the veterans benefits system should have worked equally for both women and men. Nevertheless, it became apparent in the late 1970s that this was far from the case, that these veterans benefits programs were largely irrelevant for the women veterans who were eligible for them. Looking at how this happened, reviewing the circumstances and policy decisions or nondecisions that contributed to this phenomenon, and seeking to understand the etiology is the main focus of this chapter.

It is particularly timely to analyze this situation because more and more women are going into the military services and therefore more and more women will become veterans. Women today constitute ten percent of the personnel in the military services, and there is a possibility, if the women have their way, that the percentage will grow. Interestingly enough, this increase in the proportion of women in the military forces in this country is paralleled by their rising participation in the military forces of many other nations around the world. Such an infusion of women into the military sphere has important implications and necessitates some key policy decisions not only within policy processes of the armed forces, but also those of veterans policy.

WOMEN'S SERVICE IN MILITARY

The status of "woman veteran" is a relatively modern one although women have been involved in the nation's defense since its infant days as a fledgling nation. While history textbooks mention the isolated case of a Deborah Sampson or romanticize the exploits of a Molly Pitcher, the full story of women's contributions with and in the armed forces has not been included in textbooks and hence is unknown to the general public.[1] With the resurgence of the women's movement, the development of a "feminist" history, and new departments of women's studies, an interest in women's roles has expanded. We can now observe that the role of the "woman veteran" as well as the role of the "military woman" has been a difficult one for policymakers to cope with and for society in general to accept. The women themselves sometimes have not been altogether comfortable in these roles, while women who have never assumed them are often hostile.

Women were brought into military service for the first time in large numbers in all services during World War II because they were badly needed. While the women's component was supposed to have been phased out totally after the war, policymakers took another direction and women became part of the peacetime military and continued through the Korean and Vietnam Wars to reach a current participation level of 10 percent. Women went into the military service for different reasons at different times, but throughout, they suffered calumny and unfounded negative slurs from an unsympathetic press and public. In some instances, even their military status was ambiguous. This combination of circumstances, including a self-deprecation and weak identity of the women as veterans, mitigated against development of a group that would actively pursue their rights and take their place as a power bloc either in veterans affairs or in our society.

With a country unaware and a military unmotivated to acknowledge the substantial contributions that women were making as members of the armed forces, it was easy to overlook the particular needs of the women when they left the service. Numerically, they were submerged in an overwhelmingly large male population which traditionally had been an all-male enclave. Policymakers and administrators either were unaware or indifferent to the small population of women veterans within the population, and since they themselves did not seem interested in actively pursuing their veterans benefits rights, administrators did not consider their specific needs. The result is a picture of neglect and omission based on gender that existed for almost four decades for a distinctive category of women. Particularly, the comprehensive and pioneering GI Bill of Rights package legislated during World War II for millions of returning soldiers was almost irrelevant for the almost half million women who also served.

The picture of omission and neglect was not based on legal or regulatory exclusions. First, "equal rights" was not a consideration until recently; second, there seemed to be an implicit assumption that equal status under the law would take care of "equality" objectives. The story of women veterans falling through the cracks of the established framework of veterans benefits, despite this so-called legal equality, demonstrates that in some instances this standing does not necessarily mean that all segments of the targeted population benefit. In this case, a small minority without a tradition or history within the larger group was easily overlooked. Differences based on gender may warrant some differentiated treatment in order to fulfill an equal rights commitment. Women veterans represent a group that would have benefitted from such an approach.

LACK OF DATA

It was only in the 1980s that changes altered the status quo. Before the 1980 Census, women were not queried as to their veterans status probably because conventional wisdom had it that veterans were men. That Census asked women if they were veterans and that produced a count of almost 1,200,000—more than a quarter of a million more than the Department of Defense or VA believed was the count. Not keeping statistics has been one of the major blocs to recognizing either the size of this population or its particular needs. A fact-finding review done in the late 1970s revealed that the VA was not keeping statistics on current benefit use by women and had not kept historical records.[2] Because the VA kept only 2 percent of its historical records and women were less than 2 percent of the veterans population in the World War II and Korean War periods, their records were destroyed. As a result, there is no way of getting a total picture of the women's usage of benefits in those years. It was likewise found that other government agencies which had programs relevant to women veterans did not keep statistics by gender.

How have women veterans fit into this veterans benefits system? Generally, the law setting up the veterans benefits programs did not make any distinction between men and women veterans, except in a few instances. For one, the married women veterans of both World War II and Korea did not get the same educational benefits for their spouses as did married male veterans. This inequity was finally corrected in 1972 with passage of PL 93-540.[3] There were also some inequities in death compensation benefits and in administering of home loans, which have also been corrected.[4]

One reason that a number of women veterans did not profit from the veterans benefits system was that during World War II two of the women's services were not actually part of the army, even though they were attached to it.[5] From the moment it was created in 1942, the WAAC (Women's Army Auxiliary Corps) had an ambiguous legal position; as an auxiliary, it was not considered a military body but a civilian unit. Consequently, those who served in it did not have the protections of military personnel. After the war, those who served in the WAAC—about 16,000—and had not gone into the WAC (Women's Army Corps) found that they were not eligible for veterans benefits.

Likewise, the famed WASP (Women's Air Force Service Pilots), that gallant group of approximately 1,000-plus women—expert pilots who ferried planes from factories to air bases, test-flew new aircraft, and flew planes with targets for Air Force pilots' practice—was also in an ambiguous position. When the WASP was initiated in 1943 and women were recruited and trained at Avenger Field Air Force Base in Sweetwater, Texas, it was assumed that they would be militarized. Under the conditions they were recruited, the women lived as military personnel under military discipline without the protections or advantages that the male Army Air Corps flyers had. Though the WASPs took incredible risks and suffered all the deprivations of military life, they did not have military status and attendant protections. They also had casualties. By the time the War Department went to the Congress to request military status, a complex political situation turned Congress against this proposal. Instead of commissioning them into full-fledged military status as was expected, Congress retired the WASP.[6]

There seems to have been an overall reluctance by policymakers to grant full military status to women who served with and in the military. The story of the WAAC and the WASP is only part of the iceberg. Back in World War I, the Secretary of the Navy was able to get women into the Navy as Yeomen (R) (affectionately termed Yeomenettes) through a technicality of language. General Pershing in France was not so fortunate, despite his urgent request for women to serve as telephone operators in France; he had to be content with several hundred French-speaking women who served as civilians with his forces under great hardship and under highly dangerous conditions. These groups were finally granted veterans status decades later with passage of PL 95-202 in 1977.[7]

The nurses who were part of our military history from the beginning of the republic were not granted full military status until World War II, even though the official Army Nurse Corps was formed in 1901 and the Navy Nurse Corps in 1908. During the intervening years they held "relative rank" which shortchanged them on pay and benefits, as well as status.

Indeed, the history of women's participation in the military service in this country is marked by contradictions and hassles, which confused women's perception of their roles and status and also blurred society's view of their service.[8]

VA MEDICAL CARE

One benefit that is particularly beneficial for veterans, particularly as they get older, is the VA's medical care system which provides 172 hospitals and other medical complexes such as domiciliaries and nursing homes. Development of the comprehensive medical-hospital system was predicated on the assumption that it was set up to take care of men with war-related injuries and disabilities. Yet over the years, the VA hospital system, which became an important clinical-research component of American medicine, has always ministered to the non-service-connected illnesses of America's veterans. Such treatment is accorded on a space available basis under defined priorities. Those who are hurt or disabled while in service, whether it is a war-related injury or not, are considered "service-connected" and have the first claim to hospital care. The veterans who are injured or become ill after their military service and the non-service-connected also, at least until recently, could seek medical and hospital care from the VA system, if there were resources available.

The VA, until recent policy changes to accommodate the Gramm-Rudman constraints, maintained that in order to provide the best medical care to those who were injured or disabled during their periods of service, the hospital system needed to have the patient mix of the non-service-connected and the service-connected. Because of that mix, the VA, particularly in the early decades, was able to attract the highest caliber doctors and research scientists into its ranks. Over the years, the VA hospital system became the primary health-care supplier for many of the country's veterans, whether they were war-injured or not. In 1980, almost 90 percent of VA inpatients received medical care for non-service-related illnesses; what evidence there is suggests that these were almost all males.

In 1982, the director of the VA's Department of Medical Services testified on the attack on the VA treating non-service-connected illnesses:

Should that ever happen, it would so disturb outpatient mix that our ability to continue to provide a teaching base for health manpower would be gone, and with it our ability to attract quality health professionals into the system would be gone. It would be the beginning of a reversion for an old soldiers and sailors home system so well remembered from the 1930s.[9]

How did women use the highly respected VA medical hospital health care services for which they were eligible? Despite the lack of historical data, there is considerable evidence that they were only using the system sporadically. So negligent was their participation that an important study (1977) by the National Academy of Sciences did not consider women veterans at all,[10] and a subsequent hearing by the Senate Veterans Affairs Committee on this Report (except for one organization's testimony) omitted reference to women veterans entirely. A Report on the Aging Veterans also neglected women veterans as a group.[11]

The VA, in a monograph in 1982, reported on the veterans usage of VA hospitalization benefits that the number of women seeking to use it was growing. That report also warned:

The lack of data on women veterans precludes any attempt to clarify specific future requirements in terms of services and suggests the need for an examination of patterns of use in the population which is to be served. Such information cannot be obtained from those sources currently available within the VA.[12]

PUBLIC EXPOSURE OF THE PROBLEMS

A major step was taken in correcting the omissions when, at the request of Senator Inouye, the General Accounting Office in 1982 did an investigation of women veterans' current utilization of the VA health care system.[13] The GAO report confirmed what women veterans already knew, that the hospitals were not accommodating or servicing them adequately. Bath and toilet facilities were either inappropriate or were not easily used; privacy was a major problem. There was a clear-cut lack of gynecological facilities and care for women—only one of the seven medical centers visited by the GAO investigators provided women with pelvic and breast exams, and pap smears were not taken routinely. A number of instances were cited that women were being turned away, particularly those who needed care for gynecological problems, sometimes with disastrous consequences.

Another gap was the lack of outpatient services for women veterans. "Because of restrictions on the availability of fee-basis care, non-service connected women are not eligible for outpatient gynecological treatment at these facilities even if the treatment is needed to obviate the need for hospitalization," the GAO report stated.[14] Also, in some of the psychiatric facilities, women were not admitted to specialized programs because there was not staff to supervise a sexually mixed group. Sometimes there was neither adequate privacy nor security facilities to accommodate women, so they were denied much-needed care. In its report the GAO concluded:

VA facilities have generally been sized and staffed to accommodate both service-connected and non-service-connected veterans. Thus male veterans can generally obtain needed care from a VA facility regardless of service connection. The same is not true for female veterans because of problems in insuring privacy in older facilities and variations in the availability of gynecological care.[15]

Another problem cited in the GAO report was the situation of the women who served during the Vietnam War, particularly those "in country." Vietnam veterans, after years of neglect, were recognized as suffering from the Post Traumatic Stress Disorder. Congress, in 1979, finally enacted legislation setting up the Veterans Readjustment Counselling Service with a group of Vets centers around the country to help address this disorder. The centers in their early days focussed exclusively on the male combat veterans; the women were left out entirely. However, many of the women who served in Vietnam—the vast majority of them were nurses—had been emotionally and psychologically scarred by their experiences in Vietnam, but they were not getting any help. The GAO report called attention to this fact and noted that just recently, the centers under the guidance of the Veterans Readjustment Counselling Service were beginning to service the women veterans.

Following the GAO report, the other landmarks in turning policies around for women veterans were the two sets of hearings held in March 1983 by the Health and Hospitals Subcommittee of the House Veterans Affairs Committee and the Senate Veterans Affairs Committee. These were the very first hearings to address the particular situation of women veterans vis-à-vis the VA benefits system, with special emphasis on the hospital system. Women veterans, researchers, veterans organizations, and legislators testified on the problems women had and were having in seeking to use the VA hospital system. The same problems of lack of privacy, lack of gynecological facilities and access to care, the lack of sensitivity of staff, and the lack of responsiveness in general to the needs of women veterans, enumerated in the GAO Report, were attested to by the witnesses. One study suggested that since the VA system was designed for men by men, male-biased attitudes prevailed throughout the VA health care system.[16] Altogether, a picture of benign neglect and, sometimes, active hostility toward the presence of women in VA hospitals emerged from the hearings.

Since women veterans were equally eligible to use the hospital system, under the same system of priorities, it is legitimate to ask why they hadn't made more of a stir concerning the conditions described in the GAO report and the hearings. Later studies were to show that women veterans had a much lesser awareness of their eligibility for benefits than the men. The lack of courtesy, or even responsiveness of hospital staff to women, was the kind of information that is passed through the grapevine. Women naturally were loath to put themselves in a position of being rejected or not properly treated. The fact that women veterans often deprecated the contributions they made to the country with their military service and did not expect to have anything—no less benefits—in return, also may have partially accounted for the few demands they put upon the system. Since the caseload of women veterans was so light, the hospital system was under no pressure to make changes to accommodate them.

VA ADVISORY COMMITTEE ON WOMEN

The most important instrument to bring about institutional change in the VA regarding women veterans was the VA Advisory Committee on Women Veterans, created in July 1983 by the then-administrator Henry Walters. Creation of such a committee was included in legislation offered by Senator Cranston during the March 1983 hearings. The VA had opposed making this committee statutory during those hearings, and the administrator proceeded to set up an in-house committee in July. However, Congress approved the legislation making it statutory in November 1983, with an obligation that the committee file reports to the Congress every two years on its findings and recommendations.

In its first report to the Congress a year later, the new advisory committee outlined a number of different policy steps that the VA needed to take in order to bring women veterans into the VA health-care system for which they were eligible.[17] Among the major priorities were having renovations and construction projects that would provide privacy for the women veteran patients; having a women veteran coordinator at each medical facility; emphasizing that breast and pelvic examinations and pap smears be routinely administered as part of a woman's physical examination, and seeing that there be nurse practitioners certified in gynecological care to provide some gynecological services as well as health counselling when those services are not available.

The lack of awareness of women veterans of their benefits was pinpointed as a major problem by the committee. It was recognized that all the VA information materials and outreach programs designed and run by the VA were directed to the predominantly male population.[18] Many of the women veterans had not understood that these outreach materials and programs included them because they were not identified explicitly as part of the target population. The committee urged that the VA continue an aggressive outreach program for all women veterans including publishing a separate pamphlet addressed specifically to women veterans and making efforts to educate women veterans as to their eligibility for benefits.

Even the existence of burial benefits was generally unknown to women veterans. Funeral directors and those immediately concerned with burials rarely, if ever, inquired if a women were a veteran. Therefore, the families of the woman veteran were not likely to know that she was entitled to burial benefits. The committee urged the VA to make the proper outreach and communication methods to make that fact known so that the families of women veterans would not be shortchanged.

A paucity of statistical material was noted by the committee, which recommended that all major statistical reports compiled by VA include separate breakdowns on women veterans and that all future studies of veterans include a subsample of women veterans to be analyzed separately. Furthermore, the committee requested that the VA review and revise their programs based on the newly available data on women veterans.

The issue of Agent Orange and the exposure of women veterans who served in Vietnam was of concern. Between 7,000 and 10,000 women were presumed, like the men who were in Vietnam, to have been exposed to that toxic substance. Yet women were not included in Agent Orange studies either by VA or the Centers for Disease Control because of their small numbers. The committee urged that a separate study be conducted on the women who served in South Vietnam during the time that American forces were using dioxin and other chemicals to defoliate the countryside. Furthermore, the committee urged that all women veterans who served in Vietnam should be contacted and urged to participate in the VA's Agent Orange Registry.

INSTITUTIONAL CHANGES

Leadership can make a change in institutional responsiveness. With the full commitment of the administrator behind it, the committee recommendations outlined in the first report to Congress received prompt attention. Particularly notable was the response to the lack of data emphasized by the committee which had been noted earlier by observers. Not only did the VA Office of Information Management and Statistics develop a series of monographs, but the VA also commissioned the first in-depth survey on women veterans which examined socioeconomic characteristics, health status, use of VA programs and facilities, and exposure to combat. The purpose of this VA-commissioned Louis Harris Survey was to provide information to the VA to assist them in making policy decisions on services provided by VA and in designing future programs and facilities. Women veterans began to be counted, questioned, examined, and analyzed.

It was discovered that the women veterans populations is the fastest growing segment of the veterans population. This resulted from the fact that net separation for females outnumbered deaths. On the other hand, the male veterans population has been declining steadily as male veterans deaths have surpassed net separations. The percentage of female veterans under 35 years was higher for women than for men; and the percentage of older (over 65) women veterans of the total women veterans population was also higher than for the male veterans population. As of March 31, 1986, there were 1,177,900 women veterans, making up 4.2 percent of the veterans population.[19]

The Harris survey affirmed the low usage of veterans benefits by women, particularly in the older age groups, and suggested that the low usage reflected a problem of benefit awareness rather than preference. The program most widely used by women veterans is the GI Bill, with the guaranteed home loan program next in popularity. For 11 out of the 18 programs examined, the survey found that less than half of women veterans had heard of them. "There is still a need for publicity directed at the woman veteran," suggested the Harris survey.[20]

In the two years between the first report (1984) and the second report (1986) of the advisory committee, many institutional changes came about to benefit the women. While admitting there are still areas of concern, the committee expressed satisfaction with the progress of VA in meeting the criticisms of the GAO report and in implementing its own recommendations. In particular, the second report stated, "the efforts on the part of the Department of Medicine and Surgery represent a milestone in the care of women veterans."[21] Not only are women ensured a complete physical examination, including breast and pelvic, when they come into a VA hospital, but VA medical facilities "have now ensured that gynecologic services must be available for all female veterans as well as those in VA nursing homes and domiciliaries.[22]

There is no doubt that many omissions have been recognized and many corrections have already been made by the VA in its policies for women veterans. The leadership given by the VA administrator and the oversight of the Congress have contributed to that record of correction. Another factor in the "success" story is the increased articulateness of the women veterans themselves, the proliferation of new ad hoc women veterans groups around the country, and an increased awareness and involvement of the older women veterans organizations. The move for a women veterans memorial and the drive to add a woman's statue to the current Vietnam veterans statue, also no doubt have helped raise the consciousness of these women.

POLICY IMPLICATIONS FOR THE FUTURE

Whether this "success story" will persist and whether the momentum for change will continue unabated is unknown at this point. While the resolve and commitment of the advisory committee are high, some of the conditions for success have changed. Henry Walters is no longer VA administrator, with his full commitment to turn things around for the woman veteran. Also, the post of Special Assistant to the VA Administrator which served as the Secretariat to the Advisory Committee has been abolished. Furthermore, the current stringent budget cuts and enactment of the law (PL 99-272, April 7, 1986) requiring a means test for veterans to obtain non-service-connected care from the VA Hospital System may well adversely affect women veterans.[23]

Under this law and the new terms of eligibility, the mix of service-connected and non-service-connected is going to change. Women veterans who might have been able to come to the VA hospitals, as men had, for over three decades with non-service-connected ailments, particularly as outpatients, will be restricted. This is an irony that will not be lost on women veterans. Just as the system begins to be responsive to their needs, other contingencies narrow their eligibility.

The trend towards a women veterans population, both younger and older than the male veterans population, also has policy implications. Both younger women and older women are likely to have gender-related health needs, albeit different, that are characteristic of those age groups. Furthermore, since older women's economic status in this country is way below the economic status of men of comparable age, and since many women may not be covered by private insurance plans, it is most likely that this older women veterans population is going to need VA health services.

It is particularly ironic that the call for "outreach" to women veterans comes at a time of increasingly shrinking federal resources, including VA resources. With the emphasis in 1986 on cutting back on programs, with the demands for spartan budgets to meet Gramm-Rudman requirements, there will be fewer facilities, fewer programs, fewer beds, and fewer staff personnel available to the total veterans population. Therefore, women veterans, who have been shortchanged up until very recently when they finally became aware of their benefits, may find that it is too late to use them. There is a real question whether further corrections which will require new programs and/or services, meaning allocations of money, will survive to help meet the still unmet needs of women veterans.

Within the last several years there have been efforts within the states to recognize and address the problems of women veterans. In Connecticut, early in 1986, hearings were held on legislation (which was passed) that would set up a Veterans Affairs Commission with a special component specifically to address the needs of women veterans. Both New York and New Jersey have seen bills introduced that would set up commissions to look into the problems women veterans were having in their states. In 1985, the Labor Department studied how the public employment programs were servicing women who had left military service and were seeking jobs.[24]

OTHER APPROACHES TO EQUALITY

With the pressure of the women's movement since the 1960s seeking equality in all spheres for women, public policy changes needed to take many forms. Although women have had the vote for over sixty years, equality in many areas has not been forthcoming. In reviewing national policy developments that affect the status of women, one commentator has suggested that "national policy on the status of women has been defined as involving decisions directly related to sex discrimination as it applies to legal and economic status.[25] Those decisions would include legislative actions, court decisions (national and state), and actions by the executive branch including the setting up of programs to reach this equal status. Yet those equalities are only part of the total picture.

Women veterans, despite their legal status of equality with men veterans, did not have equal access to benefits. In such a situation, they should have been able to use all the benefits programs to the same degree as the men veterans. Even in the case of health-care benefits, which were designed for those with service-connected injuries or illnesses as the primary clients, particularly until recently when non-service-connected treatment was almost routine, women could have taken advantage of their eligibility. Yet if the concept of equality implies "equality of results," one political scientist has noted, then there had been almost no equality for women veterans as far as veterans benefits are concerned until this decade.[26]

The experience of the women veterans population indicates that the legal interpretation of equality can mitigate against women's best interests. The unequalness of situations must also be taken into account in many instances. Certainly, in the medical field, biological differences between men and women call for different kinds of physical exams, different expertise, different equipment, and different facilities. Francoise Krill, one commentator, on how international humanitarian law is relevant to women, points out, "Equality could easily be transformed into injustice if it were to be applied to situations which are inherently unequal and without taking into account circumstances relating to the state of health, the age and the sex of protected persons."[27]

In many sections of the Geneva Conventions and the two additional

Protocols of 1977, Krill points out that supplementary protections for women are explicitly stated:

Countries at war generally take some measures for the benefits of persons whose weakness in one respect or another warrants special care. These measures are varied in scope and application: they may cover the granting of supplementary ration cards, facilities for medical and hospital treatment, special welfare treatment, exemption from certain forms of work, protective measures against the effects of war, evacuation, transfer to a neutral county, etc.[28]

An example is the language of the Fourth Geneva Convention: "Women shall be especially protected against any attack on their honour, in particular against rape, enforced prostitution or any form of indecent assault."[29] To make distinctions between the sexes, whether it is vulnerability or having the same advantages, is not rejecting the notion of equality. The principle of differentiated treatment, as Krill suggests, may be the only way of achieving equality of outcome.

Those who are working to achieve equality for women are often caught in the bind that the absence of legal discrimination may not produce equal results since the starting points of those who are supposedly equal are often quite different. The concept that all persons are to be treated as equals, not because they are equal in any particular respect but simply because they are human, is a welcome philosophic underpinning but does not resolve injustices when one of the groups has had a long history of not being treated as equals.[30] In other words, the rationale for affirmative action—to make up for past histories of inequalities—has merit for women as well as for minorities.

In recent years the concept of reverse discrimination, which has seen court decisions go in opposite directions, haunts the viability of affirmative action programs. Critics of affirmative action, such as Daniel Bell, claim that affirmative action introduced a new principle of rights which evolved into another kind of inequality.[31] Bell suggests that not only does the affirmative action principle lower standards but that it focuses on group identity rather than personal identity and that the principle of equal opportunity has changed and reduced all inequalities in the goal to create an equality of result.

This debate on affirmative action concerns not only how equality is to be achieved by those who have suffered inequalities, but what mode of equality is at stake. Is equality of result the social policy objective of programs like affirmative action, or is it an attempt to bring individuals or groups up to a parity that would be a more equal way for them to compete?

It should be noted that the concept of parity was at issue when the GI Bill was designed during World War II. That bill's intent was to help make up for the time lost in service and to replace lost opportunities with new ones.[32] The government, since it had drafted most of its GIs, felt an obligation to create this parity. That program was designed to give the newly separated veteran an opportunity "to catch up" with the nonveterans who remained behind, continued to work in civilian jobs, and gained experience and additional moneys, as well as seniority. That rationale for the GI Bill of Rights of World War II, which later was replicated by the other GI Bills, the Cold War GI Bill, the Korean GI Bill, and the Vietnam bills, has never been questioned. It has always been assumed that a "grateful nation" can do no less for its veterans, many of whom placed their lives on the line serving in the military forces during wartime. The entire Veterans Administration health and hospital program and all the other benefits offered to veterans by a grateful nation have continued to be cornerstones of national policy, although from time to time there have been attacks on the continuation of those programs from such sources as the AMA and the Grace Commission. The AMA periodically suggests the dismantling of the VA hospital system as being duplicative and costly. However, the premise that the nation has a debt to those veterans who contributed to the defense of the nation, to bring them to where they might have been if they had not had their lives disrupted by military service, remains intact.

Could not this concept of parity—of time lost and opportunities lost—be relevant to the women veterans, particularly in the case of the older women veterans population who did not take advantage of their benefits because of lack of awareness of them or because of flaws in the institutional processes? These women veterans are being encouraged to apply for and use programs just at the time those programs are being cut back because of current national fiscal policies. If special or additional programs are not set up, then the women will in fact be discriminated against because of past omissions. Current corrections in VA policies need to take these new realities into account.

NOTES

1. For accounts of women's early participation in America's wars, see Linda Kerber's *Women of the Republic: Intellect and Ideology in Revolutionary America* (Chapel Hill: University of North Carolina Press, 1980), Mary Beth Northon's *Liberty's Daughters* (Boston: Little Brown, 1980), and Linda De Pauw's *Seafaring Women* (Boston: Houghton-Mifflin, 1982).

2. The American Veterans Committee, Inc., under the auspices of the Ford Foundation, conducted a preliminary review of how well government agencies who administered programs for women veterans were carrying out this mandate.

3. See *Congressional Record*, February 20, 1973, pp. 877–878.

4. For details of the differences in treatment, see June A. Willenz, *Women Veterans: America's Forgotten Population* (New York: Continuum, 1983), Chapter 6.

5. Ibid. For detailed description of the WAAC founding, see Mattie Treadwell,

The Women's Army Corps (Washington, D.C.: Office of the Chief of Military History, Department of the Army, 1954).

6. See Sally Van Wagenen Keil, Those Wonderful Women with Their Flying Machines: The Unknown Heroines of World War II (New York: Rawson-Wade Publishers, 1979).

7. The WASPS and other groups lobbied for legislation for veterans status since the end of World War II. For years, the large veterans organizations lobbied against it. General "Hap" Arnold had been their strong advocate. Finally, when Senator Barry Goldwater espoused their cause, the legislation was enacted.

8. See Willenz, Chapter 4.

9. Dr. Donald Custis, remarks, Hearing of Senate Veterans Affairs Committee, 97th Congress, Second Session. VA Health Care Programs Improvement and Extension Act of 1982, p. 276.

10. "Study of Health Care for American Veterans" (Report prepared by the National Academy of Sciences, National Research Council, submitted to the Committee on Veterans Affairs, U.S. Senate, June 7, 1977).

11. "A Report on the Aging Veteran," Senate Committee Print, No. 12, January 5, 1978, p. 17.

12. "Women Veterans, Usage of VA Hospitalization," VA Report, Office of Reports and Statistics, August 1982.

13. General Accounting Office Report (HRD 82-98), "Actions Needed to Insure that Female Veterans Have Equal Access to VA Benefits," September 24, 1982.

14. Ibid.

15. Ibid.

16. Maxine Hammer, "Perceptions of Female Veterans: Their Health-Care Needs in VA Hospitals" (dissertation, University of Southern California, 1979).

17. July 1984 Report of the VA Advisory Committee on Women Veterans.

18. Ibid.

19. July 1986 Report of the VA Advisory Committee on Women Veterans.

20. Louis Harris Associates, "Executive Summary, Survey of Female Veterans— A Study of Needs, Attitudes and Experiences of Women Veterans, IM&S 79-85-7, September 1985.

21. 1986 Report of the VA Advisory Committee on Women Veterans.

22. Ibid.

23. Title XIX of the Consolidated Omnibus Budget Reconciliation Act of 1985 (Veterans Health Care Amendments of 1986), S. Prt. 99–150.

24. The Women's Bureau project carried out by the American Veterans Committee on "Employment Experiences of Women Veterans Placed by Selected Public Employment Offices," December 1985.

25. Public Policy on the Status of Women, by Irene L. Murphy.

26. Mary Lou Kendrigan, "Gender Differences: Their Impact on Public Policy" (Paper delivered to 1985 Annual Meeting of the Midwest Political Science Association, April 17–20, 1985).

27. Francoise Krill, "The Protection of Women in International Humanities Law," International Review of the Red Cross, November-December 1985.

28. Ibid.

29. Fourth Geneva Convention, Article 27, ¶2, CIV, Article 75 and 76.

30. Kendrigan, "Gender Differences."

31. Daniel Bell, "Meritocracy and Equality," in *The New Egalitarianism*, ed. David Lewis Schaefer (Port Washington, N.Y.: Kennicae Press, 1979).

32. Sar Levitan/Karen A. Cleary, *Old Wars Remain Unfinished* (Baltimore: Johns Hopkins Press, 1973).

10

THE SOCIAL WORLD AND POLITICAL COMMUNITY OF HEAD-INJURED PEOPLE: DIFFERENCE BY GENDER AND FAMILY LIFE CYCLE

SARAH SLAVIN

In this chapter Slavin deals with the gender differences that are involved in treating persons who have sustained head injuries. Head-injured persons are different. It is important to understand and evaluate the manner in which differences can be respected and considered in shaping public policy within a framework of equal treatment. This chapter shows clearly that the issue is not equality versus special treatment but rather that treatment appropriate to the circumstances is necessary for equality. One premise of this chapter is that policy making of concern to members of the social world and political community of head-injured people is influenced by gender differences. Family life cycles are different for women than men. Slavin argues that the problems of the head-injured go unnoticed and unsolved because the victims and caretakers are usually women. Gender differences can be found in dealing with: (1) elderly women as victims; (2) women in the middle as caretakers; and (3) health care professionals. Slavin evaluates the success of women-in-the-middle at political integration around the campaign against drunk drivers (through voluntary associations and interest groups). She finds that the influence of these groups on public policy is moderate and incremental.

The National Head Injury Foundation (NHIF) had as its first motto: "Life after Head Injury is Never the Same."[1] Both severe and moderate degrees of this injury have catastrophic cognitive and motoric consequences.[2] Even a minor degree of this injury appears associated with organic brain damage.[3] The morbidity presented by head injury and related expense raises numerous public funding issues. Rebecca Rimel and John Jane have found that "head injury is one of the most critical problems facing the health-care system."[4] Public policy making around health care issues and outcomes relevant to head injury is similarly critical.

One premise of this chapter is that policy making of concern to members of the social world and political community of head-injured people is influenced by gender differences. The relationship of sex and differential ability does not work favorably in the policy-making arena for those affected. Importantly, the onset of head injury similarly situates many who have not themselves sustained an injury, but who are female and close to those who have. A paucity of opportunity affects virtually all these persons. They become privatized, that is, separated from the public realm and more privileged persons. Social and political integration are not readily forthcoming, and the exercise of influence may be a foregone conclusion.

This chapter begins by outlining certain demographics of head injury. The demographics are followed by discussions of the silent epidemic, as the phenomenon of head injury sometimes is known, including concepts of social and political integration. Thereafter, discussion focuses on forms of organization that do or do not contribute to integration. A distinction is made between forms applied on behalf of the mostly female cohort highly susceptible to head injury and the mostly male cohort. The efforts of women-in-the-middle, primary caregivers of persons with chronic conditions, are suggested to be potentially important to the female cohort and shown to be critical to the success of organization on behalf of the male cohort. Outside this organization, the often close relationship of women rather than men to issues of social and political integration important to head-injured people may be treated as anomalous and not necessarily deserving favorable recognition. This marginalization generally reduces opportunities to raise issues in public arenas or to have them raised and placed on public agendas, and it may affect outcomes. Such finding reinforces and explains perceptions discussed in this book's introduction, that women and other status-deprived groups do not benefit programmatically to the extent that men in the social and political mainstream will; women's access to the good life accordingly is diminished.

Two groups of primarily Caucasian citizens are most vulnerable to head injury. One group is old.[5] Susceptible to falls, these individuals face grave difficulties upon even a minor head injury.[6] Thirty of every 10,000 persons age 75 and over sustain this injury.[7] Because of longevity patterns, females predominate among those 75 and over.[8] Health care issues among this age cohort may be properly termed women's issues.[9]

The second vulnerable group of citizens is the teenaged population. Between the ages of 15 and 19, 42 of every 10,000 of these young people sustain head trauma, making them the population most at risk.[10] Most likely, these individuals are injured in car crashes.[11] One driver in these crashes is likely to be alcohol-impaired.[12] This individual may or may not sustain the head trauma. Rimel and Jane demonstrate alcohol abuse in the backgrounds of one quarter of the head-injured persons they studied.[13] Other studies report up to 72 percent had been drinking at the time of injury.[14] Between the ages of 15 to 19, males have a much greater likelihood than females of sustaining head injury.[15] And they appear most likely to be the alcohol-impaired driver, although again, the young head-injury patient has not necessarily been drinking.[16]

Women's issues surface in the case of younger as well as older victims because the main caring relatives of head-injured people are reported most often to be mothers and wives, for 15- to 19-year-olds, clearly, mothers.[17] Mothers more than wives are likely to be in for the duration.[18]

Howard Palley and Julianne Oktay report that the caregiver for people who are old may be a "woman in the middle," and the old people cared for by women-in-the-middle are also usually women and usually have outlived their spouses.[19] A daughter or possibly a daughter-in-law, the woman-in-the-middle may be divorced—a single household head—and pulled in conflicting directions by the needs of the person with a chronic condition, by offspring, by gainful employment and, perhaps, by a spouse.[20] She also must relate to a mostly female rehabilitation staff that may characterize her as helpless, guilt ridden, dependent, resentful, competitive, and smothering.[21]

This situation is typical of women-in-the-middle related to younger as well as to older head-injury victims. It presents a set of expectations to which men mostly do not respond, and status differentials and limited mobility to which men usually are not subject.

Reasons for concern of the mostly female family members close to head-injured people include the expense of medical care and rehabilitation services. What is more, as people who sustain head injuries are likely to come from the lower socioeconomic strata, [22] the family with financial problems before the injury occurred is a family doubly burdened after the injury's occurrence.[23] Single-female-headed households are known to be likely to experience financial difficulty. However, even family members from stable financial backgrounds will be staggered by the financial implications of head injury. In short, as Mary Lou Kendrigan contends, all these women effectually may be considered part of the same economic group. Comprehensive third party insurance coverage is essential to recovery efforts as well as to the ability to cope with the situation. But, there is a vast inequality of knowledge about the complexities of insurance law and widespread reticence by insurance specialists among lawmakers to hear from those who bear the burden of medical care and rehabilitation services.

There is ample reason, then, for concern with public funding issues and outcomes accompanying head injury, regardless of which age cohort is affected. In practice, though, old age, disability, and economic impoverishment have implicated public funding mechanisms.[24] For a quarter century, through the Medicare and Medicaid programs (Titles XVIII and XIX of the Social Security Act), and also through a series of health-care-related tax deductions, the U.S. government has served as a significant source of health care for the nation.[25] All other things being equal, older people benefit most from public moneys spent on health care.[26] If only because, more even than race, old age is related to income inequality.[27] But chronic conditions tend generally to diminish a person's ability to provide self with material support, because "high medical expenses, plus inflation and decreased earnings lead to impoverishment."[28] Further, this condition is not likely to present individuals with many new opportunities for self-sufficiency. So, age per se does not appear to be as critical to status differentials related to funding in this area as do gender and the onset of head injury. Family life cycle is more useful than age in analysis pertaining to head-injured people, and women's and men's family life cycles differ.

THE SILENT EPIDEMIC

Because it affects the lives of many and no one organization, central voice, or authority is able to supervise the results, the phenomenon of head injury is known as the silent epidemic. The National Head Injury Foundation's (NHIF) excellent newsletter has stated that "supporting the NHIF with a contribution does *literally* save lives and reduce the frustration that comes from the isolation and pain of not knowing where to turn next."[29] As social scientists, we should recognize the phenomenon referred to in the newsletter as a social world. In *Invisible Lives*, David Unruh conceptualized social world usefully. He saw a social world as "a distinct form of social organization," embracing cohorts for whom social integration is believed to pose problems.[30]

Integration into a social world changes in relation to changes in life cycle.[31] *Family* life cycle may be most significant regarding the integration-related concerns of head-injured people. In fact, the medical, rehabilitation, and social services literature overall may benefit by the introduction of this variable, because it speaks to the environment in which injury occurs and in which the impact of injury is experienced. Family life cycle considers the influence of age on a person's conjugal family status and assumes systematic passage from one life cycle stage to another.[32]

Before onset of head injury, certain similarities exist in the life cycle stages of the two most susceptible cohorts. On the one hand, the family life cycle stages of the 75 and over cohort likely will demonstrate maintenance of independence, although perhaps with difficulty, and cessation of occupational activity if there were any. On the other hand, the family life cycle stage of the teenaged cohort before injury will tend to demonstrate semi-emancipation and relatively little occupational or fiscal (but probably academic) responsibility.

There are dissimilarities. For old people, reductions in familial responsibility, in mobility, and in sociability are apparent. Impairment due to pre-existing chronic conditions may contribute to the falls in which many of these head injuries are sustained. For young people, familial responsibility may vary, though mobility and sociability are likely. In some instances, socially malicious behavior in the form of drinking and driving is evident. However, many become injured through no fault of their own.

After head injury, although impairments are specific to individuals, both cohorts clearly share a life cycle stage and a social world, often marked by catastrophic cognitive and motoric consequences, increased dependency, dire financial need, isolation, and little chance for gainful employment. Both cohorts experience real need for program delivery and public funding for purposes of recovery and the prevention of something similar happening to others yet unaffected.

To keep the world meaningful as life cycle progresses, old and also teenaged victims of head injury "must struggle to keep the intense interest, physical stamina, and mental abilities often required in the face of their age peers."[33] Among the head-injured population, one's age peers are not necessarily growing old, although they may be. We have two groups forced into a similar but unfamiliar family life cycle stage after the onset of injury. But, because two different generations are involved, few may believe them to have much in common. Generation has sociohistorical connotations that age lacks.[34]

Evidence of integration or its absence is important, bearing as it does upon people's participation in both policy and society. Integration influences the degree and manner in which we manage self-identity[35] and the quality of our "membership in a political community":[36]

Head injured people are believed to be: Personally and socially a vulnerable group, often lacking means to influence policy makers in our society. By the very nature of their injuries, they are prevented from voicing their thoughts and feelings in a coherent and positive way, leaving the greater part of their burdens to be shouldered by their relatives. Fortunately, organized help from groups of relatives is developing rapidly, and the [NHIF] in the United States and Headway in Britain [and also the U.S.] seem likely to do for head-injured persons what societies for other groups of handicapped people . . . have been doing successfully for many years.[37]

In *Invisible Lives*, Unruh has stressed the significance of people's histories, opinions, and individual natures to appreciating fully the multidimensionality of integration.[38]

For Unruh, observing *forms* of social and political organization and their combination will help illuminate the meaning of social worlds.[39] The observation of organizational forms also is of direct interest to political scientists. Learning that these forms are gender or life cycle linked will increase further our ability to comment upon integration. Also, to appreciate the consequences of integration, social and political, it is necessary to examine "previous integrative status,"[40] and information about gender and family life cycle will facilitate this appreciation.

Channels of communication importantly facilitate connections between head-injured persons and their families with existing forms of social and political organization.[41] The NHIF newsletter emphasizes this point by referring to the isolation and attendant frustration that come from failure to connect. Of interest, too, are the "instrumental and expressive ends" achieved by integration.[42] For instance, having the freedom to choose one's environment, probably a home over institutional setting, may be valued highly by a head-injured individual, but material resources to make in-home living feasible may be lacking unless forthcoming from other than head-injured persons and their families.[43] This suggests that the achievement of instrumental and expressive ends may be social and political.

There is additionally the question of the decision-making process through which people order and maintain personal identities, especially those aspects of identification most prized by the individual. What goes into these decisions?[44] Suppose, for example, one consequence of head injury were cosmetic impairment. This impairment would have social (and political) costs, as well as influence one's sense of self-worth. This impairment may be significant to women, who have been taught that an attractive appearance is expected of them, but also to young men, who associate physical attractiveness with degree of success.[45] Under these circumstances, sustaining a "preferred definition of self" will stretch coping mechanisms.[46] Social integration requires and facilitates an emphasis on self in the perception of integration even as it helps provide personal meaning, and this definition of self may have political consequences, although not always the ones we anticipate.[47]

The process of political integration becomes especially interesting when a group is new and seeking equity in relation to already recognized members of the state, because a redistribution of values may be in order.[48] To quote Virginia Sapiro, "a group that has accepted the right of political self-determination, even through institutions and processes shared by others, would probably not rest content for long with a position of being an economic underclass."[49]

Sapiro's analysis focuses on "the 'significance' of sex" and may prove particularly apt for the social world of head-injured people.[50] Although both women and men occupy this world, women play a majority of its roles. If, as Sapiro argues, "women remain essentially private in the eyes of much of the public, even when they enter the public realm," this is a finding frought with significance for the future of head injury survivors, "because 'privatized' women remain anomalies in the public world of politics."[51] This may be the situation that confronts women-in-the-middle and the mostly female head-injured cohort.

The anomalous women of conventional wisdom are supposedly out of their depth in politics and politically without consequence. In this set of perceptions, any claims women would have to the right to exercise authority, that is, to legitimacy, are moral, emotional and highly personalized—meaning, primitive and antithetical to political byways of bargaining and accommodation. On any other than the neighborhood level, the political activist or leader who is a woman is supposedly not modal; she is deviant.[52] These expectations present two prescriptive problems: first, a double standard as to who should participate in public processes, and second, the paradox of "formally equal rights and... equal standards" and "pervasive and significant unequal treatment of women."[53] To see women confronting these problems, Bonnie Cook Freeman has argued that "we should give more attention to the individual and small-group dimensions of power wielding and sharing."[54] In the present study, this attention is focused on the level of a social world and its forms and on women-in-the-middle.

Gender also may figure into the amount of attention paid clientele groups: The elderly head-injured group tends to include more women than men, while the younger group, more men than women. Is the public case for the later generation made more readily than the case for the earlier, in part because of the gender of the clientele group? This is an interesting question. "The problem of [political] integration," Sapiro tells us, "is largely one of norms, values, perceptions, expectations; the links among these; and the relationships between these and political behavior."[55] What becomes telling is not the frequency of participation in elections and so on.[56] Presumably one may remain marginal to a political system even while nominally participating in it.[57] Freedom of choice must include, as Sapiro says, the freedom "to be influential," to influence outcomes.[58] And, public policy may play a large role in staking out the perimeters of this freedom.

In the next section, the situation surrounding the population of old women who sustain head injuries will be examined. Forms of social and political organization that might assist these women are shown to be ineffective or disinterested. In the section that follows, focus will shift to women-in-the-middle, as organizational activists and leaders, and to the privatization that accompanies their efforts. Finally, the role of public policy in establishing perimeters of free choice and the good life will be discussed.

ORGANIZATIONAL FORMS AND HEAD-INJURED OLD WOMEN

Bluntly put, there are no formal or semi formal organizations that focus explicitly on old women who sustain head injuries. In fact, as Doris Hammond indicates, this lack of organizational status tends to be the situation of old women overall:

With more than 1200 women's health groups throughout the nation, there is the opportunity for a strong movement dedicated to the health needs of older women. To date, the choice has not been heard to the degree we hear other organizations working toward health care improvements, such as AARP [American Association of Retired Persons], state offices on aging and the Grey Panthers.[59]

Although old women implicitly are included in the solutions of AARP, state offices on aging, and the Grey Panthers, they are included in solutions that fail specifically to consider them and hence, to meet their needs. The needs of old women often are not the same as those of old men.[60] For example, heart disease afflicts men more than women; osteoporosis is more common among women than men. Heart disease is on public health agendas; osteoporosis has not been. The latter is implicated in fractures that lead to falls, that may cause head injuries. There is a need for some differential organization and representation.

From the standpoint of triage, the old person in comparison to the young is considered limited in potential for recovery from head injury because of a "reduced capacity to learn, a less resilient vascular system, and a more limited neuronal reserve by way of alternative pathways."[61] Society also tends to *expect* old people to become weak-minded, inflexible, and conservative in orientation.[62] These expectations are taken one step further in the case of old women, who are perceived as domineering, both whimsical and conceited, dependent and passive, and in any event, eccentric.[63]

These are not always realistic perceptions, nor are these perceptions well understood. For example, Marilyn Bell and Kathleen Schwede have reported that old women may be less conflicted than young women about social norms and, left to go their own ways as they grow old, may become increasingly feminist in orientation.[64]

In conventional wisdom, though, the old woman is a conservative woman, opposed to the changes in women's and men's personal relations and in the distribution of power between them that radical feminists have sought. Conventional wisdom to the contrary, Bell and Schwede have shown that old women are complex people who effectually may collapse "the public/ private dichotomy forced upon many women."[65] Most old women no longer function actively as wives and mothers, and few are gainfully employed. The "reduction of role strain" on old women that results leaves them free to emphasize their own, not others' needs, wants, and desires.[66] They may not; countervailing expectations can be powerful. The point is that old women may become free to do so. Conventionally, this resilience has been labeled whimsical or egocentric; it is not likely to be seen as reflective of radical feminist models. Stereotypes of old women have not left room for consideration of the realities of their lives.

In general, for women and men both, aging related changes in sensory functions may alter behavioral patterns. The alterations may include all-important means of communication; understood, these changes are rational but they are not always understood as such and may be rejected by those whose sensory functions are essentially unaltered.[67] Other negative "status judgments" about those altered may also be made by those unaltered.[68] "Age-grading" itself sometimes is little more than social labeling.[69] In fact, scholarly studies of human physiology tend not to confront aging processes directly, leaving the interested observer with many inferences and nonempirically based generalizations about old people.[70] Applying a triage mentality to old people who sustain head injuries does not recommend itself. Still, in the name of "intergenerational equity," triage is applied even by a medical ethicist such as Daniel Callahan to biomedical advances and also Medicare benefits that might aid old people, including those with head injuries.[71]

Yehuda Ben-Yishay and Leonard Diller report that "as empirical evidence is accumulating, there is a growing realization that many of the mental sequelae of severe traumatic head injury resemble those encountered in varying degrees in patients with diffuse structural brain disorders of non-traumatic origin, such as aging."[72] That is, the aftereffects of head injury are something like those of growing old. Old people may receive the largest dose of these problems, but the teenagers who sustain head injuries are going to be sometimes medically more similar to old people with the same injury than to the 15- to 19-year-olds in their age cohort. Under the circumstances it is not reasonable to ignore old people in these straits. If the later generation, despite aging-like changes, may be emphasized in a search for solutions, then so may be the earlier one. As Kendrigan asserts in her introduction, if we seek equality, we seek it for all people, because of their humanness and intrinsic individual value.

Although in the search for solutions to its aftereffects, the expense of head injury overwhelms all concerned, degrees of difference are apparent. U.S. Census figures place the median income of old women 57 percent below the median income of old men; one-third of these women live below the poverty line.[73] Teenagers may not have independent incomes; but, their parent(s) probably will have, even if parents are in relatively low income brackets. Their parents may not be in as low an income bracket as old women are. And old women and men will not have parents to assist them, if not with the actual expense of care, then with obtaining access to it.

One solution to the aftereffects of head injury has to be paying the bills for relevant services and care. Old people who have paid into Social Security or Railroad Retirement, or who have paid voluntary premiums, along with people with handicapping conditions, are entitled to Medicare coverage; they also may become eligible by reasons of "actual" or medical indigence. Medical indigence occurs when health care costs basically impoverish a person, but she or he still has an income. To achieve medical indigence, people first must spend virtually everything they have acquired. This is called "spending down," and it is good for no one. Further, besides facing the inconsistency from state to state of Medicaid grants, recipients may be forced to assume some health care expense despite a need to rely on Medicaid.

Increases in required contributions to Medicare render its protection costly, too. Together with the expense of medical care generally and particularly for head injury, and the likelihood of depressed incomes for old people, especially old women, Medicare costs add up to a difficult situation. Coverage also does not extend past acute care to nursing home care, which may be required for head-injured people without caring family. Remember that old people likely have outlived the parents most likely to see head-injured individuals through the situation, although their daughters may assist them. Medicare coverage also probably will not include extended physical, occupational and speech therapies, essential to anyone's recovery efforts. Without supplementary health insurance, Medicare is not going to be enough; and poor or near poor people will not have supplementary insurance. What is more, with financial insolvency looming, Medicare's future is in doubt.

To help pay bills, unlike the person injured in a fall, the person injured in a motor vehicle crash almost always has access to either no-fault or liability (casualty) insurance, although only in states with comprehensive no-fault coverage will this be close to enough. Caps on catastrophic coverage introduce additional catastrophy. A person injured in a crash also can bring a negligence suit against the party responsible for the crash. This assumes the responsible party is not the head-injured individual and is not indigent; but an indigent driver's policy, if he has one, may include liability coverage. This also assumes the judicial system has treated seriously any charges, for example, D.W.I., against the responsible party; failure to do so occasionally has affected tort claims of injured people adversely, despite different standards of proof on the criminal and civil levels. After other insurance has paid out, teenaged head injury victims also may have access to health insurance carried by their parents. In some states victims of drinking drivers may recover under crime victim compensation acts, although not very much, and in some states, victims of car crashes may be excluded altogether from recovery.

Old people may have no grounds for a negligence suit to recover damages, which could help pay the expense of head injury. Probably neither group will be eligible for sick leave. But, the early generation often will have paid 3 cents on the dollar into Social Security and nearly 7 cents into life, fire, automobile, and health insurance.[74] The later generation, if it has paid into Social Security, has done so only for a short time and probably has not paid other premiums. Although members of either group may have access to some financial set up redistributing some of the costs of head injury,[75] old people who are head injured may be in the least favorable position to cover costs despite having paid in the most. The reality of an old person's financial situation may contribute to an already existing tendency to write her off after head injury. Admittedly, any person sustaining head injury may face the possibility of being written off. Any indigent person may face this chance. With old people, however, and particularly old women, such unjustifiable tendencies are likely to compound.

To overcome this unfavorable situation, comprehensive, sophisticated organization and integration are musts. Yet, any question of action by volunteer associations/interest groups on behalf of old people who sustain head injuries is moot, because there is no such action. The closest any group has come to this probably was in 1982 when the Older Women's League, known as OWL, founded a National Task Force on Care-Givers. Concerns about prevention of head injury and programmatic support thereafter are little articulated on old women's behalf.

The population of the social world of head-injured people includes diverse persons, but not on the same terms. No complicated procedure is involved to enter this social world—the old head-injured person soon may be lost in its vastness for want of adequate organization and integration. No authoritative body influences the situation on this group's behalf, although theoretically it comes within the National Head Injury Foundation's constituency; and NHIF seeks to assert authority. To benefit from efforts by NHIF, for example, toward relevant biomedical research, old people will first have to be redefined as capable of recovery.

The rapid rate of change characterizing the form of social organization that is a social world may confuse the person from an early generation sustaining a head injury. And, because old people are stereotyped as weak-minded, society is not going to enhance integration to any great extent after head injury occurs. Further, as Sandra Harding has discussed, society considers sex "a variable in the *distribution* of rationality," with the masculine the rational.[76] This poses yet another disadvantage for the old head-injured woman already understood to be weakminded and eccentric. Or, as Freeman has put it, the basis for women's claims to legitimacy are emotional and primitive.

Other than residential facilities and a few outpatient therapy programs, there seem to be no appropriate subworlds to moderate the flux of this social world for old people. "Shared perspectives and interests," the basis for personal involvement in the larger social world as well in certain subworlds, are effectually but not literally lacking. The nature of roles available in this social world to members of an early generation is bound to be thin and unsatisfying. Communication becomes idiosyncratic, at least in others' eyes, defeating interaction despite intentions to communicate. To an extent, idiosyncracy may assist old head-injured women to escape stereotype, but generally speaking, it will not help socially to integrate them.[77] Further, their feminism appears largely overlooked at this time by women's movement organizations, excepting OWL, although it need not be.

Compared to old men, 70 percent of whom are married, 78 percent of old women are not married.[78] Among other things, this means their most familiar settings may have been altered by widowhood. "In attempting to maintain a sense of familiarity with the settings in which they lead their daily lives the old widows must often play a passive role. They cannot control social change or the deaths, geographic mobility, or physical impairments, of friends."[79] Although the attribution of passivity may be exaggerated, after head injury the situation may be enforced and extreme. Familiar cues enable a head-injured person to order his or her environment. As a kind of communication, environment has orderliness and harmony as well as inherent consequences.[80] Any head-injured person may sustain loss in this regard; in the context of similarly injured others, given already existing losses of familiar settings, the old women probably will experience loss of an ordered environment most intensely.

Old widowed mothers tend also to be deprived of resources significant to the exercise of certain kinds of power and hence to relationships of equality; and outside their circle of friends, they may seem to lack real chances for viable relationships other than by marriage and by family.[81] For other than the independently wealthy woman and depending on her cultural background, loss of support within a family may spell a kind of powerlessness for some women that a man may not experience. Add this to the fact that head-injured persons may end up treated as a child,[82] reducing dramatically opportunities for resumption of healthy familial relationships and friendships and marking the head-injured person as unequal, and one can see that old widowed mothers who sustain head injuries are in a most unfavorable position.

Under these circumstances, the maintenance of self-esteem and identity will be compromised doubly for the old head-injured woman. As these are real people, not mannekins, the situation is not beyond negotiation. But, an already complicated situation for many old women is rendered more complicated by the onset of head injury; and little help is in sight. The privatization of these old women seems virtually complete, assuring little or no contact with political communities. These women exist on the margin: Their status as an "economic underclass" is dilatory and may tend to defeat ideas of self-assertion rather than vice versa. "The 'significance' of sex," noted by Sapiro is painfully apparent. Exercise of influence at least seems out of the question. Pushed beyond the margins of the political community, the old head-injured woman has no place to go. Further, as the different longevity patterns for women and men increase, and the "Baby Boom" population ages, chances are the population of old head-injured women is going to increase, because there are no concerted efforts to reduce the incidence of head injury in the age 75 and over cohort.

ORGANIZATIONAL FORMS AND WOMEN-IN-THE-MIDDLE

Two sets of voluntary associations/interest groups comprise subworlds of the larger social world of head-injured people. Both sets actively involve women-in-the-middle. One set focuses primarily on the deterrence of drinking drivers, who cause a preponderance of head injuries; the second set focuses primarily on recovery from head injury through research, rehabilitation, and reentry. Although by no means exclusively, prevention organizations tend to emphasize state legislative action and have centralized state legislative agendas; recovery-oriented organizations tend to emphasize federal action. In both sets of organizations, approaches to public policy making most benefit teenagers who sustain head injuries. As we have seen, the head injuries of old people are not predominantly the results of motor vehicle crashes and are defined medically as presenting poor prospects for recovery.

The Campaign against Drinking-Driving

The campaign against drinking-driving presents a subworld of the larger social world of head-injured people. For purposes of influence, which is moderate and incremental, the campaign offers one kind of authority structure, that of the voluntary association cum interest group.[83] Associational groups include Mothers Against Drunk Drivers (MADD) and A Citizen's Project to Remove Intoxicated Drivers (RID). Women founded both organizations, and most of the key officers in either group are women with dependent children at home.[84]

On May 3, 1980, a drunk driver killed 13-year-old Cari Lightner, the daughter of Candy Lightner, who in 1980 founded MADD. The driver who killed Cari left the scene of the accident; he turned out to have a valid California license and five previous drunk driving arrests. (He went on to a seventh after killing Cari Lightner and serving two and one-half years in jail for it.) By working, first, with select governing elites in California,

Lightner and MADD chapters achieved consideration of stricter penalties for D.W.I. than had existed previously. On March 14, 1983, NBC produced a movie, "Mothers Against Drunk Drivers: The Candy Lightner Story"; and on January 7, 1985, *Time* magazine ran a feature about Ms. Lightner and her efforts.

Despite the attention, attempts to marginalize MADD's impact were common. In sarcastic response to this climate, *Christian Century* ran the following personal perspective: "The unforgetting Ms. Lightner has recruited a ragtag following of soreheads from the highways and byways—mainly cripples, widows, bereft parents and other concerned men and women. Malcontents all. They want to clear the roads of drunk drivers."[85]

In a viewer's guide to its TV movie, NBC also reflected perceptions of women as anomalies in the political process and of their privatization. In a discussion section titled "Citizen Activism" came the following:

2. Candy is a novice in politics. Steven Blankenship, Steve White and Jean Moorehead all teach her about the realities of the political and social climate....
4. At one point in the story, Serena (Carl's twin sister) runs away from home. She later tells her mother that she feels that MADD has become more important to her than her family. How well does Candy deal with her young daughter's concerns?
...
6. Have you ever known a crusader, someone so committed to a single issue that other aspects of life were ignored? What were your feelings toward this person?

Frank Weed has shown that MADD chapter officers were likely to have been affected directly by drinking-driving, with 46 percent of chapter presidents coming from families in which a member has died because of a drinking driver.[86] These officers tend to be middle-aged women, with a family member sustaining a chronic condition as a result of the crash, women-in-the-middle.

By bringing together small groups already in existence in central New York in 1979, Doris Aiken founded RID. Although MADD became the most visible of the two organizations, RID was the first of them. Aiken became concerned about D.W.I. on December 4, 1977, after learning about the deaths of Karen and Tim Morris, ages 17 and 19, because of a drunk driver. Karen and Tim were the same age as Aiken's children. By garnering support from over 20 religious, volunteer, and business organizations outside RID, by reporting on relevant roll call votes of members of the New York state legislature, and by networking among RID chapters, Aiken stimulated passage in 1980 of 67 percent (4) of relevant bills before the legislature and in 1981, of 82 percent (9) of such bills. During previous years, no such legislation had passed. Aiken soon learned, though, that this was not to be an open and shut matter.

Attempts to privatize "primitive" concerns were evident. For example,

A Queen's judge had the gall to tell Anna Marie Spiro (now a RID activist) who lost her son when a drunk driver first knocked him down and then drove over his head while leaving the scene, to stay out of his court lest she become emotional and cry. When she refused, he directed her to sit in the back row.[87]

Further evidence of marginalization emerged. Doris Aiken's analysis of the situation become increasingly feminist. She criticized the influence of TV beer commercials on teenaged men. One evaluation found these commercials emphasized risk and danger as masculine, associated speed and beer consumption, and linked beer with rites of initiation into manhood; some commercials delivered their messages by portraying the sexual exploitation of women and misogynist attitudes.[88] Once RID-USA took a stand in 1984 against beer and wine ads on television, it was boycotted by the National Association of Broadcasters, a lobbying group, and it ceased to appear on network TV.[89] A subsequent study by the Harvard School of Public Health showed that after 1984, news coverage of the citizens' movement against drunk driving declined sharply.[90] Up to this point in time, according to The Project on the Citizens' Movement Against Drunk Driving, movement organizations had used media markets strategically to reach 95 percent of the U.S. population.[91]

Despite its difficulties, the campaign against drinking-driving provides one example of one "organized outlook" underlying a social world.[92] Individuals may enter this outlook because of generalized concern over the problem of drinking-driving, or because of loss or severe, moderate, or mild injury to self, a loved one, or an acquaintance. Through small chapters, typically 35 members, one-quarter of whom are victims, this subworld helps moderate the rate of change, offering constructive outlets for anger and a set of preventive solutions.[93] The outlook is often family-oriented. The population of this portion of a social world includes other than head injury survivors, but the approach is highly relevant to prevention of head injury among 15- to 19-year-olds.

It takes, then, only a cognitive identification with the need to prevent drinking-driving to come within the boundaries of this part of a social world; its boundaries are not difficult to pass through. As in the larger social world, ground for individual participation are "shared perspectives and interests."[94] The post hoc character of initiatives supported by MADD and RID may not be great incentive to participation by head-injured people. But, their participation may strengthen senses of personal efficacy, providing participants with helpful release from frustration with the fact of their injury and the disruption of their lives.

The role of association volunteer or interest group activist is more formal than roles usually provided by a social world.[95] More formal roles access political integration more readily than less formal ones and provide a level of recognition probably otherwise denied, as demonstrated by lack of emphasis in policy agendas on prevention of head injury to old women and, in the case of young men, the emphasis on prevention (as in an NHIF-supported campaign to get people to fasten their seatbelts, as well as in the anti-D.W.I. movement generally). Our ability to generalize about young men is rendered a relative proposition, though, by the marginalization of many women-in-the-middle.

Despite broadcast media boycotts, the voluntary association/interest group subworld facilitates face to face contacts that work to reduce invisibility and let voices be heard.[96] RID chapters, for example, have sponsored well-attended yearly victim speakouts; these events are reported by the print media and are also intense social and political interactions. Judges, prosecutors, and other public officials join the audience to hear the stories of people victimized by drinking drivers. A new bride's bladder incontinency becomes an open topic for discussion; a young man left mute by a head injury becomes a public speaker by using a computer's synthesized voice.

Another means to disseminate information and reduce invisibility is submission of victim impact statements to judges after a defendant's conviction and before sentencing. Use of impact statements in noncapital cases has, though, become uncertain, due to the U.S. Supreme Court's 1987 decision, *Booth* v. *Maryland*, holding unconstitutional the use of impact statements in capital cases. The Court's decision is contested vigorously by victim rights advocates.

As one organizational leader has put it, "We deal in information."[97] Many touch creatively this part of a social world, then leave it in flux.[98] Under these circumstances, information is transient: Parents, grandparents, friends of injured and dead people, injured people themselves, the police, insurance companies, high school guidance counselors and driving instructors, prosecutors, reporters, bar owners, alcoholism counselors, reformed drinking drivers, and volunteers become experts.

In this manner, MADD and RID have helped change D.W.I. laws in the 50 states, importantly encouraging the appointment in 1982 of the Presidential Commission on Drunk Driving and also contributing to passage of the Howard-Barnes Act of 1982 to stimulate and support state initiatives against D.W.I.[99] No more than 25 percent of this organizational focus is on legal change. Foci include raising public consciousness, educating young people, and changing opinions. Nor has incremental success at these endeavors lessened resistance to what MADD and RID are about.

On June 8, 1987, in *The Washington Times*, Scott Sublett referred to MADD's "hard line" that "would string offenders from the nearest tow truck" and to opposition by "card-carrying 'ACLU' " types.[100] In a divide-and-conquer tactic, Sublett presents RID as opposing MADD's interest in deterrence, although The Project on the Citizens' Movement Against Drunk Driving has found similar levels of interest in RID.[101] Expert Lawrence Ross, a member of RID's national advisory board, is quoted by Sublett as describing MADD's agenda as "moral" and not "scientific." Here again is the perception that women are bypassed in the distribution of rationality and outside political byways.

Elsewhere, Ross has argued that the risk of a crash and of injury and death is unacceptably low in relation to costs to the public of filling demands for strict treatment of D.W.I.[102] He has not, though, calculated the costs to individuals, private carriers, and also the public of the consequence of D.W.I., nor has he calculated revenue generated by fines for D.W.I. He also has overlooked the importance of achieving an acceptable balance of risks, a problem as well with TV beer commercials. This achievement is one main purpose of governmental action.[103] Although the chance of severe injury or death because of a drinking driver is 1 in 33, the chance of a driver being apprehended while drunk is 1 in 1000.[104] This is an inequitable distribution of risk, and this is a major message from women-in-the-middle, many with responsibilities with head-injured family members. The message meets with resistance outside the movement against drinking-driving, but is advanced nonetheless through integration in this part of a social world.

The NHIF

Like MADD and RID, as a subworld of a larger social world, NHIF brings with it the characteristics of a volunteer association/interest group. But, its structure may be less permeable than the structure either of MADD and RID or of the social world itself. The roles offered by NHIF also seem more formal than those forthcoming from RID and MADD and certainly those available in the larger social world. These factors simultaneously contribute to a relative degree of success at political integration for the organization, and to a lesser degree of success than NHIF wishes at social integration for head injury survivors.

NHIF was founded in Massachusetts in 1980 by Marilyn and Martin Spivack. In 1975 the Spivacks' 15-year-old daughter Debby sustained a head injury in a car crash; Debby Spivack was injured by a drinking driver. This catastrophe added incalculably to damage already done for, in 1971, the Spivacks' son had died of a head injury received in a motorcycle crash.

In 1983, on receiving an award for significant contributions on head-injured people's behalf, the Spivacks stated: "The ultimate reward for us will come when our daughter Debby and the thousands of Debbys in this country have the opportunity to live a life of dignity in an appropriate environment, to work and to play, to love and be loved."[105] A contribution envelope put out by NHIF also suggests an emphasis on the needs of younger cohorts: "Tragically, most of the victims are under the age of 34 who receive these injuries." Other NHIF materials, including legislative testimony, suggest this emphasis, too.

A focus on family involvement is evident as well in the NHIF newsletter and elsewhere, for example, in the name given its trial lawyers seminar, "Legal Implications of a Complex Medical/Rehabilitative/Family Crisis." The organization does not, though, function as a "support group" per se; and it is professionally as well as family oriented. M.D.s, Ph.D.s, and also M.A.s, specialized rehabilitation degrees, and some J.D.s follow many names mentioned in the newsletters. Cofounder Martin Spivack holds both and M.D. and a Ph.D. The M.D.s and Ph.D.s mostly are men's; M.A.s and rehabilitation degrees belong to women. This distribution of degrees by sex and field of endeavor corresponds with their distribution in society at large, with men tending to hold the most prestigious and also lucrative of them.[106] Advanced degrees do not follow the names of many women associated with the chapters, the women-in-the-middle; the names of some men are not followed by advanced degrees, either.[107]

The national organization's mailing list includes over 60,000 names, and does not cross reference names from the federation of 38 state association and affiliate, and 375 support group, membership lists. At the end of 1987, NHIF's total paid membership stood at 17,000; over half these members are head injury survivors. NHIF estimates that there are more than one million head-injured people in the United States; based on these figures, the organization involves no more than 1 percent of the total head-injured population.

The second group of paid members is made up of professionals who work with people with head injuries. To facilitate their involvement and thereby try to improve communication between clients, families, and professionals, NHIF also has a provider council of 140.

About 10 percent of NHIF's membership is involved actively. At the core of this activism are the state leaders, about an even mix of professionals and family.

Despite the enormity of a task pursued in a programmatic wasteland and the limited numbers of activists to pursue it, the organization is accomplished and growing. Among organizations working for differently abled people, NHIF ranks potentially with the most successful, including the Association for Retarded Children and the United Cerebral Palsy Association. The quality of membership of this subworld in the political community is promising. One key to this success is the high level of professional involvement NHIF has attracted.[108]

As president, formerly as executive director and vice president, founder Marilyn Price Spivack focuses full time on NHIF's development. Once a businesswomen, Mrs. Spivack states that in founding NHIF, "My intent was not to cry; my intention was to do something."[109] Rather than an angry image, Spivack says she was after an advocacy role to bring about program delivery. She began in 1980 by working through Massachusetts congresspeople; by the organization's 1986 convention in Washington, D.C., members were in direct contact with 116 congresspeople. The subjects of pictures in the organization's 1985–1986 annual report included Massachusetts Governor Michael Dukakis, U.S. Senator Edward Kennedy, Illinois Secretary of State James Edgar, and other people giving testimony to the U.S. Senate Appropriations Committee. NHIF also has become a part-time client of a Washington governmental affairs person, and Marilyn Spivack spends large segments of her time in the District. She has not escaped perceptions about women in the political process, reporting, for example, on a friend who commented in jest that he liked her best "naive and young."[110] But, the presence of professionals in the endeavor and the disavowal of protest politics seem to have softened on her the impact of gender discrimination.

Marilyn Spivack perceives that networking has been important in putting over NHIF's agenda. She explains how in making friends, she sees people develop the desire to give assistance and then respond to her requests for their expertise. Readily evident is a combination of social (networking) and political (lobbying) integration.

Curiously, despite recent improvements, pictures of people with head injuries have not appeared often in the NHIF newsletter—to this degree, in NHIF, these still are invisible, unintegrated lives. Instructive are pictures in newsletters of NHIF's national honorary cochairpersons, James Brady, the Press Secretary to President Reagan who was shot in the head during an assassination attempt, and Sarah Brady, who is married to Mr. Brady. Mrs. Brady has indicated that since his injury and because of Mr. Brady's position, she and he have received recognition—even to the point of having his meals delivered on a silver tray at the George Washington University Hospital. This particular kind of recognition has not always enabled the two to solve problems effectively. They needed recognition as head-injury survivors.

Marilyn Spivack emphasizes that "we have been educators." Public education about head injury is not a simple matter. NHIF has produced four public service announcements (PSAs) for television to heighten consciousness about the results of head injury. Such an endeavor also might help to counter the public's resistance of direct apprehension of people with handicapping conditions. But one set of the PSAs features actor Louis Jourdan. Another PSA focuses on the use of seatbelts to prevent head injuries. Opportunities for direct apprehension are limited in these PSAs. One PSA, though, features David Brady, and one talks about day-to-day concerns of head injury survivors.[111] In 1987, NHIF sought to raise public consciousness by distributing a catalogue of articles about head injury, and it also published in 1988, a new edition of a directory of rehabilitation services. Both projects seem most useful to members of the social world of head injury survivors, in particular to professionals among them and less compelling to members of the public.

Generally, NHIF's campaign is less visible than that against drinking-driving. Among other things, the organization's emphasis on the budget and appropriations processes in government is not readily visible. NHIF's major contact points—appropriations in Congress and the Office of Management and Budget—are nonetheless politically very well taken given their relation to the organization's choice of policy objectives—research, rehabilitation including training and service delivery, and reentry. These are costly undertakings.

Involvement in the appropriations process suggests the possibility of achieving categorical programming, which requires yearly decisions about spending and a continued, albeit invisible, focus on budget and appropriations. It is the case that, after their development in the 1970s, categorical health care programs lost favor to Medicare and Medicaid; but, with continuing cutbacks in Medicare and Medicaid, categorical funding again has become attractive and necessary. Further, Medicaid grants vary by state, resulting in differential benefits for people who are economically impoverished; and as we have seen, many head-injured survivors come from disadvantaged backgrounds. A categorical approach avoids the problem of variation by state in benefit structures. It is not, though, the stuff of which print and broadcast media are made.

Also to be considered, as Jonas Morris has indicated, is the fact that "while other health programs have absorbed a large share of the health care budget, the biomedical research program has remained the primary vehicle for finding solutions to health care dilemmas."[112] The process of recovering from a head injury is not entirely understood, and biomedical research has an applied dimension that translates into improved care.[113] Of interest in 1987 was the achievement by NHIF of increased funding for the National Institute on Disability and Rehabilitation Research and for the Rehabilitation Services Administration, for research and demonstration models, among other things, to help provide vocational rehabilitation services.

In another NHIF objective, training programs, the idea is to obtain adequate numbers of skilled personnel in a given field, for example, counseling or special education, and then terminate the program. With Gramm-Rudman-Hollings, presumably, more open-ended programs are things of the past. Again, the process of achieving particular objectives such as these is not visible, and it is highly specialized. Further, the impact of these achievements in their early stages may not be felt widely. As a result, political integration is going to be experienced by a small core of activists and it may be years before the marginalized clientele group, mostly members of the teenaged cohort, participates directly in its benefits.

The high level of education and dialogue of many NHIF participants also may perceptually bar participation by many head injury survivors, who may not be so well-off educationally, socially, or economically. The frequency in the newsletter and other printed materials with which photographs of people in formal wear appear at least suggests the involvement of a select population that in itself may be offsetting.

An example of this dilemma is provided by a column called "First Person," in the fall 1985 NHIF newsletter. A female single head of household from a small midwestern town wrote about her experiences after her 16-year old son received a severe head injury because of a drinking driver. After the crash her son was able to recognize her with a smile, retained some movement in one arm, and could swallow. Neither Medicaid nor her insurance would pay for maintenance-level care, and she herself was paying to keep him near home in a nursing care facility. The home state of this mother and son has no medically needy program and narrow eligibility standards for Medicaid. It will buy into Medicare for those on Medicaid. This mother said in the newsletter that:

One of the things you never seem to mention in your "happy" stories is the cost of care and rehabilitation of those who have sustained head injuries.... This is important to me....
   I try not to be bitter, but it is hard....
   His hopes, my hopes and prayers are all in your people to keep doing what you are doing.

This personal testimony effectively demonstrates the concerns of many women-in-the-middle and the limited source of outlet for these concerns, along with their frequent disregard. These women and their families are not well integrated into the NHIF and even alienated by some of the organization's emphases, however sophisticated they may be. Yet, the NHIF is mostly what there is for them, as this woman recognizes. She is caught in-between.

NHIF's lack of success with social integration is reflected in the formation of local splinter groups to represent head injury survivors. Splinter groups may articulate an understandable interest in a personally supportive environment. Put off in the medical world by many physicians and intruded upon by interventionist-minded therapists and social workers, head injury survivors may long for the understanding of people in similar situations. In relation to NHIF, these groups may appear parochial, but they really are not. Uniformly, activists in the head injury policy arena are well informed and sophisticated, if somewhat cynical. Splinter groups, though, may prove even less inclusive than NHIF because of "inbreeding" and close relationships among active members. Likely they do not perceive having excluded anyone.

Ironically, NHIF's relative success may be in part the consequence of limited social integration. Within this constraint, women such as Marilyn Spivack bring forward a battery of professionals with all the prestige that professionalism connotes. Professionalism also helps to diminish the impact on NHIF's efforts of social stereotyping of women in the organization's forefront and of differently abled people, especially those from lower income brackets. Professionalism, though, is not a gender neutral phenomenon, and it also contributes to social stratification in a manner not directly helpful to the economically taxed survivors of head injury.[114] In short, it has its costs.

CLIENTS, CAREGIVERS, AND THE GOOD LIFE

Head injury is a catastrophic event. It is here viewed by way of social and political organizations. Although these are tendencies and not absolutes, head injury presents a world divided on the one hand into mostly teenaged men and mostly old women. Members of both cohorts are likely to come from "lower" socioeconomic backgrounds and to be single. On the other hand, significant to each cohort are women as caring family members; these women tend to be middle-aged, gainfully employed, and single—women-in-the-middle.

Those entering the social organization that is the world of head-injured people find no barriers to their entry. If not injury, then cognitive identification brings people within the boundaries of the social world as well as into any of the subworlds herein discussed. Coping in this world is not as simple. At this point in time, a desirable equality of results and the "good" life may be inconceivable for many within the boundaries of the social world of head-injured people.

A major premise underlying the collection of chapters in this volume is that "society's very concern for the good life of its members determines which differences and which similarities it must respect."[115] A second premise relates to the significance of an equality of results, which in turn requires an emphasis on outcomes in the policy process. In considering, in this chapter's context, the good life and an equality of results, it will be recalled that the social world under discussion extends de facto to at least one million people with head injuries. De jure, identification of this population is subject to definition, testing and evaluation, registration, and needs assessment—to the demonstration of difference. The ability to cope with the injury's aftereffects depends not on the almost uniformly diminished status imposed upon head injury survivors by virtue of difference or association with difference, but in large part on policy outcomes that contribute to an equalization of status across the head-injured population and throughout society.

Authority structures such as those in the subworlds presented by NHIF, RID, and MADD contribute importantly to effective access to decision-making points in the policy process. Otherwise, a social world may prove nonsystematic and not only to a person with a head injury. Available family members must work their ways through a confusing labyrinth of regulations and bureaucratic structures to make meaningful access to program delivery and its financing. Individual and family alike may face unmitigated loneliness and feelings of alienation, and greater or lesser degrees of sociopolitical isolation, without the assistance of authority structures such as those found in NHIF, RID, and MADD.

A social world is constantly in flux. However, voluntary associations/interest groups that work for prevention and program delivery help moderate flux and thereby stabilize rates of change. For example, NHIF founder Marilyn Spivack cites the accumulation of newly head-injured persons over the last decade and a half; but RID and MADD both can cite over-time reductions in deaths and severe injuries on the highway in conjunction with increases by law in the drinking age in 38 states since 1981. The accumulation of newly injured persons to which Spivack refers is the result of improved care in the immediate aftermath of trauma. The reductions in deaths influenced by MADD and RID currently are threatened, however, by federally approved increases in speed on interstate highways in areas of relatively low population density, the areas with the greatest risks of mortality as a result of car crashes.[116] As stated previously, the influence exercised by these subworlds is moderate and incremental.

As another example of the ability of voluntary associations/interest groups to help moderate flux and stabilize rates of change, NHIF came on the scene because no one advocated systematically in the policy-making process for head injury survivors. Certain needs of these persons now are on federal agendas, including the U.S. Office of Special Education and Rehabilitation Services, which spans the National Institute of Handicapped Research and the Rehabilitation Services Administration, the National Institute of Mental Health, the National Institute of Communicative Disorders and Stroke, and the Department of Special Education and Developmental Disabilities. The language is there; the funding may not be. In 1987, NHIF became an organizational member of the President's Committee on Employment of the Handicapped. Marilyn Spivack is NHIF's official representative on the committee and serves on the Employment Preparation Subcommittee, whose job it is to improve education, vocational preparation, and work experiences for people with handicapping conditions, including those with head injuries.

Yet, as members of a social world, head-injured individuals do not experience an easy transition to political community, although they seem likely to discern inequity in their status. For people who have sustained head injuries, accepting "the right of political self-determination" may be problematic because of the aftereffects of trauma but also because of outsiders' perceptions (and their own) about lack of independence. To separate out self-fulfilling prophecies from the consequences of brain damage is not easy. This serious problem is exacerbated for old women in the clientele group. An interaction between gender role expectations and family life cycle is burdensome for this group, and at least noticeable for the teenaged one—the supposed bad boys—as well.

These individuals may be represented usefully by caring family, usually women-in-the-middle, and by concerned professionals. This representation, nonetheless, heightens the vicarious character of representation. For example, access to long-term respite care is much sought by some family members of people with head injuries. A desire to reduce the stress and responsibility of caring for a head-injured person must be considered valid; and sometimes a person's condition may not permit in-home care. Further, in-home care for individuals with severe damage is more expensive than institutionalization. Yet, institutionalization and separation from caring family can result in regression for the person with a head injury. Recommendations of rehabilitation therapists may be limited by failure to grasp all facets of the situation. Insurance companies want the cheapest solution. In short, competing interests are at work. To fashion maximally feasible solutions, these competing interests must be weighed. The interests of insurance companies and even of rehabilitation therapists cannot be permitted to outweigh those of people with head injuries, regardless of sex and family life cycle stage, and of women-in-the-middle. Yet, at present, this is the situation. There is not, as the editor of this volume has indicated, "enough equality of condition to allow more equal participation in citizenship,"[117] in short, to facilitate political integration.

For head injury survivors, getting out from under *economically* depends on a complex of factors, including but not limited to comprehensive third party coverage. Payment on claims needs to be strictly enforced. Allowing a claimant to collect a high rate of interest after 30 days on claims unreasonably denied is helpful. The courts need to continue to discourage use of consultants whose business is assistance in denying claims. Use of rehabilitation nurses as liaison between claimee and claimant must be monitored and regulated: These nurses are not advocates for claimant; they may contribute to delay or worse. In any event, they are not objective parties.

Partly at issue is the high cost of technology, but not necessarily technology itself.[118] Complaints about medicotechnological advance in this field may come from those not appreciating the potential for meaningful lives of most head injury survivors. The problem is particularly acute for old women who sustain head injuries. Analyzing costs without benefits is futile.

At least initially, the ever-increasing costs of hospitalization and physicians' fees will be significant to economic standing. The aftereffects of head injury are, however, chronic. For the long run, nursing care expense is a great concern. One key to recovery is quality nursing care. However, without reform in Medicare and Medicaid and without sanction by health care delivery agencies of the move by nurses toward fee-for-service status, nurses may become less accessible than at present to the person with a head injury.

Failure to treat medical indigency will reinforce any tendency by family members not to get involved. Further, I.R.S. regulations forbid deducting the injured person as a dependent if payments on claims by outside coverage exceed family support; yet family may spend thousands of dollars yearly. Also, insurance companies may seek to exploit families with limited resources, banking on the likelihood they will, first, lack access to attorneys and, second, be unable to pay them to challenge unreasonable denials of claims. Low family income or socioeconomic status and the feminization of poverty also may be used implicitly as a justification for not investing in aspects of a claimant's future.

Equally undesirable are spend-down provisions that leave caring family unable even to care for themselves in the event of their own serious illness: The rigors of caring for a person with a head injury may take their toll on certain aspects of family health.[119] In the case of married couples, where one individual has sustained a head injury, the two may divorce to protect the uninjured family member from losing everything previously compiled. Where there are dependent children in these situations, the necessity of saving something for their needs may make divorce highly likely.

As the editor of this volume has written, economic reforms alone will not result in adequate political integration. Social institutions need to change. Among other things, failure to provide helpful, sensitive community support services to head injury survivors continues the unreasonable burdens they bear. Failure to provide extended rehabilitation services mutes possibilities for renewed levels of independence and hopes for self-sufficiency; it also heightens further the responsibility family members must take and acts to discourage family members from taking responsibility. Special education and independent living/vocational rehabilitation are at issue too, and must not be forced upon people with head injuries at the expense of other rehabilitation therapies; otherwise, failure at special education and independent living/vocational rehabilitation may be preordained. Inadequate consideration of factors such as these reinforces any tendency to see institutionalization as a final solution and to focus policy agendas accordingly.

More even than old men, old women experience "economic underclass" status and lack social and political means to confront it. In combination with head injury, interaction between gender role expectations and family life cycle stage, which are social institutions, works to defeat old women's lessened concern with social norms and increased self-assertion through feminism. This defeat depresses the old woman's means for confrontation.

Care for old women and for the teenaged cohort as well tends to devolve onto women-in-the-middle. These women are at a life cycle stage torn by cross-cutting demands, are subject to harmful social stereotyping by gender, and may be perceived as political anomalies. Their marginalization can be reduced overall by networking with professionals in the head injury specialties. However, the presence of these professionals in voluntary associations/interest groups relevant to head-injured people may work to discourage participation by many head injury survivors. From the standpoint of either self-identification and its management, or the quality of membership in a political community that leads to an equality of results, there are many reasons for concern about the status of head-injured people overall and particularly of the old women among them, and about the state of women-in-the-middle.

NOTES

This chapter is a revised version of a paper presented to the annual meeting of the American Political Science Association, Washington, D.C., 1986. I acknowledge the inspiration of my son, Victor Hale Schramm, who has faced the aftermath of head injury constructively and with necessary determination to overcome it.

1. A multimedia public awareness program based on this motto was developed for NHIF by Rossen, Greenberg, Seronick, and Hill of Boston and released in late 1983. A public service announcement produced in 1985, and featuring Louis Jourdan, concluded with a revised motto: "For the survivors of head injury, life may never be the same."

2. H. S. Levin et al., "Long-term Neuropsychological Outcome of Closed Head Injury," *Journal of Neurosurgery* 56 (1982): 19–25; Rebecca W. Rimel et al., "Moderate Head Injury: Completing the Clinical Spectrum of Brain Trauma," *Neurosurgery* 2, no. 3 (1982): 344–345.

3. In cases of minor damage, prediction to outcome is not so determined by severity of injury as in cases of severe or moderate damage. John A. Jane et al., "Outcome and Pathology of Head Injury," in *Head Injury: Basic and Clinical Aspects*, ed. R. G. Grossman and P. L. Gildenberg, pp. 229–237 (New York: Raven Press, 1982).

4. Rebecca W. Rimel and John A. Jane, "Characteristics of the Head Injured Person," in *Rehabilitation of the Head Injured Adult*, ed. Mitchell Rosenthal et al., p. 9 (Philadelphia: F. A. Davis Company, 1983).

5. With severity of injury, age is believed a predictor to outcome of injury. See Jane, "Outcome and Pathology," in *Head Injury*, p. 1.

6. Seymour Eisenberg, "Communication with Elderly Patients: Effects of Illness and Medication on Mentation, Memory, and Communication," in *The Aging Brain: Communication with the Elderly*, ed. Hanna K. Ulatowska, p. 71, also Table 6-1 at p. 72 (San Diego, Calif.: College-Hill Press, 1985).

7. Rimel and Jane, "Characteristics of the Head-Injured Person," in *Rehabilitation of the Head Injured Adult*, p. 1.

8. Doris B. Hammond, "Health Care for Older Women: Curing the Disease," *Women & Politics* 6, no. 2 (1987): p. 1.

9. Ibid.

10. Rimel and Jane, "Characteristics of the Head-Injured Person," in *Rehabilitation of the Head Injured Adult*, p. 1.

11. Ibid., p. 14. Further, two-thirds of these crashes overall result in the head injury (p. 9).

12. William Haddon, Jr., and Murray Blumenthal, "Foreword," in *Deterring the Drinking Driver*, ed. H. Laurence Ross (Lexington, Mass.: Lexington Books, 1982), p. xiv.

13. Rimel and Jane, "Characteristics of the Head-Injured Person in *Rehabilitation of the Head Injured Adult*, p. 13.

14. Michael R. Bond, "Effects on the Family System," in *Rehabilitation of the Head Injured Adult*, ed. Rosenthal et al., p. 213.

15. Ibid., p. 11.

16. Ross, *Deterring the Drinking Driver*, p. 4.

17. Bond, "Effects on the Family System," in *Rehabilitation of the Head Injured Adult*, p. 213.

18. Ibid., p. 215.

19. Howard A. Palley and Julianne S. Oktay, *The Chronically Limited Elderly: The Case for a National Policy for In-Home and Supportive Community-Based Services* (New York: Haworth Press, 1983), pp. 8, 16. The term "woman in the middle" is attributed to Elaine M. Brody, "Women in the Middle and Family Help for Older People," *The Gerontologist* 21 (October 1981): 471–480.

20. Palley and Oktay, *Chronically Limited Elderly*, p. 8. See also Nadine Brozan, "Infirm Relatives' Care: A New Women's Issue," *New York Times*, November 3, 1986, p. C1.

21. See Ann Marie McLaughlin and Vicki Schaffer, "Rehabilitate or Remold?: Family Involvement in Head Trauma Recovery," *Cognitive Rehabilitation, A Publication for the Therapist, Family and Patient* 3 (January-February 1985): 14–17. The authors offer a qualitative typology of developmental stage, head trauma recovery, family reaction (remolding), and family response to staff. There is no indication of the size of population observed, no discussion of probabilities, and no overt treatment of the category, staff response to family.

22. Bond, "Effects on the Family System," in *Rehabilitation of the Head Injured Adult*, p. 209.

23. Mitchell Rosenthal and Craig A. Muir, "Methods of Family Intervention," in *Rehabilitation of the Head Injured Adult*, ed. Rosenthal et al., p. 412.

24. Jonas Morris, *Searching for a Cure: National Health Policy Considered* (New York: Pica Press, 1984), p. 32.

25. Ibid., pp. 23, 176–177.

26. Stephen M. Davidson and Theodore R. Marmor, *The Cost of Living Longer* (Lexington, Mass.: Lexington Books, 1980), p. 6.

27. Erdman Palmore and Kenneth Manton, "Ageism Compared to Racism and Sexism," *Journal of Gerontology* 28 (1973): 363–380.

28. Palley and Oktay, *Chronically Limited Elderly*, p. 36.

29. *National Head Injury Foundation Newsletter*, 3:1, Summer 1983, p. 2.

30. David R. Unruh, *Invisible Lives: Social Worlds of the Aged* (Beverly Hills, Calif.: Sage, 1983), pp. 13, 14.

31. See Ibid., p. 17.

32. John B. Lansing and Leslie Kish, "Family Life Cycle as an Independent Variable," *American Sociological Review* 22 (August 1957): 512–513.

33. See Unruh, *Invisible Lives*, p. 17.

34. See Virginia Sapiro, "News from the Front: Inter-sex and Intergenerational Conflict over the Status of Women," *Western Political Quarterly* 22 (June 1980): 260–277.

35. Sarah H. Matthews, *The Social World of Old Women: Management of Self-Identity* (Beverly Hills, Calif.: Sage, 1979).

36. Virginia Sapiro, *The Political Integration of Women: Roles, Socialization and Politics* (Urbana: University of Illinois Press, 1983).

37. Michael R. Bond, "Conclusion," in *Rehabilitation of the Head Injured Adult*, ed. Rosenthal et al., p. 33.

38. Unruh, *Invisible Lives*, p. 26.

39. Ibid., pp. 26–27.

40. Ibid., p. 27.

41. Ibid., p. 28.

42. Ibid., p. 29.

43. See Palley and Oktay, *Chronically Limited Elderly*, p. 48.

44. See Unruh, *Invisible Lives*, pp. 29–30.

45. See Ann O'M. Bowman, "Physical Attractiveness and Electability: Looks and Votes," *Women & Politics* 4 (Winter 1984): 55–65.

46. See, for example, Fred Davis, "Deviance Disavowal: The Management of Strained Interaction by the Visibly Handicapped," *Social Problems* 9 (1961): 120–132.

47. See Bowman, "Physical Attractiveness and Electability."

48. See Sapiro, *Political Integration of Women*, p. 27.

49. Ibid., p. 28.

50. Ibid., p. 29.

51. Ibid., p. 32. See also Bonnie Cook Freeman, "Power, Patriarchy, and 'Political Primitives,' " in *Beyond Intellectual Sexism: A New Woman, A New Reality*, pp. 241–264 (New York: McKay, 1976).

52. Freeman, "Power, Patriarchy, and 'Political Primitives'," in *Beyond Intellectual Sexism*, ed. Joan Roberts, pp. 242–243, 245, 251.

53. Ibid., p. 247.

54. Ibid., p. 258.

55. Ibid., p. 33.

56. Ibid., p. 107.

57. Ibid., p. 138.

58. Ibid., p. 139.

59. Hammond, "Health Care for Older Women," p. 45.

60. Ibid., pp. 11, 8–9.

61. Bryan Jennett, "Scale and Scope of the Problem," in *Rehabilitation of the Head Injured Adult*, ed. Rosenthal et al., p. 6.

62. Hanna K. Ulatowska, "Introduction," in *Aging Brain*, ed. Ulatowska, p. 5.

63. See discussion in Marilyn J. Bell and Kathleen M. Schwede, "Roles, Feminist Attitudes and Older Women," *Women & Politics* 5 (Spring 1985): 7–13.

64. Ibid., p. 19.

65. Ibid., p. 18.

66. Ibid., p. 19; see also Marilyn J. Bell, ed., *Women as Elders: The Feminist Politics of Aging* (New York: Harrington Park Press, 1986).

67. M. Powell Lawton, "Sociology and Ecology of Aging: Environment as Communication," in *Aging Brain*, ed. Ulatowska, pp. 8–12.

68. Ibid., p. 10.

69. Andrea Fontana, *The Last Frontier: The Social Meaning of Growing Old* (Beverly Hills, Calif.: Sage, 1977), pp. 26–29.

70. Ibid., p. 25.

71. Daniel Callahan, *Setting Limits* (New York: Simon & Schuster, 1987).

72. Yehuda Ben-Yishay and Leonard Diller, "Cognitive Deficits," in *Rehabilitation of the Head Injured Adult*, ed. Rosenthal et al., p. 171.

73. See Hammond, "Health Care for Older Women," pp. 41–42.

74. Andrew Tobias, *Invisible Bankers* (New York: Linden Press/Simon & Schuster, 1982), pp. 19–20.

75. This arrangement constitutes one definition of insurance; a second definition refers to the legally binding agreement of one party to compensate a second party for losses incurred. See Mark S. Dorfman, *Introduction to Insurance* (Englewood Cliffs, N.J.: Prentice-Hall, 1978), pp. 3–5.

76. Sandra Harding, "Is Gender a Variable in Conceptions of Rationality? A Survey of Issues," in *Beyond Domination: New Perspectives on Women and Philosophy*, ed. Carol C. Gould, pp. 43–44 (Totawa, N.J.: Rowman and Allanheld, 1983).

77. See Matthews, *Social World of Old Women*, pp. 90–92.

78. See Hammond, "Health Care for Older Women," p. 42.

79. Matthews, *Social World of Old Women*, pp. 103–105.

80. A. J. DeLong, "Synthesis and Synergy: Developing Models in Man-Environment Relations," in *Aging and the Environment: Theoretical Approaches*, ed. M. P. Lawton et al., pp. 19–32 (New York: Spring Publishing Company, 1982).

81. See Matthews, *Social World of Old Women*, pp. 133–136.

82. Robin McNery, "Deficits in Acts of Daily Living," in *Rehabilitation of the Head Injured Adult*, ed. Rosenthal et al., pp. 150–151.

83. See Unruh, *Invisible Lives*, pp. 34–35, p. 31, Figure 1.1.

84. John D. McCarthy, Mark Wolfson, and Debra S. Harvey, "Chapter Survey Report of The Project on The Citizens' Movement Against Drunk Driving," Center for the Study of Youth Development, The Catholic University of America, 1987.

85. Karen Lindskoog, "They Call Themselves MADD? Well, We Are DDAM Mad!" *Christian Century*, June 2, 1982, pp. 655–656.

86. Frank J. Week, "Grass-roots Activism and the Drunk Driving Issue: A Survey of MADD Chapters" (Paper presented to the annual convention of the American Sociological Association, 1985).

87. Bill Aiken, "How Can I Help?" (Schenectady, N.Y.: RID-USA, Inc., n.d.), p. 2.

88. See "Are Beer Commercials Sending Young Men a Dangerous Message?" *Status Report of the Insurance Institute for Highway Safety*, December 26, 1987, p. 7.

89. John Gannon, "RID vs. MADD-The Battle Over Booze Ads on TV, Radio," *Sacramento Bee*, June 17, 1987.

90. Matthew L. Wald, "New Campaign Set on Driving Drunk," *New York Times*, December 6, 1987. In a defensive posture, Michael Kinsley wrote for *Time* on February 22, 1988: "No doubt it is as boring to hear once again as it is to point out that the First Amendment exists to protect unpopular views—even rightly unpopular views. Unpopular views are, in fact, the only kind that need its protection. No one is trying to shut down Mothers Against Drunk Driving" (p. 96).

91. McCarthy, Wolfson, and Harvey, "Chapter Survey Report."

92. See Tamotsu Shibutani, *Society and Personality* (Englewood Cliffs, N.J.: Prentice-Hall, 1971), quoted in Unruh, *Invisible Lives*, p. 32.

93. Unruh, *Invisible Lives*, p. 31, Figure 1.1.

94. Ibid.

95. Ibid.

96. Ibid.

97. Aiken, "How Can I Help?" p. 5.

98. Unruh, *Invisible Lives*, p. 34.

99. See "A Checklist of Selected Drinking and Driving Counter-measures Adopted by the 50 States, the District of Columbia, and Puerto Rico," in the *Status Report of the Insurance Institute for Highway Safety*, March 22, 1986, p. 5.

100. Scott Sublett, "Conflict over Drinking and Driving," *The Washington Times*, June 8, 1987, p. 1B.

101. McCarthy, Wolfson, and Harvey, "Chapter Survey Report."

102. Ross, *Deterring the Drinking Driver*, p. 112.

103. See Nicholas Rescher, *Risk: A Philosophical Introduction to the Theory of Risk Evaluation and Management* (Washington, D.C.: University Press of America, 1983), ch. 12.

104. See Ross, *Deterring the Drinking Driver*, p. 107.

105. *NHIF Newsletter*, Summer 1983, p. 10.

106. Although the focus of this chapter is not on it, a third group of women in the social world and political community of people with head injuries comes from the health care professions. The fields of nursing, social work, special education, and occupational, physical and speech therapies have attracted more women than men. These professions receive less responsibility, status, and remuneration than medicine, a profession including fewer women than men. Controversy over these differentials is long-standing. A focus on the professional status differentials of these women, and on the inequity sometimes visited by these individuals on women-in-the-middle, is overdue.

107. This author will not forget a supportive hospital visit paid by an NHIF member, the male parent of a man who had sustained a head injury, after her own son was injured.

108. See also Joyce Gelb and Alice Sardell, "Organizing the Poor: A Brief Analysis of the Welfare Rights Movement," *Policy Studies Journal* 3 (Summer 1975): 349–350. The authors find professional allies a source of "money, technical knowledge, and skills, that may be otherwise unavailable to the client group, and also of intercession with significant decision makers to influence helpful responses."

109. Telephone interview with Marilyn Spivack by Sarah Slavin, May 2, 1986.

110. Ibid.

111. PSAs are available for $10 each from the NHIF, POB 567, Framingham, MA 00100.

112. *Searching for a Cure*, p. 22.

113. Bryan Jennett, "Scale and Scope of the Problem," in *Rehabilitation of the Head Injured Adult*, ed. Rosenthal et al., p. 6.

114. David G. Allen, "Professionalism, Occupational Segregation by Gender and the Control of Nursing," *Women & Politics* 6, no. 3 (1987): 1–24, argues that professionalism fails to confront issues of class and gender and, further, continues certain undesirable features of the health care system. One undesirable feature is the concealment "of social values behind a claim of scientific neutrality," (p. 6).

115. Mary Lou Kendrigan, "Understanding Equality" in *Gender Differences*.

116. See "An Editorial by William H. Foege, M.D., *The New England Journal*

of Medicine, reprinted in *Status Report of the Insurance Institute for Highway Safety*, June 27, 1987, p. 2.

117. Kendrigan, "Understanding Equality."

118. But see Morris, *Searching for a Cure*, pp. 113–114, 204, on computerized axial tomagraphy (CAT scan).

119. See Carol Armstrong, "Abstract of the Three D's of Head Injury: Depression, Denial and Disability," NYS Head Injury Association Newsletter, Spring 1987, p. 2. See also Bond, "Effects on the Family System," in *Rehabilitation of the Head Injured Adult*, ed. Rosenthal et al., p. 213 passim.

11

WHY EQUALITY OF RESULTS?

MARY LOU KENDRIGAN

The main theme of this book is that, while treating women the same as men would provide a significant improvement in the lives of many women, treating men and women the same will not solve the problems of institutional discrimination. In such a stratified society, similar treatment is inherently unequal treatment.[1] The evidence presented in these chapters shows that if equality is presumed to mean simply treating everyone the same, or simply eliminating obstacles to equal opportunity, public policy may lead to the improvement in the lives of some women. However, for most women, the inequalities due to gender will increase and be further legitimated. Inequalities are so deeply entrenched in society that it is essential that any definition of equality must be similarly pervasive.

Such an understanding of equality must utilize empirical analysis. Surely normative conclusions can never be reached simply through empirical observation. Nonetheless, normative values must be compared and tested with the best understanding of the real world that empirical observation can produce. Today, for example, the fashionable question seems to be: Should gender differences be considered at all? Much of the current discussion about gender differences would be fairly quickly cleared up if such discussions were linked to empirical analysis. When the implications of social stratification, institutional racism, and institutional sexism are evaluated, we can see why treating people the same or eliminating obstacles to equal opportunity is not enough. If we understand the significance of institutional discrimination, we will realize the limitations of many of the normative arguments concerning equality. As we have seen, any definition of equality that does not consider such institutional discrimination simply becomes a justification for existing inequalities. Even more significantly, empirical observations can only have value to the extent that they contribute to normative analysis. Analysis of institutional discrimination is valuable only if it can provide some guidelines towards a further understanding of equality. In each chapter of this book, empirical analysis is directed towards developing this understanding.

As demonstrated throughout this book, a proper understanding of equality must take into consideration differences, must focus on public-policy outcomes, and must see such public-policy issues within their social context. Equality of results is the only understanding of equality that provides an adequate assessment of existing inequalities. Prescriptions based on the equality of results would seek to minimize differences not only in the articulation of the problem but in the conception and implementation of the policy. They would also urge a concern with minimizing differences in the outcomes of policies. This standard of equality leads us to question: Which public policies lead to more and which to less equality between members of the society?[2]

Equality of results is regularly misunderstood to mean that equality is only possible when everyone has the same amount of society's resources and status. Since such a goal is so impossible to achieve and possibly not even desirable, such interpretations lessen the credibility of equality conceived as equality of results. I have tried to devise a different term to avoid that problem. I considered such terms as equality of respect or equality of concern, but neither of those terms is comprehensive enough to deal with the nature of existing inequalities. Equality must mean decreasing the discrepancies between those who have and those who do not have. Otherwise, all but a few (possibly exceptional) persons will remain at the bottom of the social pyramid.

Equality does not involve treating people the same. Equality requires treating people equally well. But what does "equally well" mean? It is impossible to come up with a precise answer to this question. It is not that equality means certain specific results—that when we have them, we have equality. It is simply that, because of the complexity and durability of gender differences, any policy or procedure must be continually evaluated and reevaluated to assess its impact on existing inequalities.

A demand for equality of results requires significant social change and constant vigilance in order to achieve a society that guarantees a certain level of physical and economic security for all members.[3] Those at the bottom of the social structure must insist on decreasing the discrepancy between those who have and those who do not have. The justification for this demand is its affirmation of equality of being or belonging.[4] People are valued as ends in themselves. We recognize something that is highly and equally valuable in all persons but having nothing to do with their merit.[5] It is this recognition that constitutes the claim for equal rights. For example, while head-injured persons are certainly different, they should be seen as not less valuable.

Claims for equality cannot be based on merit.[6] If we cling to merit, equality is impossible. Merit comes more easily to the person who has a good family, goes to the best schools, and lives in a supportive environment. Institutional discrimination influences our evaluation of merit: what we consider as meritorious and how merit is achieved. If women do not look for higher paying jobs or are not as aggressive about veterans' benefits or crime victims' benefits, that is not sufficient justification for the enormous existing inequalities. If black students do not score as high as other students on entrance exams, this should not be used to keep them out of universities or graduate schools. An egalitarian should rather ask: Is behavior congruent with benefits? What can be done to change such behavior? All persons are to be treated as equals, not because they are equal in some particular respect, but simply because they are human.[7] This does not mean that we admit everyone to schools or provide social service benefits with no screenings. It does mean we take into consideration how privilege leads to further privilege while disadvantages build on existing disadvantages. It also means that we try to use public policy to compensate for such tendencies.

But what about the danger of lowering standards and diminishing quality? When inequalities are lessened—when women are better trained, when disadvantaged persons have access to better opportunities—the formerly disadvantaged will become more meritorious. When a friend once asked me what I thought would have been the impact on the potential John Miltons if we worked towards more equality, I wondered how many Miltons have been discouraged because of inequalities? *Paradise Lost* could have been written even in a more egalitarian society. Surely a society with greater equality would have many more people who could enjoy Milton's work![8]

In an attempt to create more equality, I see at least three advantages to defining equality as equality of results: (1) Equality of results presumes that differences must be considered in any attempts to achieve greater equality; (2) Because equality is so elusive in this very unequal world, equality of results presumes that we must always evaluate outcomes; (3) Since inequalities are so intransigent, any changes in existing patterns of inequalities must not be evaluated in isolation but must be seen within their social context.

An adequate definition of equality must be based on the understanding that equal concern for the good lives of its members requires a society to treat people differently. This is, of course, a very dangerous idea. There is real danger involved in arguing that women are to be treated differently in order to be treated equally. As our contributors have demonstrated, human beings have always been treated differently. Those differences have usually reinforced advantages to the advantaged and disadvantages to the disadvantaged. The fact that women have a different societal role than men traditionally has been used to keep women in a lesser status than men. When women were treated differently, they were treated less well. Women's role was understood to be different from men's, and those differences were translated into enormous inequalities for women. The existence of gender differences was used to keep women in a subservient position.[9]

Clearly moves towards greater equality require opposing some differences. Certainly differences that perpetuate and continue existing inequalities should be opposed. In addition, more demanding requirements for women must also be opposed. Willenz notes that married women veterans of both World War II and Korea did not receive the same educational benefits for their spouses as married male veterans. At that time, there were also some inequities in death benefits and in the administration of home loans. Richard found that training programs for female jobs required a high school diploma or a GED certificate. Similar programs for male jobs included training for the GED. Such differences do not, of course, enhance equality.

Because of this fear of different treatment, one obvious response to discriminatory behavior is to demand that people be treated the same. It is, however, very dangerous to leap from an understanding of the manner in which differences have been manipulated in the past to a rejection of all claims to gender differences. A major advantage of treating people the same is simplicity. H. L. Mencken once remarked, however, that for every difficult problem there is a quick and easy answer: quick, easy—and wrong.

Social stratification, institutional racism, and institutional sexism illustrate why any analysis of equality must consider differences. It is only with an understanding of these concepts that the pervasiveness of differential treatment becomes clear. These concepts also illustrate why such a definition must concentrate on outcomes. The dominant ideology can and does use both difference and similarities between the sexes to maintain the advantages of the privileged. Because inequalities are so entrenched in society, claims of "no differences" can be manipulated just as easily as claims of differences. Class, race, and gender play a crucial role in the determination of differential treatment.

Racism and sexism are more than, and sometimes different from, unpleasant, unfair, nasty, or rotten behavior. Racism and sexism involve acts of domination and subordination. Racist and sexist acts can be performed by nice people. Our contributors provide several illustrations of the manner in which domination and subordination on the basis of race, gender, and class operate in all aspects of life. As each of the chapters in this book illustrates, the way out is not to ignore claims of differences in the hope of avoiding their dangers. Such dangers exist not because of the recognition of differences but because of the nature of inequality. If we are to achieve more equality, we must shift the grounds of analysis. We must ask in what ways gender differences should be considered in order to create more equality.

As this book shows, public policy usually reinforces existing inequalities. Sometimes policies specifically favor men. More often, seemingly neutral laws ignore the different role women play in society. Certainly in public-policy outcomes, many gender differences can be identified. Programs that appear to be neutral have in fact discriminated against women. Rules that are applied similarly in different situations cannot ensure equality.

Our contributors demonstrate that treating people the same when their situations are not the same will lead to increased inequalities. Women are victims of different kinds of crime. Biological differences between men and women veterans call for different kinds of physical exams, different expertise, different equipment, and different facilities in veterans' hospitals. Unemployment affects women differently from men. Job training programs that deal with women must be organized differently. Men's and women's family life cycles are different. Likewise, gender-neutral tax laws are not neutral in their effects. Men and women fit differently into the economy and respond differently to incentives and disincentives. Corporate taxation affects men and women differently because women are employed in low-paying jobs in competitive industries and benefit less from tax credits. Thus, as Ruttenberg and McCarthy show, tax laws have a different impact on women. The primary beneficiaries of governmental tourism policy have been men. Tax concessions for business travel subsidize activities that remain 75 percent male. Government primarily subsidizes vacation travel of interest to men. Any move toward greater equality must take these differences into consideration.[10]

This analysis was directed to the issue of equality between the sexes, but inequalities on the basis of gender are not the only significant inequalities. Slavin points out that the elderly are more likely to suffer head injuries. Beckett's study suggests that perhaps young workers are more likely to be forced to deal with plant closings. Race and social class are, of course, also crucial factors in explanations of existing social inequalities. Because feminists come to their understanding of equality and inequality on the basis of their experience with inequalities of gender, it is most appropriate that they emphasize those inequalities. This emphasis does not exclude other kinds of inequalities. It simply requires that due attention be given to gender inequalities.

Differences do not necessarily denote superiority and inferiority. People are so varied in their needs, aspirations, talents, and interests that different treatment is both necessary and unavoidable. What constitutes the good life for one person may not do so for another.[11] One may be a talented violinist;

another may be a skilled lawyer or a football player. If differences are ignored, it is impossible to achieve significant progress towards more equality.

Equality of results, on the other hand, recognizes that it is not different treatment that is the problem. It is different treatment that leads to greater inequalities that must be avoided. Equality of results requires treating people differently in order to treat them equally well. For any increased equality it is essential that we understand this distinction.

The differences that exist between men and women today are significant in perpetuating greater inequalities. Certainly, gender differences will not disappear in the foreseeable future, and any understanding of equality must take them into consideration. However, any commitment to differences must be based on an understanding that with equal treatment some differences will become less relevant to an analysis of social inequality. If gender differences lessen, perhaps class differences will become more important. Nevertheless, differences will still have to be considered in a society that values equality. Efforts to treat people equally well must not be based on the false assumption that equal treatment requires that we ignore all differences.

A second advantage of defining equality as equality of results is that it directs us to look at policy outcomes. Where ideology can use similarities or differences, the question should not be whether men and women are treated the same or differently, but what is the outcome of that treatment? Because treating people differently in order to treat them equally well is far more challenging than treating everyone the same, programs to create more equality must be continually evaluated.

We are so far from equality that it is hard to see what it would look like. Furthermore, it is too easy to develop all sorts of arguments against such a radical disruption of existing realities. Discussions of absolute quality not only do not further the quest for greater equality but may well seem so impossible to attain that they become justifications for the present system of existing inequalities. Since we are so far away from absolute equality, such discussions unnecessarily cloud a more relevant issue: How can we achieve gender equality than we have now? Which public policies lead to more equality among members of society?

A policy of equality of results may lead to more questions than answers. We do not have all the answers—but that does not mean that we have *no* answers. While it is impossible to state precisely what equal outcomes might be, there are some parameters. Perhaps it is not possible or even desirable that everyone have access to the same amount or the same kind of societal rewards. The society needs only so many eye surgeons, concert pianists, entrepreneurs. The society also needs people in more modest positions with more modest rewards. If we are to value equality, however, we must assert that everyone should have access to food, clothing, shelter, medical care, education, and opportunities for further self-development. If we are to re-alize more equal distribution of resources, we must also demand that the gap between the haves and the have-nots, if not entirely erased, must surely be narrowed. There must be changes in the existing social institutions that reinforce oppressed peoples' acceptance of their secondary status. If race and gender are not to be obstacles to access to the advantages of society, public policy must be directed towards lessening the obstacles of race and gender. African-Americans should have no more obstacles than the average white person. The average women should have no more obstacles than the average male. The desired outcome is the elimination of all internal and external barriers to women and minorities attaining full personhood.[12]

Each of the chapters in this book shows the advantages of looking at policy outcomes if we are to understand the operations of existing ine-qualities and/or to evaluate the policies that are helpful in creating more equality. Deitch, Nowak, and Snyder trace the history of the Equal Em-ployment Opportunity Commission to show that those federal policies most explicitly concerned with women's employment opportunities were not con-ceived or formulated with the specific needs of women in mind. Deitch, Nowak, and Snyder and also Beckett explain that while men and women are differently affected by plant shutdowns, the problem is usually defined in exclusively male terms. Willenz identifies the manner in which women were ignored in veterans' outreach programs and in the studies of Agent Orange. Slavin argues that the problems of the head-injured go unnoticed and unsolved because the victims and the caretakers are usually women. Compensation programs were developed to help victims of crime, but the major crimes that victimize women were virtually excluded from the pro-grams. Benefits were often determined in ways that were of greater advan-tage to male victims. Eligibility was determined in ways disadvantageous to women. Similar patterns have been identified in unemployment compen-sation programs.[13]

Such discrimination is usually not noticed because women are often in-visible in the conception, development, and evaluation of programs. Na-tional monuments and historic sites have routinely ignored women's cultural, artistic, scientific, and commercial achievements. Women have not yet been allowed to be part of the Vietnam War Memorial. As Richter points out, women are not only invisible in monuments and museums, but also in the collection of data on the impact of public policy. Willenz also found women missing from the collection of data on veterans. Women's rate of unemployment exceeded men all through the 1950s, the 1960s and the 1970s. Women make up 40 percent of the discouraged workers. Despite this, programs geared to the unemployed have focused on men.

While public policy usually ignores the concerns of women, eventually some of the dimensions of such gender discrimination are recognized. For example, the compensation programs for victims of crime initially ignored the plight of rape victims. More recent legislation has accommodated some of those victims. Nonetheless, these programs are seldom quite as effective for women as for men. Women are often less aware of benefits and less knowledgeable on how to get them. Women expect to get little and make few demands on the system. Willenz found that one of the major drawbacks facing women veterans was that they discount their contributions to their country, are unaware of the benefits that they deserve, and do not ask for them. We found similar patterns in studying compensation for victims of crime. Women victims do not know of the program and do not demand that it meet their needs.

Thus even when programs are useful to women, they are not as useful as programs that do not affect women. Willenz points out that parity with nonveterans was the goal of the GI Bill. Neither veterans' programs to benefit women nor other programs of assistance to women have aspired to such a goal. Bella Abzug had parity in mind when she recommended an affirmative action program for Congress. She suggested that one of the two senators from each state should be female, and every open seat in the House of Representatives should be given to a woman until women comprise half that body.[14] Deitch, Nowak, and Snyder document how useful the Equal Employment Opportunity Commission has been to women. However, while the EEOC was useful in certain cases, it has not been as effective as the Voting Rights Act. The Voting Rights Law has stronger enforcement aspects than does the Equal Employment Opportunity Act. I do not mean to imply that women are more discriminated against than other groups. I simply wish to point out that even in programs devised to help women, the breadth and vision of that assistance must continue to be evaluated critically.

Nonetheless, if existing forms of discrimination are to be counteracted, disadvantaged groups must look to public policy to compensate for some of the inequalities in both public and private life. Richter explains that bad policies, budget shortages, and other political failures take their heaviest toll on women. She explains that women, as the most economically disadvantaged class, may be the most affected positively or negatively by the type of tourism the government encourages, the scale of tourism sought, and the ways in which government spending for tourism is allocated and revenues from tourism are spent. Deitch, Nowak, and Snyder argue that public policy must be adopted to counteract the effects of market forces. For it is, indeed, these market forces that create inequalities in the economy.

Thus, politics must fit within our understanding of the parameters of equality. If women do not have political power, social change will come at their expense. Certainly greater equality includes the removal of obstacles to greater participation in public life. Effective public policy to meet needs is not easy. Treating people differently can only result in more equality if the people so treated have some political power.[15] Inequalities entail dif-

ferential power, and the powerful work to maintain their power. Furthermore, they are usually successful.

Women's lack of representation in shaping policy means that public policy
is not as effective as it might be in creating more equality. This has been
true in veterans' benefit programs, in job training programs, and in the
development of tourism policies. When women are not involved in the
shaping of policy, the right questions are not asked. This was clearly true
in the case of compensation programs for victims of crime. No one asked:
What about victims of rape or domestic abuse?

Feminists must demand increased political participation by women.
Women and men who are feminists must be involved in the development
of policies, in their implementation, and in the evaluation of their effectiveness. Willenz attributes much of the success of women in winning veterans' benefits largely to the increased articulateness of the women veterans
themselves, the proliferation of the new and ad hoc women veterans' groups
around the country, and an increased awareness and involvement of the
older women veterans' organizations.

It is not, however, simply participation that counts, but certain kinds of
participation with specific results. Participation is a necessary but not a
sufficient condition for equality of results. Slavin describes the struggle involved in meeting the public policy needs of citizens who have suffered head
injuries. She evaluates the success of persons involved in that struggle and
the role gender plays in limiting those successes. Slavin explains that one
may be marginal to the political system even while participating. The goal,
she explains, is the freedom "to be influential."

When feminists are influential, it can matter. Public policy can help alleviate inequalities in other sectors of life and soften the impact of social
stratification, institutional racism, and institutional sexism. Although public
policy usually reinforces existing inequalities, there are exceptions. As Richard explains, access to adequate day care does open options in job training
and employment for women. The Comprehensive Employment and Training
Act (CETA) was more helpful to women who needed job training than the
Job Training Partnership Act (JTPA). The Massachusetts education and
training program has helped women. Beckett's study shows that the devastating effects of plant shutdowns can be minimized when certain policies
are adopted to assist the affected workers. Deitch, Nowak, and Snyder
explain that in the 1970s a small but significant number of women entered
higher paying, blue-collar work and improved their positions in these industries. These gains in the steel industry were as a result of Title VII and
litigation. The steel plan included goals, quotas, and timetables. It mandated
future hiring and recruitment, training and transfers, promotions, local enforcement committees, and data collection and reporting. It was not a perfect
plan, but it led to real and significant gains. Slavin argues that public policy

can matter to victims of head injuries and their caretakers. She urges stricter law-enforcement efforts to combat people driving under the influence of liquor. She advocates comprehensive third-party insurance coverage, enforced payments of insurance claims, and the regulation of insurance. There must also be quality medical care and changes in the social institutions for victims of head injuries. Richter identifies the reasons why it is important that women influence governmental policy concerning leisure.

Furthermore, the advantages that any disadvantaged groups achieve are always tenuous and they may be short-lived. The Veterans Administration became aware of discrimination against women in the veterans hospitals. However, just as women veterans began to learn about their benefits, the sympathetic veterans administrator left office, and stringent budget cuts led to means tests for non-service-related illness. When the system had begun responding to women veterans' needs, other contingencies narrowed their eligibility. When equal treatment became available to women, treatment for all veterans was seriously curtailed. Deitch, Nowak, and Snyder found a similar pattern in their study of the effectiveness of the Equal Employment Opportunity Commission. They found that the EEOC's usefulness was limited when times changed. Many of the features that made the affirmative action plan in the steel industry effective were the same policies that courts, the Civil Rights Commission, and the Justice Department under the Reagan administration have reversed and declared illegal.

We must make the moral claim that equality requires minimizing the socially significant differences among persons in order to provide all citizens with similar access to participation in public life. Furthermore, we need to be aware of the ends we wish to achieve and continually evaluate the rules to see how well they accomplish those ends. It must be presumed that the normal functioning of social institutions works to maintain and perpetuate inequalities. The rules we adopt to modify those inequalities must continually be evaluated with that knowledge in mind.

A third advantage of adopting equality of results as our standard is that the analyst who applies it must avoid looking at any one program in isolation. No one program can overcome existing inequalities. The interactions among existing inequalities are complex. We try to keep programs from reinforcing existing inequalities. We attempt to make modest improvements against blatant discrimination. The only check on that possibility is constant awareness of the goals and constant evaluation of the policies. Policies that seem to be useful in achieving greater equality might become meaningless or even counterproductive. No particular changes are adequate in themselves to meet the goals feminists wish to achieve. Any procedures can be manipulated to maintain inequalities. No matter how sensible, desirable, or functional any one program sounds, because of women's limited political power or of the rigidity of existing inequalities and opposition to change, it is more than likely that such a program will not lead to increased equality.[16] The only check on that possibility is constant awareness of the goals and constant evaluation of the policies.

The social context is important. Ruttenberg and McCarthy point out that tax policy does not operate in a vacuum. The interactions are complex. Affirmative action can have little impact when plants are closing. As Deitch, Nowak, and Snyder point out, affirmative action is necessary—but not enough. Feminists must not confuse change with progress.[17] We can anticipate that social change will most harshly affect the most vulnerable members of society. The privileged are better able to adapt to such changes. Deitch, Nowak, and Snyder explain how just when women were able to gain admittance to well-paying blue-collar jobs, deindustrialization accelerated. Better paying blue-collar jobs that women gained in the 1970s are disappearing while the expanding areas of women's employment are in lower paying, nonunion, predominantly female, service industries.

Furthermore, changes must not be seen in isolation. Changes in one aspect of life will be related to changes in many other aspects as well. While the kinds of jobs that are available to women are changing, women's role in the family is also evolving in ways that make women more dependent on such jobs. With more low-paying jobs, the need will increase for better health care, different kinds of funding for day care, housing subsidies, and more creative retirement benefits. Feminists must understand the complexity of differences in all aspects of the efforts to deal with social change.

Any one public policy must be evaluated in its context. Ruttenberg and McCarthy explain that the dependent-care tax credit does little to offset the high cost of private day care. Meanwhile, federal and state programs to assist in child care have been cut. Federal policy to assist with day care is helpful to the more affluent and counterproductive for those in greatest need. Deitch, and Nowak, Snyder argue that without a full-employment policy, affirmative action and equal-opportunity employment can do little to protect women workers in their short-term goals.

People who are less than equal have fewer options in manipulating the laws, norms, and symbols of society to their advantage. They also have limited options in other areas. Deitch, Nowak, and Snyder explain that laid-off steel workers find themselves in a locality where the options for blue-collar workers are extremely limited. Richard found illustrations of limited options among the applicants for job training that she studied. Slavin shows us the limited options available to head-injury victims and their caretakers. As these studies indicate, citizens with limited options must rely on effective public policy to meet their needs.

My intention in presenting these studies is to show that any one program must be evaluated in a larger perspective that favors not only affirmative action or compensation for victims of rape, but true equality. If race and gender are not to limit access to the advantages of society, public policy must be directed to lessening the impact of institutional racism and institutional sexism. Such public policy must be based on an understanding that the society in all its ordinary operations works towards providing greater advantages to the advantaged and increased disadvantages to the disadvantaged. The only check on such tendencies towards increased inequalities is constant awareness of the goals and constant evaluation of the policies. While an understanding of equality as equality of results will not avoid the problems of institutional discrimination, this understanding can compensate for such discrimination by asking those concerned with equality to look to what the program accomplished and to avoid excessive commitment to any one program.

We can anticipate that any movement towards equality will be marginal. Even minor revisions in existing inequalities take enormous effort. Such marginal change can, however, be very important to the persons involved. Furthermore, if we do not look at the outcomes, continued and perhaps greater inequalities are to be expected. The normal functioning of society's institutions continues to create further inequalities. If equality is not properly understood, there is a danger that existing inequalities will not only be perpetuated, but that they will be perpetuated in the name of equality.

The aim must be a society in which no person should be so powerless that she or he has no control over her or his own life, a society in which no person should be so powerful that he or she can force others to do her or his bidding without taking others into account, [18] a society in which all those vitally affected by a decision of the community have an effective voice in that decision.[19] Such goals are more than utopian dreams. They are the only hope that any society has for taking significant steps away from existing institutional discrimination and towards more equality. We must act as if such goals are possible. Such actions create some possibilities. If we fail to assert such goals or work towards them, inequalities will be perpetuated and intensified. Any understanding of equality that aims for less may simply mean that divorced women would lose their right to financial support and custody of their children, while they gained the right to be drafted!

NOTES

1. Mary Lou Kendrigan, *Political Equality in a Democratic Society: Women in the United States* (Westport, Conn.: Greenwood Press, 1984).

2. Herbert Gans, *More Equality* (New York: Vintage Books, 1973), p. iv.

3. John H. Schaar, "Equality of Opportunity and Beyond" in *Nomos IX: Equality*, ed. J. Roland Pennock and John W. Chapman, p. 247 (New York: Atherton Press, 1967).

4. Schaar, "Equality of Opportunity," p. 247. See also Jean Bethke Elshtain, "The Feminist Movement and the Question of Equality," *Polity* 7 no. 4 (Summer 1975).

5. Ronald Dworkin, *Taking Rights Seriously* (Cambridge, Mass.: Harvard University Press, 1977).

6. Robert E. Goodin, *Reasons for Welfare: The Political Theory of the Welfare State* (Princeton, N.J.: Princeton University Press, 1988), esp. Chapter 3.

7. Willian K. Frankena, "The Concept of Social Justice," in *Social Justice*, ed. Richard B. Brandt, p. 19 (Englewood Cliffs, N.J.: Prentice-Hall, 1962).

8. As Thomas Gray wrote in *Elegy Written in a Country Churchyard* (1742– 1750): "Full many a gem of purest ray serene, / The dark unfathom'd caves of ocean bear: / Full many a flower is born to blush unseen, / And waste its sweetness on the desert air. / ... / Some village-Hampden, that with dauntless breast / The little tyrant of his fields withstood; / Some mute inglorious Milton here may rest, / Some Cromwell guiltless of his country's blood."

9. Kendrigan, *Political Equality*, pp. 47–61.

10. Hester Eisenstein and Alice Jardine, eds., *The Future of Differences* (Boston, Mass.: G. K. Hall & Co., 1986).

11. "It is what justifies, for example, giving C a banjo, D a guitar, and E a skin-diving outfit," notes Willian Frankena. "Although C, D and E are treated differently, they are not dealt with unequally, since their differing needs and capacities so far as these relate to the good life are equally considered and equally well cared for." Frankena, "Concepts of Social Justice," p. 20.

12. Daniel C. Maguire, *A New American Justice: Ending the White Male Monopolies* (New York: Doubleday & Co., Inc., 1980).

13. Diane Pearce, "Toil and Trouble: Women Workers and Unemployment Compensation," *Signs* (Spring 1985): 439–459.

14. Bella Abzug, "Address to Women and the Constitution: A Bicentennial Perspective," Atlanta, February 10–12, 1988.

15. Kendrigan, *Political Equality*, pp. 47–64.

16. Kendrigan, *Political Equality*, pp. 91–115.

17. Kendrigan, *Political Equality*, pp. 80–84.

18. Gans, *More Equality*, p. 10.

19. C. Wright Mills, *The Sociological Imagination* (London: Oxford University Press, 1959).

SELECT BIBLIOGRAPHY

Baer, Judith. *The Chains of Protection: The Judicial Response to Women's Labor Legislation*. Westport, Conn.: Greenwood Press, 1978.

Barber, Benjamin. *The Conquest of Politics: Liberal Philosophy in Democratic Times*. Princeton, N.J.: Princeton University Press, 1988.

Beitz, Charles. *Political Equality: An Essay in Democratic Theory*. Princeton, N.J.: Princeton University Press, 1989.

Boneparth, Ellen, and Emily Stoper. *Women, Power and Policy*. Riverside, N.J.: Pergamon Press, 1988.

Bookman, Ann, and Sandra Morgan, eds. *Women and the Politics of Empowerment*. Philadelphia: Temple University Press, 1988.

Bowie, Norman, ed. *Equal Opportunity*. Boulder, Colo.: Westview Press, 1988.

Brown, Wendy. *Manhood and Politics: A Feminist Reading in Political Theory*. Totowa, N.J.: Rowman and Littlefield, 1988.

Bumiller, Kristin. *The Civil Rights Society: The Social Construction of Victims*. Baltimore: Johns Hopkins University Press, 1988.

Conway, Jill K., Susan C. Bourque, and Joan W. Scott, eds. *Learning about Women: Gender, Politics, and Power*. Ann Arbor: University of Michigan Press, 1987.

Crites, Laura L., and Winifred L. Hipperle, eds. *Women, the Courts and Equality*. Beverly Hills, Calif.: Sage Publishing, 1987.

Dahl, Robert A. *Democracy, Liberty, and Equality*. (New York: Oxford University Press, 1988.

Dworkin, Ronald. *Taking Rights Seriously*. Cambridge, Mass.: Harvard University Press, 1977.

Eisenstein, Hester, and Alice Jardine, eds. *The Future of Differences*. Boston: G. K. Hall & Co., 1986.

Eisenstein, Zillah R. *The Female Body and the Law*. Berkeley: University of California Press, 1988.

Evans, Judith, ed. *Feminism and Political Theory*. Beverly Hills, Calif.: Sage Publishing, 1986.

Evans, Sara M., and Barbara J. Nelson. *Wage Justice: Comparable Worth and the Paradox of Technocratic Reform*. Chicago: University of Chicago Press, 1989.

Fraser, Nancy. *Unruly Practices: Power, Discourse, and Gender in Contemporary Social Theory*. Minneapolis: University of Minnesota Press, 1989.

Goodin, Robert E. *Reasons for Welfare: The Political Theory of the Welfare State* Princeton, N.J.: Princeton University Press, 1988.

Gordon, Linda. *Heroes of Their Own Lives: The Politics and History of Family Violence, Boston, 1880–1960*. New York: Viking Press, 1988.

Gould, Carol C. *Rethinking Democracy*. New York: Cambridge University Press, 1988.

Greene, Katherine W. *Affirmative Action and Principle of Justice*. Westport, Conn.: Greenwood Press, 1989.

Gunnell, John G. *Between Philosophy and Politics: The Alienation of Political Theory*. Amherst, Mass.: University of Massachusetts Press, 1986.

Hale, Mary M., and Rita Mae Kelly, eds. *Gender, Bureaucracy, and Democracy: Careers and Equal Opportunity in the Public Sector*. Westport, Conn.: Greenwood Press, 1989.

Harrison, Cynthia. *On Account of Sex: The Politics of Women's Issues, 1945–1968*. Berkeley: University of California Press, 1988.

Held, Virginia. *Rights and Goods: Justifying Social Action*. Chicago: University of Chicago Press, 1989.

Jones, Kathleen, and Anna G. Jonasdotter. *The Political Interests of Gender*. Beverly Hills, Calif.: Sage Publishing, 1985.

Kelly, Rita Mae, and Jane Bayes, eds. *Comparable Worth, Pay Equity and Public Policy*. Westport, Conn.: Greenwood Press, 1988.

Kendrigan, Mary Lou. *Political Equality in a Democratic Society: Women in the United States*. Westport, Conn.: Greenwood Press, 1984.

MacKinnon, Catharine. *Toward a Feminist Theory of the State*. Cambridge: Harvard University Press, 1989.

Maguire, Daniel C. *A New American Justice: Ending the White Male Monopolies*. New York: Doubleday & Co., 1980.

Malson, Micheline, Jean O'Barr, Sarah Westphal-Wihl, and Mary Wyer. *Feminist Theory in Practice and Process*. Chicago: University of Chicago Press, 1989.

Mezey, Susan Gluck. *No Longer Disabled: The Federal Courts and the Politics of Social Security Disability*. Westport, Conn.: Greenwood Press, 1988.

Milkman, Ruth. *Gender at Work: The Dynamics of Job Segregation by Sex During World War II*. Urbana: University of Illinois Press, 1987.

Okin, Susan Moller. *Justice, Gender and the Family* (New York: Basic Books, 1989.

O'Neill, William L. *Feminism in America: A History*. 2nd rev. ed. New Brunswick, N.J.: Transaction Publishers, 1989.

Ozawa, Martha, ed. *Women's Life Cycle and Economic Insecurity: Problems and Proposals*. Westport, Conn.: Greenwood Press, 1989.

Pateman, Carole. *The Sexual Contract*. Stanford, Calif.: Stanford University Press, 1988.

Pateman, Carole, and Elizabeth Gross, eds. *Feminist Challenges, Social and Political Theory*. Boston: Northeastern University Press, 1986.

Pearce, Diane. "Toil and Trouble: Women Workers and Unemployment Compensation." *Signs* (Spring 1985): 439–459.

Phillips, Anne, ed. *Feminism and Equality*. New York: New York University Press, 1987.

Rhode, Deborah I. *Justice and Gender*. Cambridge, Mass.: Harvard University Press, 1989.

———. *Theoretical Perspectives on Sexual Differences*. New Haven, Conn.: Yale University Press, 1990.

Sidel, Ruth. *Women and Children Last: The Plight of Poor Women in Affluent America*. New York: Penguin Books, 1987.

Weitzman, Lenore J. *The Divorce Revolution: The Unexpected Social and Economic Consequences for Women and Children in America*. New York: The Free Press, 1985.

INDEX

Job Training Partnership Act, case study: background of, 111–113; classroom training, 116; evaluation of, 117–118; findings of study, 115–117; on-the-job-training placements, 115–116; program participants, 113–115; relocation, 116; Tri-County Community Action Agency and, 112, 113, 116, 117–118
Jourdan, Louis, 207

Kamerman, Sheila B., 106
Kanter, Rosabeth, 58, 59
Kasl, Stanislav V., 68–69
Kendrigan, Mary Lou, 53, 191
Kennedy, Edward, 207
Kenya, tourism in, 157
Knoxville, Tennessee, tourism in, 164
Krill, Francoise, 184, 185

Labor force participation, increase of women in, 104–105
Leisure time, impact of the increase in, 155
Lightner, Candy, 201–202
Lightner, Cari, 201
Lincoln, Abraham, 3, 133
Local taxes, state and, 145–147

McCarthy, Amy A., 225, 231
MADD, 201–202, 203–205, 211
Manpower Demonstration Research Corp., 111
Manpower Development and Training Act, 107
Manufacturers Hanover Trust Co., 143
Marcos, Ferdinand, 156
Marx, Karl, 133
Massachusetts' ET Choices, 118–120
Medical indigence, 198
Medicare, 198
Michigan. See Victim-compensation programs in Michigan and Wisconsin
Mick, Stephen S., 49, 50
Monk-Turner, Elizabeth, 55
Morris, Jonas, 208
Morris, Karen, 202

Morris, Tim, 202
Mothers Against Drunk Drivers (MADD), 201–202, 203–205, 211
"Mothers Against Drunk Drivers: The Candy Lightner Story," 202

Nash, June, 39
National Academy of Sciences, National Research Council of: pay for women and, 106; women veterans and, 178
National Association for the Advancement of Colored People (NAACP), 43, 45
National Asssociation of Broadcasters, 203
National Crime Survey, 13
National Head Injury Foundation (NHIF): creation of, 205, 206–207; function of, 192, 193, 194, 199, 205–206, 207–208, 211; membership of, 206; motto of, 190; problems with, 208–210. See also Head injuries
National Institute on Disability and Rehabilitation Research, 208
National Organization for Women, 45
National Task Force on Care-Givers, 199
National Tourism Policy Act, 157
Navy Nurse Corps, 177
NBC, 202
Nelson, Susan C., 107
New Jersey: employment and training programs in, 120; women veterans in, 184
New Orleans, tourism in, 164
New York, women veterans in, 184
NHIF. See National Head Injury Foundation
Nowak, Thomas C., 47, 48, 49, 50, 51, 227, 228, 229, 230, 231
Nurses, military status of, 177

Occupational distribution differences, 106
Oktay, Julianne, 191
Older Women's League (OWL), 199

CONTRIBUTORS

JOYCE O. BECKETT is Professor of Social Work at Virginia Common-
wealth University. She has written extensively on the employment of older
and minority women, mental health intervention with black families and
women, and female addiction. She was formerly a clinical and psychiatric
social worker.

CYNTHIA DEITCH teaches in the Department of Sociology at George
Washington University in Washington, D.C.

MARY LOU KENDRIGAN is in the Social Science Department at Lansing
Community College, Lansing, Michigan. She is the author of *Political Equality in a Democratic Society: Women in the United States* and the forthcoming
Political Equality, Women, and the Military. She is presently at work on
studies of the political economy of state politics and the political philosophy
of Belle LaFollette.

AMY A. McCARTHY is a Senior Associate at Ruttenberg, Kilgallon &
Associates, Washington, D.C. She was formerly chair of the Department of
Economics of Trinity College.

ELIZABETH MONK-TURNER is Adjunct Professor of Sociology at Old
Dominion University in Norfolk, Virginia. She is the author of several ar-
ticles, whose titles include "Dual Career Academic Couples: Analysis of
Problems"; "Sex and Voting Behavior in the United States"; and "Sex

Differentials in Unemployment Rates in Male-dominated Occupations and
Industries during Periods of Economic Downturn."

THOMAS C. NOWAK is Professor of Sociology at Indiana University of
Pennsylvania. He is the author of several publications concerning sex differences in the impact of plant shutdowns, job loss and demoralization, and
displaced factory women and public policy.

PATRICIA BAYER RICHARD is a Professor in the Department of Political
Science at Ohio University. Her areas of specialization include electoral and
legislative politics; women, law, and politics; and science policy. She is the
author of more than two dozen articles and papers on such topics as the
impact of Reaganomics on women, abortion policy and reproductive rights
issues, and voting behavior. Her writings have appeared in such journals
as *Women's Studies Quarterly*, *Appalachian Journal*, and *Western Political
Quarterly*.

LINDA K. RICHTER is Associate Professor of Political Science at Kansas
State University, where she teaches public policy, sex and politics, and public
administration. Her publications include over 30 articles on the politics of
tourism, women in South and Southeast Asia, and Philippine politics. She
is the author of *Land Reform and Tourism Development: Policy Making
in the Philippines* and has testified before Congress on issues concerning
women and Philippine development aid.

RUTH RUTTENBERG is President of Ruth Ruttenberg and Associates, Inc.
She was formerly Senior Associate of Ruttenberg, Kilgallon & Associates,
Washington, D.C. She has appeared as an expert witness on behalf of trade
unions at arbitrations. She has conducted research projects, testified, and
published on such topics as occupational safety and health, military waste,
tax policy, national policy on raw materials, international trade and multinational corporations, manpower, and collective bargaining.

SARAH SLAVIN is an Assistant Professor at the State University College
at Buffalo. She specializes in constitutional law, judicial process and behavior, women in American government, and minorities and U.S. politics.
She was editor of *Women and Politics* for seven years. She has written and
edited numerous publications addressing the impact gender differences have
on public policy, feminism and the F.C.C., and other topics related to
women's studies.

KAY A. SNYDER is a Professor in the Department of Sociology and An-
thropology at Indiana University of Pennsylvania. Her areas of specialization

include social stratification, racial and ethnic inequality, the sociology of unemployment, sexual inequality, and industrial and political sociology.

MARY ANN E. STEGER is an Associate Professor in the Department of Political Science at Northern Arizona University. Her research interests include nonprofit community-based organizations, citizen participation in policy issues that are scientifically and technically complex, and worker/community mobilization in response to industrial plant closings. She has published in *Urban Affairs Quarterly, Justice System Journal, Research in Urban Policy,* and *Urban Interest.* She presently is collaborating on a research project investigating the use of scientific and technical information by environmental interest groups in Canada and the United States.

JUNE A. WILLENZ is the author of *Women Veterans: America's Forgotten Heroines.* She is the executive director of the American Veterans Committee. She is chair and cofounder of the newly formed Committee on Women of the World Veterans Federation. She is also a writer and lecturer. She has appeared on numerous radio and television programs and serves on the President's Committee on Employment of the Handicapped Subcommittee on Disabled Veterans.